HYPEROBJECTS

posthumanities

Cary Wolfe SERIES EDITOR

(continued on page 233)

HYPEROBJECTS

Philosophy and Ecology after the End of the World

TIMOTHY MORTON

posthumanities 27

UNIVERSITY OF MINNESOTA PRESS

MINNEAPOLIS • LONDON

The University of Minnesota Press gratefully acknowledges financial assistance provided for the publication of this book by Rice University.

"Midnight Oil" by Sheryl St. Germain reprinted by permission of the poet. Portions of *A House Is a House for Me* by Mary Ann Hoberman, copyright 1978 by Mary Ann Hoberman, reprinted by permission of Viking Penguin, a division of Penguin Group (USA) Inc. "Styrofoam Cup" by Brenda Hillman reprinted by permission of the poet.

Published by the University of Minnesota Press
111 Third Avenue South, Suite 290
Minneapolis, MN 55401-2520
http://www.upress.umn.edu

Library of Congress Cataloging-in-Publication Data
Morton, Timothy.
Hyperobjects : philosophy and ecology after the end of the world / Timothy Morton. (Posthumanities ; 27) Includes bibliographical references and index.
ISBN 978-0-8166-8922-4 (hc)
ISBN 978-0-8166-8923-1 (pb)
1. Object (Philosophy) 2. Future, The. I. Title.
BD336.M67 2013
110–dc23
2013028374

Printed in the United States of America on acid-free paper

The University of Minnesota is an equal-opportunity educator and employer.

20 19 18 17 16 15 14   11 10 9 8 7 6 5 4 3

To

MY EXTENDED FAMILIES

I am become death, the shatterer of worlds.

—ROBERT OPPENHEIMER,
after the Bhagavad Gita

Contents

Acknowledgments

Cary Wolfe (the Posthumanities series editor) and Douglas Armato (the director of the University of Minnesota Press) deserve deep thanks for their support of this project, as does Steven Shaviro, whose kind reading of the book was both helpful and inspiring. Associate editor Danielle Kasprzak ably saw the book through production. Thanks also to Nicolas Shumway, dean of the School of Humanities at Rice University, for research fund assistance.

I was very lucky to have been able to road test many of the ideas here in a number of fora: the California Institute of the Arts; the Second Object-Oriented Ontology Symposium, UCLA; the Architectural Association, London; the National Institute for Experimental Arts, Sydney; the University of Melbourne Law School; Dialogues with Tomorrow, New Zealand; Tunghai University and National Chung-Hsing University, Taiwan; the Rocky Mountain Modern Language Association, Albuquerque; Loyola University, New Orleans; Rice University; Rutgers University; the Georgia Institute of Technology; the Design and Sustainability Symposium at the New School, New York; Temple University; the Department of Philosophy at De Paul University ; the Royal College of Art, London; Columbia College, Chicago; the Royal Academy of Art, London; the Climate Change and Critical Theory Conference at the University of Exeter; and the Emergent Environments Conference, Queen Mary University of London. A number of journals have also helped me to crystallize my thoughts: *Qui Parle, Speculations, World Picture, Adbusters, Graz Architectural Magazine, English Language Notes, Helvete,* and *Romantic Circles Praxis.* The websites Fractured Politics and Figure/Ground interviewed me on hyperobjects and the Contemporary Condition solicited a short essay on the subject.

To my colleagues in object-oriented ontology I am profoundly grateful for the chance to share the exciting work of thinking. I am very grateful to Dirk Felleman, who over the last two years has been an invaluable source of feedback and information, thinking things through alongside me. Thanks to Larry Butz and Ben Levaton, who provided invaluable research assistance. I am thankful to all my kind hosts and colleagues over these last two years for helping me to think hyperobjects: Jane Bennett, Jill Bennett, Hannes Bergthaller, Steven Blevins, Eliza Bonham-Carter, Alan Braddock, Kuei-fen Chiu, William Connolly, Arne DeBoever, Carl Douglas, Rick Elmore, Paul Ennis, Jarrod Fowler, William Fox, Nathan Gale, Peter Gratton, Jairus Grove, Liam Heneghan, Robert Jackson, Sophie Jerram, Adeline Johns-Putra, Douglas Kahn, Michelle Leh, Kevin Love, Dugal MacKinnon, Jorge Marcone, Lin Mu, Judy Natal, Connal Parsley Alexander Regier, David Reid, Ken Reinhard, Julia Reinhard Lupton, Gerhard Richter, Chris Schaberg, Janelle Schwartz, Sam Solnick, Cameron Tonkinwise, Hent Vinckier, Jonathan Watts, and Andrew Whatley.

This book is dedicated to my extended families. Hyperobjects make you think about how families are fuzzy sets of beings, distributed over spaces and times wider than me and my immediate surroundings.

A Quake in Being

An Introduction to Hyperobjects

In *The Ecological Thought* I coined the term *hyperobjects* to refer to things that are massively distributed in time and space relative to humans.[1] A hyperobject could be a black hole. A hyperobject could be the Lago Agrio oil field in Ecuador, or the Florida Everglades. A hyperobject could be the biosphere, or the Solar System. A hyperobject could be the sum total of all the nuclear materials on Earth; or just the plutonium, or the uranium. A hyperobject could be the very long-lasting product of direct human manufacture, such as Styrofoam or plastic bags, or the sum of all the whirring machinery of capitalism. Hyperobjects, then, are "hyper" in relation to some other entity, whether they are directly manufactured by humans or not.

Hyperobjects have numerous properties in common. They are *viscous,* which means that they "stick" to beings that are involved with them. They are *nonlocal;* in other words, any "local manifestation" of a hyperobject is not directly the hyperobject.[2] They involve profoundly different temporalities than the human-scale ones we are used to. In particular, some very large hyperobjects, such as planets, have genuinely *Gaussian* temporality: they generate spacetime vortices, due to general relativity. Hyperobjects occupy a high-dimensional phase space that results in their being invisible to humans for stretches of time. And they exhibit their effects *interobjectively;* that is, they can be detected in a space that consists of interrelationships between aesthetic properties of objects.

The hyperobject is not a function of our knowledge: it's *hyper* relative to worms, lemons, and ultraviolet rays, as well as humans.

Hyperobjects have already had a significant impact on human social and psychic space. Hyperobjects are directly responsible for what I call *the end of the world,* rendering both denialism and apocalyptic environmentalism obsolete. Hyperobjects have already ushered in a new human phase of *hypocrisy, weakness,* and *lameness*: these terms have a very specific resonance in this study, and I shall explore them in depth. *Hypocrisy* results from the conditions of the impossibility of a metalanguage (and as I shall explain, we are now freshly aware of these conditions because of the ecological emergency); *weakness* from the gap between phenomenon and thing, which the hyperobject makes disturbingly visible; and *lameness* from the fact that all entities are fragile (as a condition of possibility for their existence), and hyperobjects make this fragility conspicuous.[3] Hyperobjects are also changing human art and experience (the aesthetic dimension). We are now in what I call *the Age of Asymmetry.*

Hyperobjects are not just collections, systems, or assemblages of other objects. They are objects in their own right, objects in a special sense that I shall elucidate as we proceed through this book. The special sense of *object* derives from *object-oriented ontology* (OOO), an emerging philosophical movement committed to a unique form of realism and nonanthropocentric thinking. Least of all, then, would it be right to say that hyperobjects are figments of the (human) imagination, whether we think imagination as a bundling of associations in the style of Hume, or as the possibility for synthetic judgments a priori, with Kant. Hyperobjects are real whether or not someone is thinking of them. Indeed, for reasons given in this study, hyperobjects end the possibility of transcendental leaps "outside" physical reality. Hyperobjects force us to acknowledge the immanence of thinking to the physical. But this does not mean that we are "embedded" in a "lifeworld."

Hyperobjects thus present philosophy with a difficult, double task. The first task is to abolish the idea of the possibility of a metalanguage that could account for things while remaining uncontaminated by them. For reasons I shall explore, poststructuralist thinking has failed to do this in some respects, or rather, it didn't complete the job. The second task is to establish what phenomenological "experience" is in the absence of anything meaningfully like a "world" at all: hence the subtitle, "Philosophy and Ecology after the End of the World."

I have divided this book into two parts. Since there is a radical split between the object and its appearance-for some other entity, it seems appropriate to divide the book in this manner. Hyperobjects require direct philosophical, historical, and cultural explication, and this suits the first part of the book. But then we must move on to the human appropriation of hyperobjects, which occupies the second part.

Throughout *Hyperobjects* I frequently write in a style that the reader may find "personal"—sometimes provocatively or frustratingly so. This decision to write somewhat "personally" was influenced by Alphonso Lingis's risky and rewarding phenomenology. It seems appropriate. I am one of the entities caught in the hyperobject I here call *global warming* (another decision—I don't subscribe to calling it *climate change*: see Figure 1); one of the entities I know quite well. And as an object-oriented ontologist I hold that all entities (including "myself") are shy, retiring octopuses that squirt out a dissembling ink as they withdraw into the

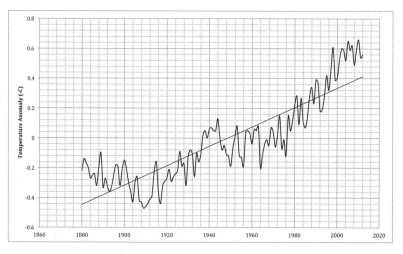

FIGURE 1. Global warming cannot be directly seen, but it can be thought and computed, as this graph demonstrates. Data from NASA Godard Institute for Space Studies; graph by Larry Butz.

ontological shadows. Thus, no discourse is truly "objective," if that means that it is a master language that sits "meta" to what it is talking about. There is also a necessarily iterative, circling style of thought in this book. This is because one only sees pieces of a hyperobject at any one moment. Thinking them is intrinsically tricky.

This line of reasoning makes me seem like a postmodernist, though for reasons that will become clear, the emerging ecological age gets the idea that "there is no metalanguage" much more powerfully and nakedly than postmodernism ever did.[4] Since for postmodernism "everything is a metaphor" in some strong sense, all metaphors are equally bad. But since for me, and indeed for all humans as we transition into the Age of Asymmetry there are real things for sure, just not as we know them or knew them, so some metaphors are better than others.[5] Yet because there is nowhere to stand outside of things altogether, it turns out that we know the truth of "there is no metalanguage" more deeply than its inventors. The globalizing sureness with which "there is no metalanguage" and "everything is a metaphor" are spoken in postmodernism means that postmodernism is nothing like what it takes itself to be, and is indeed just another version of the (white, Western, male) historical project. The ultimate goal of this project, it seems, was to set up a weird transit lounge outside of history in which the characters and technologies and ideas of the ages mill around in a state of mild, semiblissful confusion.

Slowly, however, we discovered that the transit lounge was built on Earth, which is different from saying that it was part of Nature. (Throughout this book, I capitalize *Nature* precisely to "denature" it, as one would do to a protein by cooking it.) "The actual Earth," as Thoreau puts it, now contains throughout its circumference a thin layer of radioactive materials, deposited since 1945.[6] The deposition of this layer marks a decisive geological moment in the *Anthropocene,* a geological time marked by the decisive human "terraforming" of Earth as such.[7] The first significant marks were laid down in 1784, when carbon from coal-fired industries began to be deposited worldwide, including in the Arctic, thanks to the invention of the steam engine by James Watt. The birth of the steam engine, an all-purpose machine whose all-purpose quality (as noted in its patent) was precisely what precipitated the industrial age, was an event whose significance was not lost on Marx.[8] This universal machine (uncanny harbinger of the computer, an even more general machine) could be connected to vast assemblages of other machines to supply their motive power, thus giving rise to the assemblages of assemblages that turn the industrial age into a weird cybernetic system, a primitive artificial intelligence of a sort—to wit, industrial capitalism, with the vampire-like downward causality of the emergent machine level, with its related machine-like qualities of abstract value, sucking away at the humans on the levels beneath. After 1945 there began *the Great Acceleration,* in which the geological transformation of Earth by humans increased by vivid orders of magnitude.

Yet like everyone else until about a decade ago, Marx missed the even bigger picture. Think about it: a geological time (vast, almost unthinkable), juxtaposed in one word with very specific, immediate things— 1784, soot, 1945, Hiroshima, Nagasaki, plutonium. This is not only a historical age but also a geological one. Or better: we are no longer able to think history as exclusively human, for the very reason that we are in the Anthropocene. A strange name indeed, since in this period nonhumans make decisive contact with humans, even the ones busy shoring up differences between humans and the rest.

The thinking style (and thus the writing style) that this turn of events necessitates is one in which the normal certainties are inverted, or even dissolved. No longer are my intimate impressions "personal" in the sense that they are "merely mine" or "subjective only": they are footprints of hyperobjects, distorted as they always must be by the entity in which they make their mark—that is, me. I become (and so do you) a litmus test of the time of hyperobjects. I am scooped out from the inside. My situatedness and the rhetoric of situatedness in this case is not a place of defensive self-certainty but precisely its opposite.[9] That is, situatedness is now a very uncanny place to be, like being the protagonist of a Wordsworth poem or a character in *Blade Runner.* I am unable to go beyond what I have elsewhere called *ecomimesis,* the (often) first-person rendering of situatedness "in."[10] This is not to endorse ecomimesis, but to recognize that there is no outside, no metalanguage. At every turn, however, the reader will discover that the prose in this book sways somewhat sickeningly between phenomenological narrative and scientific reason. Yet just as I am hollowed out by the hyperobject, so by the very same token the language of science is deprived of its ideological status as cool impersonality. The more we know about hyperobjects, the stranger they become. Thus hyperobjects embody a truth about what I once thought only applied to lifeforms, the truth of the *strange stranger*.[11]

What this book seeks then is a weird ecomimesis that tugs at the limits of the rhetorical mode, seeking out its hypocrisy. For reasons I give later, the term *hypocrisy* is very carefully chosen. *The time of hyperobjects is a time of hypocrisy.* Yet, for the same reasons, seeking out hypocrisy cannot be done from the point of view of cynicism. If there is no metalanguage, then cynical distance, the dominant ideological mode of the left, is in very bad shape, and will not be able to cope with the time of hyperobjects.

There is a further reason why Alphonso Lingis is central to this project. Lingis's book *The Imperative* is a remarkable reworking of Kantian ethics, taking phenomenology into account. The phenomenology in question is Lingis's own, developed from years of study and affiliation with Emmanuel Levinas, and very different from the Husserlian phenomenology that is its great-grandparent. In particular, Lingis makes it possible to think a truly ecological ethics. Many of his most potent examples are drawn from ethical dilemmas concerning ecological action. In the later sections of this book (contained in part 2: "The Time of Hyperobjects"), I explore in depth why a Lingis-inspired view of ethics is essential for ecological action. In particular, the section entitled "Hypocrisies" deals extensively with Lingis's thought.

Hyperobjects are what have brought about the end of the world. Clearly, planet Earth has not exploded. But the concept *world* is no longer operational, and hyperobjects are what brought about its demise. The idea of the end of the world is very active in environmentalism. Yet I argue that this idea is not effective, since, to all intents and purposes, the being that we are to supposed to feel anxiety about and care for is gone. This does not mean that there is no hope for ecological politics and ethics. Far from it. Indeed, as I shall argue, the strongly held belief that the world is about to end "unless we act now" is paradoxically one of the most powerful factors that inhibit a full engagement with our ecological coexistence here on Earth. The strategy of this book, then, is to awaken us from the dream that the world is about to end, because action on Earth (the real Earth) depends on it.

The end of the world has already occurred. We can be uncannily precise about the date on which the world ended. Convenience is not readily associated with historiography, nor indeed with geological time. But in this case, it is uncannily clear. It was April 1784, when James Watt patented the steam engine, an act that commenced the depositing of carbon in Earth's crust—namely, the inception of humanity as a geophysical force on a planetary scale. Since for something to happen it often needs to happen twice, the world also ended in 1945, in Trinity, New Mexico, where the Manhattan Project tested the Gadget, the first of the atom bombs, and later that year when two nuclear bombs were dropped on Hiroshima and Nagasaki (Figure 2). These events mark the logarithmic increase in the actions of humans as a geophysical force.[12] They are of "world-historical" importance for humans—and indeed for any lifeform within range of the fallout— demarcating a geological period, the largest-scale terrestrial era. I put "world-historical" in quotation marks because it is indeed the fate of the concept *world* that is at issue. For what comes into view for humans at this moment is precisely the end of the world, brought about by the encroachment of hyperobjects, one of which is assuredly Earth itself, and its geological cycles demand a *geophilosophy* that doesn't think simply in terms of human events and human significance.

The end of the world is correlated with the Anthropocene, its global warming and subsequent drastic climate change, whose precise scope remains uncertain while its reality is verified beyond question. Throughout *Hyperobjects* I shall be calling it *global warming* and not *climate change*. Why? Whatever the scientific and social reasons for the predominance of the term *climate change* over *global warming* for naming this particular hyperobject, the effect in social and political discourse is plain enough. There has been a decrease in appropriate levels of concern. Indeed, denialism is able to claim that using the term *climate change* is merely the rebranding of a fabrication, nay evidence of this fabrication in flagrante delicto. On the terrain of media and the sociopolitical realm, the phrase *climate change* has been such a failure that one is tempted to see the term itself as a kind of denial, a reaction to the radical trauma of unprecedented global warming. That the terms are presented as choices rather than as a package is a symptom of this failure, since logically it is correct to say "climate change as a result of global warming," where "climate change" is just a compression of a more detailed phrase, a metonymy.

If this is not the case, then *climate change* as a *substitute* for *global warming* is like "cultural change" as a substitute for *Renaissance,* or "change in living conditions" as a substitute for *Holocaust. Climate change* as substitute enables cynical reason (both right wing and left) to say that the "climate has always been changing," which to my ears sounds like using "people have always been killing one another" as a fatuous reason not to control the sale of machine guns. What we desperately need is an appropriate level of shock and anxiety concerning a specific ecological

FIGURE 2. Trinity test at 0.016 seconds, July 16, 1945. For some time this picture was banned, since it was considered far more provocative than the habitual mushroom cloud. The tiny shapes on the horizon are trees. Los Alamos National Laboratory.

trauma—indeed, *the* ecological trauma of our age, the very thing that defines the Anthropocene as such. This is why I shall be sticking with the phrase *global warming* in this book.

Numerous philosophical approaches have recently arisen as if in response to the daunting, indeed horrifying, coincidence of human history and terrestrial geology. *Speculative realism* is the umbrella term for a movement that comprises such scholars as Graham Harman, Jane Bennett, Quentin Meillassoux, Patricia Clough, Iain Hamilton Grant, Levi Bryant, Ian Bogost, Steven Shaviro, Reza Negarestani, Ray Brassier, and an emerging host of others such as Ben Woodard and Paul Ennis. All are determined to break the spell that descended on philosophy since the Romantic period. The spell is known as *correlationism,* the notion that philosophy can only talk within a narrow bandwidth, restricted to the human–world correlate: meaning is only possible between a human mind and what it thinks, its "objects," flimsy and tenuous as they are. The problem as correlationism sees it is, is the light on in the fridge when you close the door?

It's not quite idealism, but it could tend that way. But the problem goes back further than the Romantic period, all the way back to the beginning of the modern period. (Unlike Latour, I do believe that we have "been modern," and that this has had effects on human and nonhuman beings.)[13] The restriction of philosophy's bandwidth attempts to resolve a conundrum that has been obsessing European thinking since at least the uncritical inheritance by Descartes of the scholastic view of substances—that they are basic lumps decorated with accidents.[14] Despite his revolutionary rationalism—brilliantly deriving reality from his confidence in his (doubting) mental faculties—Descartes uncritically imported the very scholasticism his work undermined, imported it into the area that mattered most, the area of ontology. Since then, even to say the word *ontology* has been to say something with a whiff of scholasticism about it. Epistemology gradually took over: How can I know that there are (or are not) real things? What gives me (or denies me) access to the real? What defines the possibility of access? The possibility of possibility? These thoughts even affect those who strove against the trend, such as Schelling and Heidegger, and the original phenomenologists, whose slogan was "To the things themselves!" Speculating outside of the human became a minor trend, exemplified by the marginalization of Alfred North Whitehead, who thanks to speculative realism has been enjoying a recent resurgence.

Speculative realism has a healthy impulse to break free of the correlationist circle, the small island of meaning to which philosophy has confined itself. It is as if, since the seventeenth century, thinking has been cowed by science. Yet science not only cries out for "interpretation"—and heaven knows some defenses of the humanities these days go as far as to argue that science needs the humanities for PR purposes. Beyond this, science doesn't necessarily know what it is about. For a neo-Darwinist, reality is mechanisms and algorithmic procedures. For a quantum physicist, things might be very different. Reality might indeed entail a form of correlationism: the Copenhagen Interpretation is just that. Or everything is made of mind.[15] So what is it? Which is it? Asleep at the switch, philosophy has allowed the default ontology to persist: there are things, which are basically featureless lumps, and these things have accidental properties, like cupcakes decorated with colored sprinkles.

This thinking—or the lack thereof—is not unrelated to the eventual manufacture, testing, and dropping of Little Boy and Fat Man. Epistemological panic is not unrelated to a sclerotic syndrome of "burying the world in nullity . . . in order to prove it."[16] This thinking still continues, despite the fact that thought has already made it irrelevant. The thinking reaches the more than merely paradoxical idea that if I can evaporate it in an atomic energy flash, it must be real. The thinking is acted out daily in drilling, and now "fracking" for oil. The year 1900 or thereabouts witnessed a number of "prequels" to the realization of the Anthropocene and the coming of the Great Acceleration. These prequels occurred within human thinking itself, but it is only in retrospect that humans can fully appreciate them. Quantum theory, relativity theory, and phenomenology were all born then. Quantum theory blew a huge hole in the idea of particles as little Ping-Pong balls. Relativity theory destroyed the idea of consistent objects: things that are identical with themselves and constantly present all the way down. (Both theories will be discussed at length in later sections.) Extreme forms of realism in narrative began to set streams of consciousness free from the people who were having them, and the hand-holding benevolent narrator vanished. Monet began to allow colors and brushstrokes to liberate themselves from specific forms, and the water in which the water lilies floated, exhibited on the curving walls of the Orangerie, became the true subject of his painting. Expressionism abolished the comforting aesthetic distances of Romanticism, causing disturbing, ugly beings to crowd towards the viewer.

What did the "discoveries of 1900" have in common? Water, quanta, spacetime began to be seen. They were autonomous entities that had all kinds of strange, unexpected properties. Even consciousness itself was no longer just a neutral medium: phenomenology made good on the major philosophical discovery of the Romantic period, the fact of consciousness that "has" a content of some kind.[17] Monet had started painting water lilies; or rather, he had started to paint the space in which water lilies float; or rather, he had started to paint the rippling, reflective object in which the lilies float—the water. Just as Einstein discovered a rippling, flowing spacetime, where previously objects had just floated in a void, Monet discovered the sensuous spaciousness of the canvas itself, just as later Tarkovsky was to discover the sensuous material of film stock. All this had been prefigured in the Romantic period with the development of blank verse narratives, meandering through autobiographical detours. Suddenly a whole lot more paper was involved.

Around 1900 Edmund Husserl discovered something strange about objects. No matter how many times you turned around a coin, you never saw the other side as the other side. The coin had a dark side that was seemingly irreducible. This irreducibility could easily apply to the ways in which another object, say a speck of dust, interacted with the coin. If you thought this through a little more, you saw that all objects were in some sense irreducibly withdrawn. Yet this made no sense, since we encounter them every waking moment. And this strange dark side applied equally to the "intentional objects" commonly known as thoughts, a weird confirmation of the Kantian gap between phenomenon and thing. Kant's own example of this gap is highly appropriate for a study of hyperobjects. Consider raindrops: you can feel them on your head—but you can't perceive the actual raindrop in itself.[18] You only ever perceive your particular, anthropomorphic translation of the raindrops. Isn't this similar to

the rift between weather, which I can feel falling on my head, and global
climate, not the older idea of local patterns of weather, but the entire system? I can think and compute climate in this sense, but I can't directly
see or touch it. The gap between phenomenon and thing yawns open,
disturbing my sense of presence and being in the world. But it is worse
still than even that. Raindrops are raindroppy, not gumdroppy—more's
the pity. Yet raindrop phenomena are not raindrop things. I cannot
locate the gap between phenomenon and thing anywhere in my given,
phenomenal, experiential, or indeed scientific space. Unfortunately raindrops don't come with little dotted lines on them and a little drawing
of scissors saying "cut here"—despite the insistence of philosophy from
Plato up until Hume and Kant that there is some kind of dotted line
somewhere on a thing, and that the job of a philosopher is to locate
this dotted line and cut carefully. Because they so massively outscale us,
hyperobjects have magnified this weirdness of things for our inspection:
things are themselves, but we can't point to them directly.

Around 1900 Einstein discovered something strange about objects.
The speed of light was constant, and this meant that objects couldn't be
thought of as rigid, extended bodies that maintained their shape. Lorentz
had noticed that electromagnetic waves shrank mysteriously, as if foreshortened, as they approached light speed. By the time you reach the end
of a pencil with your following eyes, the other end has tapered off somewhere. If you put tiny clocks on your eyelids, they would tell a different
time than the tiny clocks on your feet lying still beneath the table as
you twirl the pencil in your fingers, the tiny clocks in each fingernail
registering ever so slightly different times. Of course you wouldn't see
this very clearly, but if you were moving close to the speed of light,
objects would appear to become translucent and strangely compressed
until they finally disappeared altogether. Spacetime appeared, rippling
and curved like Monet's water lilies paintings. And there must then be
regions of spacetime that are unavailable to my perception, even though
they are thinkable: another strange confirmation of the Kantian gap between phenomenon and thing.

Around 1900 Max Planck discovered something strange about objects.
If you tried to measure the energy in an enclosed object (like an oven) by

summing all the waves, you reached absurd results that rocketed toward infinity above a certain temperature range: the blackbody radiation problem. But if you thought of the energy as distributed into packets, encapsulated in discrete quanta, you got the right result. This accuracy was bought at the terrible price of realizing the existence of a bizarre quantum world in which objects appeared to be smeared into one another, occupying indeterminate areas and capable of penetrating through seemingly solid walls. And this is yet another confirmation of the phenomenon–thing gap opened up by Kant, for the simple reason that to measure a quantum, you must fire some other quanta at it—to measure is to deflect, so that position and momentum are not measurable at the same time.

The Kantian gap between phenomenon and thing places the idea of substances decorated with accidents under extreme pressure. Drawing on the breakthroughs of the phenomenologist Husserl, Heidegger perhaps came closest to solving the problem. Heidegger realized that the cupcakes of substance and the sprinkles of accidence were products of an "objective presencing" that resulted from a confusion within (human) being, or *Dasein,* as he put it. Heidegger, however, is a correlationist who asserts that without Dasein, it makes no sense whatsoever to talk of the truth of things, which for him implies their very existence: "Only as long as Dasein *is,* 'is there' *[gibt es]* being . . . it can neither be said that beings *are,* nor that they are not."[19] How much more correlationist do you want? The refrigerator itself, let alone the light inside it, only exists when I am there to open the door. This isn't quite Berkeleyan *esse est percipi,* but it comes close. Heidegger is the one who from within correlationism descends to a magnificent depth. Yet he is unwilling to step outside the human–world correlation, and so for him idealism, not realism, holds the key to philosophy: "If the term idealism amounts to an understanding of the fact that being is never explicable by beings, but is always already the 'transcendental' for every being, then the sole correct possibility for a philosophical problematic lies in idealism."[20]

Heidegger had his own confusion, not the least of which is exemplified by his brush with Nazism, which is intimately related to his insight and blindness about being. Graham Harman, to whose object-oriented ontology I subscribe, discovered a gigantic coral reef of sparkling things beneath the Heideggerian U-boat. The U-boat was already traveling at a profound ontological depth, and any serious attempt to break through in philosophy must traverse these depths, or risk being stuck in the cupcake aisle of the ontological supermarket.

Harman achieved this discovery in two ways. The first way is simple flexibility. Harman was simply ready to drop the specialness of Dasein, its unique applicability to the human, in particular to German humans. This readiness is itself a symptom of the ecological era into which we have entered, the time of hyperobjects. To this effect, Harman was unwilling to concede Heidegger the point that the physical reality described in Newton's laws did not exist before Newton.[21] This line of Heidegger's thought is even more correlationist than Kant's. The second way in which Harman attacked the problem was by a thorough reading of the startling tool-analysis in the opening sections of Heidegger's *Being and Time*. This reading demonstrates that nothing in the "later" Heidegger, its plangency notwithstanding, topples the tool-analysis from the apex of Heidegger's thinking. Heidegger, in other words, was not quite conscious of the astonishing implications of the discovery he made in the toolanalysis: that when equipment—which for all intents and purposes could be anything at all—is functioning, or "executing" *(Vollzug)*, it withdraws from access *(Entzug)*; that it is only when a tool is broken that it seems to become present-at-hand *(vorhanden)*. This can only mean, argues Harman, that there is a vast plenum of unique entities, one of whose essential properties is *withdrawal*—no other entity can fully account for them. These entities must exist in a relatively *flat ontology* in which there is hardly any difference between a person and a pincushion. And relationships between them, including causal ones, must be *vicarious* and hence *aesthetic* in nature.

If we are to take seriously the ontological difference between being and beings, argues Harman, then what this means is twofold:

(1) No realism is tenable that only bases its findings on "ontic" data that are pregiven. This would be like thinking with prepackaged concepts—it would not be like thinking at all.

(2) Idealism, however, is unworkable, since there exist real things whose core reality is withdrawn from access, even by themselves.

Point (1), incidentally, is the trouble with science. Despite the refreshing and necessary skepticism and ruthless doubt of science, scientific discoveries are necessarily based on a decision about what real things are.[22] Point (2) is the primary assertion of OOO, Harman's coral reef beneath the Heideggerian U-boat.

It will become increasingly clear as this book proceeds that hyperobjects are not simply mental (or otherwise ideal) constructs, but are real entities whose primordial reality is withdrawn from humans. Hyperobjects give us a platform for thinking what Harman calls *objects* in general. This introduction is not quite the right moment for a full explication of OOO. Outlining OOO might mean that we never got around to hyperobjects themselves. And, more significantly, the subtlety of OOO itself requires a thorough examination of hyperobjects. Moreover, it seems like good practice to start with the things at hand and feel our way forward—in this I join Lingis. Yet I trust that by the end of the book the reader will have a reasonable grasp of how one might use this powerful new philosophical approach for finding out real things about real things.

So, let's begin to think about hyperobjects in some depth. What is the most striking thing about their appearance in the human world? Naturally humans have been aware of enormous entities—some real, some imagined—for as long as they have existed. But this book is arguing that there is something quite special about the recently discovered entities, such as climate. These entities cause us to reflect on our very place on Earth and in the cosmos. Perhaps this is the most fundamental issue— hyperobjects seem to force something on us, something that affects some core ideas of what it means to exist, what Earth is, what society is.

What is special about hyperobjects? There's no doubt that cosmic phenomena such as meteors and blood-red Moons, tsunamis, tornadoes, and earthquakes have terrified humans in the past. Meteors and comets were known as *disasters*. Literally, a disaster is a fallen, dysfunctional, or dangerous, or evil, star *(dis-astron)*. But such disasters take place against a stable background in at least two senses. There is the

Ptolemaic–Aristotelian machinery of the spheres, which hold the fixed stars in place. This system was common to Christian, Muslim, and Jewish cosmology in the Middle Ages. To be a disaster, a "star" such as a meteor must deviate from this harmonious arrangement or celestial machinery. Meanwhile, back on Earth, the shooting star is a portent that makes sense as a trace on the relatively stable horizon of earth and sky. Perhaps the apocalypse will happen. But not just yet. Likewise, other cultures seemed to have relatively coherent ways of explaining catastrophes. In Japanese Shinto, a tsunami is the vengeance of a *Kami* who has been angered in some way.

It seems as if there is something about hyperobjects that is more deeply challenging than these "disasters." They are entities that become visible through post-Humean statistical causality—a causality that is actually *better* for realism than simply positing the existence of glass spheres on which the fixed stars rotate, to give one example. This point never fails to be lost on global warming deniers, who assert, rightly, that one can never directly prove the human causes of global warming, just as I never prove that this bullet you fire into my head will kill me. But the extreme statistical likelihood of anthropogenic global warming is better than simply asserting a causal factoid. Global warming denial is also in denial about what causality is after Hume and Kant—namely a feature of phenomena, rather than things in themselves.

What does this mean to nascent ecological awareness? It means that humans are not totally in charge of assigning significance and value to events that can be statistically measured. The worry is not whether the world will end, as in the old model of the *dis-astron,* but whether the end of the world is already happening, or whether perhaps *it might already have taken place.* A deep shuddering of temporality occurs. Furthermore, hyperobjects seem to continue what Sigmund Freud considered the great humiliation of the human following Copernicus and Darwin. Jacques Derrida rightly adds Freud to the list of humiliators—after all he displaces the human from the very center of psychic activity. But we might also add Marx, who displaces human social life with economic organization. And we could add Heidegger and Derrida himself, who in related though subtly different ways displace the human from the center of meaning-making. We might further expand the list by bringing in Nietzsche and his lineage, which now runs through Deleuze and Guattari to Brassier: "Who gave us the sponge to wipe away the entire horizon?" (Nietzsche).[23] And in a different vein, we might add that OOO radically displaces the human by insisting that my being is not everything it's cracked up to be—or rather that the being of a paper cup is as profound as mine.

Is it that hyperobjects seem to push this work of humiliation to a yet more extreme limit? What is this limit? Copernicus, it is said, is all about displacement. This was first taken to mean an exhilarating jump into cognitive hyperspace. But what if the hyperobjects force us to forget even this exit strategy? What if hyperobjects finally force us to realize the truth of the word *humiliation* itself, which means being brought low, being brought down to earth? Hyperobjects, in effect, seem to push us into a double displacement. For now the possibility that we have loosed the shackles of the earthly to touch the face of the "human form divine" (Blake) seems like a wish fulfillment.[24] According to hyperobjects themselves, who seem to act a little bit like the gigantic boot at the end of the *Monty Python* credits, outer space is a figment of our imagination: *we are always inside an object.*

What we have then, before and up to the time of hyperobjects from the sixteenth century on, is the truth of Copernicanism, if we can call it that—there is no center and we don't inhabit it. Yet added to this is another twist: there is no edge! We can't jump out of the universe. Queen Mab can't take Ianthe out of her bed, put her in a spaceship, and whisk her to the edge of time to see everything perfectly (Percy Shelley's fantasy). Synthetic judgments a priori are made inside an object, not in some transcendental sphere of pure freedom. Quentin Meillassoux describes Kant's self-described Copernican turn a Ptolemaic counterrevolution, shutting knowing up in the finitude of the correlation between (human) subject and world.[25] But for me, it is the idea of a privileged transcendental sphere that constitutes the problem, not the finitude of the human–world correlation. Kant imagines that although we are limited in this way, our transcendental faculties are at least metaphorically floating in space beyond the edge of the universe, an argument to which Meillassoux himself cleaves in his assertion that reality is finally knowable exclusively by (human) subjectivity. And *that* is the problem, the problem called anthropocentrism.

It is Kant who shows, at the very inception of the Anthropocene, that things never coincide with their phenomena. All we need to do is extend this revolutionary insight beyond the human–world gap. Unlike Meillassoux, we are not going to try to bust through human finitude, but to place that finitude in a universe of trillions of finitudes, as many as there are things—because a thing just is a rift between what it is and how it appears, for any entity whatsoever, not simply for that special entity called the (human) subject. What ecological thought must do, then, is unground the human by forcing it back onto the ground, which is to say, standing on a gigantic object called *Earth* inside a gigantic entity called *biosphere*. This grounding of Kant began in 1900. Phenomenology per se is what begins to bring Kantianism down to Earth, but it's hyperobjects and OOO that really convince me that it's impossible to escape the gravitational field of "sincerity," "ingenuousness," being-there.[26] Not because there is a *there*—we have already let go of that. Here I must part company with ecophenomenology, which insists on regressing to fantasies of embeddedness. No: we are not in the center of the universe, but we are not in the VIP box beyond the edge, either. To say the least, this is a profoundly disturbing realization. It is the true content of ecological awareness. Harman puts it this way:

> On the one hand, scientism insists that human consciousness is nothing special, and should be naturalized just like everything else. On the other hand, it also wants to preserve knowledge as a special kind of relation to the world quite different from the relations that raindrops and lizards have to the world. . . . For all their gloating over the fact that people are pieces of matter just like everything else, they also want to claim that the very status of that utterance is somehow special. For them, raindrops know nothing and lizards know very little, and some humans are more knowledgeable than others. This is only possible because thought is given a unique ability to negate and transcend immediate experience, which inanimate matter is never allowed to do in such theories, of course. In short,

for all its *noir* claims that the human doesn't exist, it elevates the structure of human *thought* to the ontological pinnacle.[27]

The effect of this double denial of human supremacy is not unlike one of Hitchcock's signature cinematic techniques, the pull focus. By simultaneously zooming and pulling away, we appear to be in the same place, yet the place seems to distort beyond our control. The two contradictory motions don't cancel one another out. Rather, they reestablish the way we experience "here." The double denial doesn't do away with human experience. Rather, it drastically modifies it in a dizzying manner.

The ecological thought that thinks hyperobjects is not one in which individuals are embedded in a nebulous overarching system, or conversely, one in which something vaster than individuals extrudes itself into the temporary shapes of individuals. Hyperobjects provoke *irreductionist* thinking, that is, they present us with scalar dilemmas in which ontotheological statements about which thing is the most real (ecosystem, world, environment, or conversely, individual) become impossible.[28] Likewise, irony qua absolute distance also becomes inoperative. Rather than a vertiginous antirealist abyss, irony presents us with intimacy with existing nonhumans.

The discovery of hyperobjects and OOO are symptoms of a fundamental shaking of being, a *being-quake*. The ground of being is shaken. There we were, trolling along in the age of industry, capitalism, and technology, and all of a sudden we received information from aliens, information that even the most hardheaded could not ignore, because the form in which the information was delivered was precisely the instrumental and mathematical formulas of modernity itself. The Titanic of modernity hits the iceberg of hyperobjects. The problem of hyperobjects, I argue, is not a problem that modernity can solve. Unlike Latour then, although I share many of his basic philosophical concerns, I believe that we *have* been modern, and that we are only just learning how not to be.

Because modernity banks on certain forms of ontology and epistemology to secure its coordinates, the iceberg of hyperobjects thrusts a genuine and profound philosophical problem into view. It is to address these problems head on that this book exists. This book is part of the apparatus of the Titanic, but one that has decided to dash itself against the hyperobject. This rogue machinery—call it speculative realism, or OOO—has decided to crash the machine, in the name of a social and cognitive configuration to come, whose outlines are only faintly visible in the Arctic mist of hyperobjects. In this respect, hyperobjects have done us a favor. Reality itself intervenes on the side of objects that from the prevalent modern point of view—an emulsion of blank nothingness and tiny particles—are decidedly medium-sized. It turns out that these medium-sized objects are fascinating, horrifying, and powerful.

For one thing, we are inside them, like Jonah in the Whale. This means that every decision we make is in some sense related to hyperobjects. These decisions are not limited to sentences in texts about hyperobjects. When I turn the key in the ignition of my car, I am relating to global warming. When a novelist writes about emigration to Mars, he is relating to global warming. Yet my turning of the key in the ignition is intimately related to philosophical and ideological decisions stemming from the mathematization of knowing and the view of space and time as flat, universal containers (Descartes, Newton). The reason why I am turning my key—the reason why the key turn sends a signal to the fuel injection system, which starts the motor—is one result of a series of decisions about objects, motion, space, and time. Ontology, then, is a vital and contested political terrain. It is on this terrain that this study will concentrate a significant amount of attention. In the menacing shadow of hyperobjects, contemporary decisions to ground ethics and politics in somewhat hastily cobbled together forms of process thinking and relationism might not simply be rash—they might be part of the problem.

The "towering-through" (Heidegger) of the hyperobject into the misty transcendentalism of modernity interrupts the supposed "progress" that thinking has been making toward assimilating the entire universe to a late capitalism-friendly version of *Macbeth,* in which (in the phrase Marx quotes) "all that is solid melts into air."[29] For at the very point at which the melting into air occurs, we catch the first glimpses of the all-too-solid iceberg within the mist. For reasons I give in the second part of this book, I doubt gravely whether capitalism is entirely up for the job of processing hyperobjects. I have argued elsewhere that since the raw machinery of capitalism is reactive rather than proactive, it might contain a flaw that makes it unable to address the ecological emergency fully.[30] Capitalism builds on existing objects such as "raw materials" (whatever comes in at the factory door). The retroactive style of capitalism is reflected in the ideology of "the consumer" and its "demands" that capital then "meets."

The ship of modernity is equipped with powerful lasers and nuclear weapons. But these very devices set off chain reactions that generate yet more hyperobjects that thrust themselves between us and the extrapolated, predicted future. Science itself becomes the emergency break that brings the adventure of modernity to a shuddering halt. But this halt is not in front of the iceberg. *The halting is (an aspect of) the iceberg.* The fury of the engines is precisely how they cease to function, seized up by the ice that is already inside them. The future, a time "after the end of the world," has arrived too early.

Hyperobjects are a good candidate for what Heidegger calls "the last god," or what the poet Hölderlin calls "the saving power" that grows alongside the dangerous power.[31] We were perhaps expecting an eschatological solution from the sky, or a revolution in consciousness—or, indeed, a people's army seizing control of the state. What we got instead came too soon for us to anticipate it. Hyperobjects have dispensed with two hundred years of careful correlationist calibration. The panic and denial and right-wing absurdity about global warming are understandable. Hyperobjects pose numerous threats to individualism, nationalism, anti-intellectualism, racism, speciesism, anthropocentrism, you name it. Possibly even capitalism itself.

With a view to explicating how hyperobjects are already here, this book consists of a diptych that folds around its middle. First, the basic shock of hyperobjects is elucidated: the iceberg appears. In this way, the book preserves the feeling that we humans are playing catch-up with reality. In part 1, "What Are Hyperobjects?," I explore the scope and depth of the quake in being from the viewpoint of "objective" description, trying to evoke the *objectness* of hyperobjects, which consists primordially in their being prior to thinking. The book then cuts ruthlessly to the "reaction shot"—how the dawn of hyperobjects appears for us humans, its implications for our social coexistence, and the thinking that goes along with this coexistence. Hyperobjects are the harbingers of a truly "post-modern" age.[32] Thus part 2 is entitled "The Time of Hyperobjects." All humans, I shall argue, are now aware that they have entered a new phase of history in which nonhumans are no longer excluded or merely decorative features of their social, psychic, and philosophical space. From the most vulnerable Pacific Islander to the most hardened eliminative materialist, everyone must reckon with the power of rising waves and ultraviolet light. This phase is characterized by a traumatic loss of coordinates, "the end of the world." It also consists of an embarrassing shock to the shock troops of critique, in the form of an all-encompassing *hypocrisy* that demonstrates, physically and without compromise, the weirdness of the Lacanian truth that "there is no metalanguage."[33] This truth was by no means secured by poststructuralist and postmodern thinking.

Humans have entered an age of *hypocrisy, weakness,* and *lameness,* terms that have a specific valence and definition that I elucidate in part 2. The overall aesthetic "feel" of the time of hyperobjects is a sense of *asymmetry* between the infinite powers of cognition and the infinite being of things. There occurs a crazy arms race between *what we know* and *what is,* in which the technology of what we know is turned against itself. The arms race sets new parameters for aesthetic experience and action, which I take in the widest possible sense to mean the ways in which relations between beings play out. Very significant consequences for art emerge, and the book ends by outlining some of them.

The frequent visitor to my writing will perhaps be somewhat puzzled, even disconcerted, by the substantial use of Heidegger. In the past I have described Heideggerian philosophy as regressive and unsuitable for thinking some of the more significant features of what I have called *ecology without Nature.* I have come to recognize that it is not so much Heidegger as a type of Heideggerianism against which I have been reacting. If anyone gives us a vivid sense of the uncanny strangeness of coexistence, it is Heidegger. I have also come to understand, against Levinas, that it is indeed on the terrain of ontology that many of the urgent ecological battles need to be fought.

The reasons for my turn to Heidegger are, without doubt, not accept-able to Heideggerianism at large, and this means that certain strands of thinking in Heidegger are also rejected. The concept *world* remains deeply problematic, as the subsection on that concept in part 2 makes clear. The frankly ontotheological positing of humans as the most important entity, and of German humans as the quintessence of this importance, is also ruthlessly rejected. It is through OOO that this book owes its debt to Heidegger. There is something attractive—perhaps suspiciously so, as it resonates with a Christian image—in the idea of a stone that the builders rejected becoming the cornerstone of new thinking. The time of hyperobjects makes use of what appears merely to be a broken tool lying around in the workshop of thinking—I refer to Heidegger's tool-analysis, which until Harman's strikingly innovative appropriation of it, lay around in the shop, halfheartedly handled by pragmatism and ignored by deconstruction. The turn to the tool-analysis in OOO and in "thing theory" is welcome.[34]

By some strange, non-Hegelian magic of the negative, it is this very tool that is the "saving power" of which Hölderlin and Heidegger speak, a mute, brutal thing resonant with all the anthropocentric force of accu-mulated human prejudice. The Pixar movie *Wall•E* is the story of how broken tools save the Earth.[35] So is this book. In *Wall•E,* the broken tools are two obsessive robots: one, the protagonist, with his melancholy col-lection of human trinkets; the other, a cleaning robot whose compulsion to wipe every surface forces him between two closing sliding doors at a crucial juncture. In this book, the two robots are the two parts of the book. Part 1 of *Hyperobjects* is the obsessive melancholic that catalogs the surfaces and dimensions of the hyperobject. Part 2 is the compulsive robot that holds open the sliding doors of history just as they appear to be snapping shut, imprisoning us in modernity forever.

Since it is not possible for me not to anthropomorphize, since I am a human, the first part of the book will also contain some thoughts on hyperobjects as they pertain to humans. Yet since I am not totally stuck "inside" some casket-like space of humanness, the second part of the book will contain some further details on the qualities of hyperobjects themselves. Hyperobjects seem to have five interrelated qualities. Or rather these qualities provide more and more accurate modes of human attunement to hyperobjects. Part 1 thus starts with an overall quality of hyperobjects *(viscosity)* and moves through three categories until we arrive at the fifth section (on *interobjectivity*), in which it becomes clear that hyperobjects force us to rethink what we mean by *object*. The three categories are *nonlocality, temporal undulation,* and *phasing*.

The human reaction to the time of hyperobjects takes three basic forms, which I designate using the three sections in part 2. The first form of reaction is the dissolution of the notion of *world*. The second reaction is the impossibility of maintaining cynical distance, the dominant ideological mode of our age (or rather, the time *before* the time of hyperobjects). The third reaction has to do with what kinds of aesthetic experience and practice are now thinkable in the time of hyperobjects. Throughout part 2, I argue that the time of hyperobjects is an age of *hypocrisy, weakness,* and *lameness*.

PART I

What Are Hyperobjects?

The awful shadow of some unseen power.
—PERCY SHELLEY

Viscosity

I do not access hyperobjects across a distance, through some transparent medium. Hyperobjects are here, right here in my social and experiential space. Like faces pressed against a window, they leer at me menacingly: their very nearness is what menaces. From the center of the galaxy, a supermassive black hole impinges on my awareness, as if it were sitting in the car next to me at the traffic lights. Every day, global warming burns the skin on the back of my neck, making me itch with physical discomfort and inner anxiety. Evolution unfolds in my genome as my cells divide and mutate, as my body clones itself, as one of my sperm cells mixes it up with an egg. As I reach for the iPhone charger plugged into the dashboard, I reach into evolution, into the *extended phenotype* that doesn't stop at the edge of my skin but continues into all the spaces my humanness has colonized.[1]

On every right side mirror of every American car is engraved an ontological slogan that is highly appropriate for our time: OBJECTS IN MIRROR ARE CLOSER THAN THEY APPEAR. Not only do I fail to access hyperobjects at a distance, but it also becomes clearer with every passing day that "distance" is only a psychic and ideological construct designed to protect me from the nearness of things. There is a reason why they call it "the schizophrenic defense" when someone has a psychotic break. Could it be that the very attempt to distance is not a product of some true assessment of things, but is and was always a defense mechanism against

a threatening proximity? So is that environmentalist speech that demands that we "get back to Nature"—that is, achieve a greater intimacy
with things—only half right? Is there is nothing to "get back to," since the
problem is not that things are truly distant, but that they are in our face—
they *are* our face? Is this very environmentalism caught up in warding
off the threatening nearness of things? That the concept *Nature* is an
"object in mirror" whose referents are much, much closer than a view
from the front seat of an SUV careering across the Tibetan plateau; or
from behind a camera while I stand in the Arches National Park, Utah;
or even as I unzip my tent flap in the middle of "it"?

In the sections that compose part 1, I attempt to specify hyperobjects
with greater and greater accuracy. There is a logic to the sequence, beginning with this section, in which I describe hyperobjects as *viscous*.

While hyperobjects are near, they are also very uncanny. Some days,
global warming fails to heat me up. It is strangely cool or violently stormy.
My intimate sensation of prickling heat at the back of my neck is only a
distorted print of the hot hand of global warming. I do not feel "at home"
in the biosphere. Yet it surrounds me and penetrates me, like the Force
in *Star Wars*. The more I know about global warming, the more I realize
how pervasive it is. The more I discover about evolution, the more I realize how my entire physical being is caught in its meshwork. Immediate,
intimate symptoms of hyperobjects are vivid and often painful, yet they
carry with them a trace of unreality. I am not sure where I am anymore.
I am at home in feeling not at home. Hyperobjects, not some hobbit hole,
not some national myth of the homeland, have finally forced me to see
the truth in Heidegger.

The more I struggle to understand hyperobjects, the more I discover
that I am stuck to them. They are all over me. They are me. I feel like Neo
in *The Matrix,* lifting to his face in horrified wonder his hand coated in
the mirrorlike substance into which the doorknob has dissolved, as his
virtual body begins to disintegrate. "Objects in mirror are closer than
they appear." The mirror itself has become part of my flesh. Or rather,
I have become part of the mirror's flesh, reflecting hyperobjects everywhere. I can see data on the mercury and other toxins in my blood. At
Taipei Airport, a few weeks after the Fukushima disaster, I am scanned

for radiation since I have just transited in Tokyo. Every attempt to pull myself free by some act of cognition renders me more hopelessly stuck to hyperobjects. Why?

They are already here. I come across them later, I find myself poisoned with them, I find my hair falling out. Like an evil character in a David Lynch production, or a ghost in M. Knight Shyamalan's *The Sixth Sense,* hyperobjects haunt my social and psychic space with an always-already. My normal sense of time as a container, or a racetrack, or a street, prevents me from noticing this always-already, from which time oozes and flows, as I shall discuss in a later section ("Temporal Undulation"). What the demonic *Twin Peaks* character Bob reveals, for our purposes, is something about hyperobjects, perhaps about objects in general.[2] Hyperobjects are agents.[3] They are indeed more than a little demonic, in the sense that they appear to straddle worlds and times, like fiber optic cables or electromagnetic fields. And they are demonic in that through them causalities flow like electricity.

We haven't thought this way about things since the days of Plato. What Ion and Socrates call a *daimon,* we call electromagnetic waves, which amplify plucked guitar strings and broadcast them through a PA system.[4] Since the beginning of the Anthropocene, but particularly since the start of the Great Acceleration (the 1940s), these demonic channels have become more and more powerful. Human artists have become rhapsodes: Jackson Pollock, John Cage, William Burroughs. Under these circumstances, it becomes possible to understand why many have thought art to be a domain of evil.

When I listen to My Bloody Valentine, I do not reach out toward the sound—instead, I am assaulted from the inside by a pulsation that is also sound, a physical force that almost lifts me off the floor. Kevin Shields's guitar sears into me like an x-ray, scanning me, strafing me. The chords lurch around one another sickeningly, gliding in and out of tune, amassing towers of harmonics through dissonance. Distortion pulps and fragments the sound into a welter of gravel and thick oil. Yet try as I might, I can't tear my ears away. The music is so beautiful. I wonder how Odysseus felt, strapped to the mast as he heard the Sirens. I think I can hear singing, a quiet, wistful song. Inside the bubble is the pattering ooze of guitar distortion washed with cymbals. I think that this music could liquefy my internal organs, make my ears bleed (this has actually occurred), send me into seizures. Perhaps it could kill me. To be killed by intense beauty, what a Keatsian way to die. I think of the planet-destroying sound system of the band Disaster Area in Douglas Adams's *The Hitchhiker's Guide to the Galaxy,* which begins Ursula Heise's discussion of planetary consciousness.[5]

My Bloody Valentine's singer, Belinda Butcher, places her voice on either side of the stereo image, at extreme right and left. Her voice becomes the fragile bubble container for the onslaught of glittering guitar fog from Kevin Shields. It becomes ambient (the Latin *ambo* means "on both sides"). We hardly hear it. It's as if her voice contained a hyperobject, the surging, sickening slides, lurches, and poundings of guitar. In this sense My Bloody Valentine's music is more truly ecological than representational "nature" music, and more uncompromising than quiet ambient music.

Kant argues that aesthetic experience is an attunement *(Stimmung).*[6] But I do not attune to My Bloody Valentine. Rather, My Bloody Valentine tunes to me, pursuing my innards, searching out the resonant frequencies of my stomach, my intestines, the pockets of gristle in my face. Yet always with those beautiful chords, the ones that lash you to the mast. The walls of feedback that the Velvet Underground inaugurated in "Heroin" are sound as hyperobject, a sound from which I can't escape, a viscous sonic latex. It hurts me. A strange masochistic dimension of aesthetic experience opens up underneath the one in which the "art object" and I appear to be held in a perfect Kantian mind meld. Prior to this appearance of the beautiful, there must already be a sticky mesh of viscosity in which I find myself tuned by the object, an aesthetic uterus that subtends even my supposed acts of transcendence. Hyperobjective art makes visible, audible, and legible this intrauterine experience that Sartre loathed, the "sly solidarity" between things: "The slimy is myself."[7] Viscosity for Sartre is how a hand feels when it plunges into a large jar of honey—it begins to dissolve: "The sugary death of the For-itself (like that of a wasp which sinks into the jam and drowns in it)."[8] The old art theories that separated sweetness and power collapse.[9] For sweetness, it turns out, just is power: the most powerful thing.

It is possible to imagine a sound so piercing that it could rearrange our inner structure and result in our death, and no doubt the Pentagon is now developing, and possibly even deploying, such sound weapons. When the inside of a thing coincides perfectly with its outside, that is called *dissolution* or *death*. Given a large enough hyperobject (say the entropy of the entire universe) all beings exist in the jaws of some form of death, which is why Buddhist thangkas of the Wheel of Life depict the six realms of existence cycling around within the open, toothy mouth of Yama, the Lord of Death. Reza Negarestani imagines the machinations of Earth below its surface as a series of agents that humans unwittingly unleash on themselves and the rest of Earth, in a demonic parody of environmentalist nonfiction: "The surface biosphere has never been separate from the cthulhoid architecture of the nether."[10] Dust and wind are imagined as swirling beings that generate a "mistmare," enveloping humans in a literal "fog of war" in which America and the Middle East haplessly wage war on behalf of cthonic agents they do not understand: weather as monster.[11]

A baby vomits curdled milk. She learns to distinguish between the vomit and the not-vomit, and comes to know the not-vomit as self.[12] Every subject is formed at the expense of some viscous, slightly poisoned substance, possibly teeming with bacteria, rank with stomach acid. The parent scoops up the mucky milk in a tissue and flushes the wadded package down the toilet. Now we know where it goes. For some time we may have thought that the U-bend in the toilet was a convenient curvature of ontological space that took whatever we flush down it into a totally different dimension called *Away*, leaving things clean over here. Now we know better: instead of the mythical land Away, we know the waste goes to the Pacific Ocean or the wastewater treatment facility. Knowledge of the hyperobject Earth, and of the hyperobject biosphere, presents us with viscous surfaces from which nothing can be forcibly peeled. There is no Away on this surface, no here and no there. In effect, the entire Earth is a wadded tissue of vomited milk.

The very attempt to introduce coherence in psychic and social space has resulted in the return of this wadded tissue, not the revenge of Gaia but something far more disturbingly prosaic yet also hauntingly weird.[13] Light itself is the most viscous thing of all, since nothing can surpass its speed. Radiation is Sartre's jar of honey par excellence, a luminous honey that reveals our bone structure as it seeps around us. Again, it's not a matter of making some suicidal leap into the honey, but of discovering that we are already inside it. This is it folks, this is ecological interconnectedness, come in and join the fun! But I see, you are already here. Hyperobjects are *viscous.*

Along with this vivid intimacy goes a sense of unreality. Thus, there emerges the fully demonic quality of contemporary ecological experience, mimed in post-1945 art. The intensity of the hyperobject's aesthetic trace seems unreal in its very luminosity. The vastness of the hyperobject's scale makes smaller beings—people, countries, even continents—seem like an illusion, or a small colored patch on a large dark surface. How can we know it is real? What does *real* mean? The threat of global warming is not only political, but also ontological. The threat of unreality is the very sign of reality itself. Like a nightmare that brings news of some real psychic intensity, the shadow of the hyperobject announces the existence of the hyperobject.

We find ourselves caught in them. The name of this trap is *viscosity.* In the final episode of *Twin Peaks,* Dale Cooper enters the demonic Black Lodge. He is offered a cup of coffee, his favorite beverage, the drink with which we often mark time (as with the coffee break or morning coffee). Yet when he tries to drink it, he finds that the coffee has frozen into a solid plastic lump of darkness. It is as if time has stopped. Then he tries to pour it again, and it spills on his legs, burning him. Time flows at a human speed. Then when he pours it once again, it oozes out of the cup like the "burnt engine oil" whose smell coats the surface of the entrance to the Black Lodge. What is real? It is as if we are seeing the same events happening from the points of view of different beings, with very different temporalities. The prophetic dreams and dreamlike sequences (and how can we truly distinguish between what is a dream and what is merely "dreamlike"?) in *Twin Peaks* are of a piece with this molten time. Cooper warns Laura Palmer before she has even been murdered, speaking to her from inside the Black Lodge. Viscosity is a feature of the way in which time emanates from objects, rather than being a continuum in which they float.

When the BP Deepwater Horizon disaster happened in 2010, non-humans and humans alike were coated with a layer of oil, inside and outside their bodies (Figure 3). While the media has moved on to other spectacles, the oil continues to act. Around Chernobyl there is an uncanny dead zone, the Zone of Alienation, named the Red Forest for when the trees had become ginger brown and died (the notion of *zones* will become a significant analytical tool later in this book). In 2002 three wandering woodcutters in a north Georgian forest near the village of Liya discovered two small cylinders of radioactive strontium-90 that kept them warm for a few hours' sleep before they succumbed to radiation

FIGURE 3. Deepwater Horizon oil spill captured by NASA's Terra satellite on May 24, 2010. Humans now have the ability to track gigantic fluid forms such as this— and the ability to make them.

sickness and burning.[14] Strontium-90 emits beta rays, quanta that can pass through skin; beta rays release a great deal of heat when they strike other quanta. The exposed strontium-90 sources emitted thirty-five thousand curies each, giving a fatal dose of radiation in two minutes. The strontium-90 was used in radiothermal generators of electricity: the Soviet Union employed many in remote locations, while there are radio-thermal batteries aboard Voyagers 1 and 2, which are now exiting the Solar System, passing through the heliosheath, a hyperobject consisting of slowed, turbulent solar winds formed into million-mile-wide bubbles as they interact with the interstellar medium.

In 2006, beagles encased in concrete were dug up near to the exit of the highway that leads to the University of California at Davis. From the 1960s to the 1980s in the Laboratory for Energy Related Research, sci-entists had exposed the dogs throughout their necessarily brief lives to strontium-90 and radium-226. Feeding began twenty-one days into ges-tation (the dogs were fed "by maternal administration"). The dogs who ingested the maximum 12 microcuries per day, died after a median 5.2 years.[15] One microcurie is the radiation activity of a millionth of a gram of radium-226. The most spectacular scalar discrepancies exist between the size of an ionizing particle emitted by an isotope and the long-term effects of radiation on lifeforms and other entities.

At the Trinity Test Site in New Mexico, weird light-green glass (trini-tite) was formed when the nuclear explosion fused sand to ten thousand times hotter than the surface of the sun (Figure 4). Robert Oppenheimer named it Trinity after one of John Donne's Holy Sonnets: "Batter my heart, three-personed God."[16] Oppenheimer thought of Shiva after the explosion: "I am become death, the shatterer of worlds."[17] Oppenheimer had not become death. That role goes fair and square to the hyperobject.

It's oil we must thank for burning a hole in the notion of *world*. What kind of hole? A sticky hole, like a ball of tar. Return to the scene in which Neo touches a mirror in *The Matrix*, the mirror seems to melt and coat his flesh, and he raises his hand and regards it with fascinated horror. The mirror has ceased to be merely a reflective surface; it has become a viscous substance that adheres to his hand. The very thing that we use to reflect becomes an object in its own right, liquid and dark like oil in the dim light of the room in which Neo has taken the red pill. The usual reading of this scene is that Neo's reality is dissolving. If we stay on the level of the sticky, oily mirror, however, we obtain an equally powerful reading. It's not reality but the subject that dissolves, the very capacity to "mirror" things, to be separate from the world like someone looking at a reflection in a mirror—removed from it by an ontological sheath of reflective glass. The sticky mirror demonstrates the truth of what phenomenology calls *ingenuousness* or *sincerity*.[18] Objects are what they are, in the sense that no matter what we are aware of, or how, there they are, impossible to shake off. In the midst of irony, there you are, being ironic. Even mirrors are what they are, no matter what they reflect.[19] In its sincerity, reality envelops us like a film of oil. The mirror becomes a *substance*, an object. Hyperobjects push the reset button on sincerity, just as Neo discovers that the mirror no longer distances his image from him in a nice, aesthetically manageable way, but sticks to him.

FIGURE 4. Trinitite, an entirely new mineral formed by the explosion of the Gadget, the first nuclear device. Photograph by Shaddack.

The more we fight phenomenological sincerity with our reason, the more glued we figure out we are, which is what it feels like to live in *risk society*: a society in which growing scientific awareness of risk (from toxic chemicals, for instance) changes the nature of democracy itself.[20] But it also means that we have exited modernity. The beautiful reversibility of the oily, melting mirror speaks to something that is happening in a global warming age, precisely because of hyperobjects: the simultaneous dissolution of reality and the overwhelming presence of hyperobjects, which stick to us, which are us. The Greeks called it *miasma,* the way bloodguilt sticks to you.[21] What Husserl noticed—that objects can't be exhausted by perception—has a viscous consequence. There is no Goldilocks position that's just right from which to view objects. What OOO asserts is that one can extend this insight to nonhuman entities. In a sense, all objects are caught in the sticky goo of viscosity, because they never ontologically exhaust one another even when they smack headlong into one another. A good example of viscosity would be radioactive materials. The more you try to get rid of them, the more you realize you can't get rid of them. They seriously undermine the notion of "away." Out of sight is no longer out of mind, because if you bury them in Yucca Mountain, you know that they will leach into the water table. And where will that mountain be 24.1 thousand years from now?

Neo's melting mirror is a perfect rendition of the phenomenological sincerity inherent in the Great Acceleration, when we humans find ourselves embedded in earthly reality, not circling above it in geostationary orbit. This discovery is made precisely through our advanced technology and measuring instruments, not through worn peasant shoes and back-to-Nature festivals: "By coming to terms with an increasing range of objects, human beings do not become nihilistic princes of darkness, but actually the most sincere creatures the earth has ever seen."[22] The fact that "there is no metalanguage" (according to Lacan) does not mean that we are forever floating in outer space, but quite the opposite: we are glued to our phenomenological situation.[23]

The mirror of science melts and sticks to our hand. The very tools we were using to objectify things, to cover Earth's surface with shrink wrap, become a blowtorch that burns away the glass screen separating humans from Earth, since every measurement is now known as an alteration, as quantum-scale measurements make clear. Quantum objects are viscous. Complementarity means that when you nudge a quantum, it sticks to the nudging device such that you can't disentangle them. Rather than dissolving objects into nothingness, quantum theory makes them sticky. If you stretch this stickiness, how far would it go? At the quantum level, *to measure* is just *to deflect* with a photon or electron (and so forth). Thus complemenarity ensues, in which what we see is glued to the equipment that sees it.

Niels Bohr took this to be a warning not to think of quantum phenomena as real, but as correlations to (human) instruments. Instruments and quanta form a whole that cannot be further analyzed.[24] To this extent, as Bohr puts it, "There is no quantum world."[25] But an equally plausible view breaks the taboo on ontological interpretations and argues that the entanglement of equipment and quanta happens because of some deep further fact about the quantum (or even subquantum) level.[26] Likewise, Einstein's relativity has been taken to give a green light to relativism. Yet relativity plausibly frees nonhuman objects from their exclusive tie to humans, in a blow to anthropocentrism that continues the Copernican Revolution. The perspective of any human on the universe, whether they are on Earth or on a starship, is now known for sure to be only one of a vast plenitude of perspectives based on relative position and velocity.

Nonlocality

When I look at the sun gleaming on the solar panels on my roof, I am watching global warming unfold. Carbon compounds and other molecules in the upper atmosphere magnify the burning intensity of the sun in the Great Central Valley of California. Yet I do not see global warming as such. I see this brilliant blade of sunlight, burning the top of my head as I watch it with half-closed eyes reflecting off the burnished, sapphire surface of the solar panels. The manifold that I witness is not merely a "subjective impression," but is rather just this collusion between sunlight, solar panels, roof, and eyes. Yet global warming is not here. Hyperobjects are *nonlocal*.

Nuclear radiation is not visible to humans. The nuclear accidents at Chernobyl and Fukushima bathed beings thousands of miles away in unseen alpha, beta, and gamma particles, as radioactive specks floated in air currents across Europe and the Pacific. Days, weeks, months, or years later, some humans die of radiation sickness. Strange mutagenic flowers grow.

Likewise, endocrine disruptors penetrate my body through my skin, my lungs, and my food. The disruptors in pesticides such as Roundup, a cousin of Agent Orange (also made by Monsanto), often dioxins of some kind, start cascading reactions in my body, interfering with the production and circulation of hormones. I have no idea what it was that I ate, or whether it was that field I walked through in Norfolk, England, the air redolent with the potent pungency of pesticide—one could almost see it glistening on the stalks in the rich arable land of a teenage holiday. Perhaps it was some other less vividly recalled moment. Yet statistics tell me, obliquely, never able to point to a direct causal link, that my cancer may have come from an endocrine disruptor. Hyperobjects seem to inhabit a Humean causal system in which association, correlation, and probability are the only things we have to go on, for now. That's why it's so easy for Big Tobacco and global warming deniers: of course there is no direct proof of a causal link.

Post-Humean causality is by no means a matter of "objective" versus "subjective" impressions, let alone a matter of human reality versus nonhuman reality. Rather it's a matter of different levels of causality. It's a matter of how entities manifest for other entities, whether they are human, or sentient, or not. Nuclear radiation-for the flower turns its leaves a strange shade of red. Global warming-for the tomato farmer rots the tomatoes. Plastic-for the bird strangles it as it becomes entangled in a set of six-pack rings. What we are dealing with here are aesthetic effects that are directly causal. The octopus of the hyperobject emits a cloud of ink as it withdraws from access. Yet this cloud of ink is a cloud of effects and affects. These phenomena are not themselves global warming or radiation: action at a distance is involved. A gamma particle is a wonderful example of a profound confusion of *aisthēsis* and *praxis,* perceiving and doing. A gamma particle is an ultra-high-frequency photon. In illuminating things, it alters things: flesh, paper, brains.

The subject of gamma rays brings up the source of the title of this section: quantum theory. Quantum theory is a nonmaterialist theory of physical substances. Antirealism appropriates quantum theory, since quantum theory supposedly shows reality is fuzzy or deeply correlated with perception and so forth. Quantum theory is the only existing theory to establish firmly that things really do exist beyond our mind (or any mind). Quantum theory positively guarantees that real objects exist! Not only that—these objects exist beyond one another. Quantum theory does this by viewing phenomena as quanta, as discrete "units" as described in *Unit Operations* by OOO philosopher Ian Bogost.[1] "Units" strongly resemble OOO "objects."[2] Thinking in terms of units counteracts problematic features of thinking in terms of systems. Consider the so-called black body radiation problem. Classical thermodynamics essentially combines the energy of different waves to figure out the total energy of a system. The black box in question is a form of oven. As the temperature in the oven increases, results given by summing the wave states according to classical theory become absurd, tending to infinity.

By seeing the energy in the black box as discrete quanta ("units"), the correct result is obtained. Max Planck's discovery of this approach gave birth to quantum theory. Now consider perception, for the sake of which antirealism usually cites quantum theory. What does quantum theory show about our mental interactions with things? Perceptual, sensual phenomena, such as hardness and brilliance, are at bottom quantum mechanical effects. I can't put my hand through this table because it is statistically beyond unlikely that the quanta at the tip of my finger could penetrate the resistance wells in the quanta on the table's surface. *That's what solidity is.* It's an averagely correct experience of an aggregate of discrete quanta. This statistical quality, far from being a problem, is the first time humans have been able to formalize supposedly experiential phenomena such as solidity. What some people find disturbing about quantum theory (once in a gajillion times I can put my finger through the table) is precisely evidence for the *reality* of things.[3]

Quantum theory specifies that quanta withdraw from one another, including the quanta with which we measure them. In other words, quanta really are discrete, and one mark of this discreteness is the constant translation or mistranslation of one quantum by another. Thus, when you set up quanta to measure the position of a quantum, its momentum withdraws, and vice versa. Heisenberg's uncertainty principle states that when an "observer"—not a subject per se, but a measuring device involving photons or electrons (or whatever)—makes an observation, at least one aspect of the observed is occluded.[4] Observation is as much part of the universe of objects as the observable, not some ontologically different state (say of a subject). More generally, what Bohr called complementarity ensures that no quantum has total access to any other quantum. Just as a focusing lens makes one object appear sharper while others appear blurrier, one quantum variable comes into sharp definition at the expense of others.[5] This isn't about how a human knows an object, but how a photon interacts with a photosensitive molecule. Some phenomena are irreducibly undecidable, both wavelike and particle-like. The way an electron encounters the nucleus of an atom involves a dark side. Objects withdraw from each other at a profound physical level. OOO is deeply congruent with the most profound, accurate, and testable theory of physical reality available. Actually it would be better to say it the other way around: quantum theory works because it's object-oriented.

Probing the quantum world is a form of auto-affection: one is using quanta to explore quanta. Bohr argued that quantum phenomena don't simply concatenate themselves with their measuring devices. They're *identical* to them: the equipment and the phenomena form an indivisible whole.[6] This "quantum coherence" applies at temperatures close to absolute zero, where particles become the "same" thing (Bose–Einstein condensates), or in a very hot plasma (Fermi–Dirac condensates). To an electron, an ultracold or ultrahot substance may appear transparent, as if it didn't exist at all.[7] Macroscale objects approximate separate-seeming entities that in some deeper sense are the same thing. Nanoscale cogwheels get stuck because when tiny things approach one another, Casimir forces glue them together. The cogs become indistinguishable.[8] They no longer function mechanically, as external to one another.[9] Nothing is radically external to anything else: particles don't clunk onto each other like little metal balls in an executive's toy.[10] Rough approximations notwithstanding, reality is not a machine.[11] Quantum theory extends the nonmechanism inherent in relativity theory: "The classical idea of the separability of the world into distinct but interacting parts is no longer valid or relevant."[12] Quantum theory is performative too: if it walks and quacks like an electron, it is one.[13] Quantum performativity strongly resembles evolutionary performativity, commonly called "satisficing": as a duck, you just have to look and quack enough like a duck to pass on your genes.[14] What hyperobjects do is make us acknowledge the reality of what OOO calls *execution*.

Nonlocality is a technical term in quantum theory. Alain Aspect, Einstein's student David Bohm, Anton Zeilinger, and others have shown that the Einstein-Podolsky-Rosen paradox concerning quantum theory is an empirical fact.[15] Einstein, Rosen, and Podolsky argued that if quantum theory were telling us something true about the universe, then you would be able to entangle particles.[16] You can then send one particle some information (make it spin a certain way), and the other(s) will instantly spin in complementary ways. This works to an arbitrary distance—that is, whether two yards, two miles or two light years apart. According to the accepted view, this should fail to happen, since it implies signals traveling faster than light. Zeilinger has demonstrated nonlocal phenomena using entangled particles on either side of Vienna, between two Canary Islands, and between orbiting satellites.[17]

Unless you want to believe that the speed of light can be violated—a notion that gives physicists the jitters—you might have to accept that reality just is nonlocal. Nonlocality deals a crushing blow to the idea of discrete tiny things floating around in an infinite void, since there is strictly no "around" in which these things float: one is unable to locate them in a specific region of spacetime. This void is a remnant of Christian ontology left over from a condemnation by the Bishop of Paris in 1277 (with Pope John XXI's blessing) of doctrines that limited the power of God: Thou shalt not imagine that God couldn't create anything he likes. God is powerful enough to create an infinite void; therefore, he did.[18] Seventeenth-century science adopted this idea, for no well-worked-out reason. In some deep sense there's no (single, firm, separate) photon as such. If biology discovers how entangled lifeforms are, quantum entanglement opens a more profound interconnectedness.

Nonlocality means something is profoundly wrong with atomism.[19] Moreover, objects have blurred boundaries at scales considerably larger than we used to think. Photosynthesizing molecules in chloroplasts, the symbiotic bacteria that make plants green, put photons into coherence. When a photon enters the molecule the photon occupies many positions at once.[20] Other recent developments have shown nonlocality to operate in objects as large as molecules and the buckyball-shaped fullerenes. These objects are huge compared with electrons and photons, about as huge compared to electrons as you and I are compared with fullerenes. In early 2010 Aaron O'Connell and other physicists at the University of

California, Santa Barbara, established quantum coherence in an object visible to the eye: a tiny fork vibrating and not vibrating simultaneously.[21] O'Connell and others put the fork thirty microns long into its ground state by cooling it down to almost absolute zero, then they ran a phonon—a quantum of vibration—through it. Their naked eyes could see it vibrating and not vibrating simultaneously, a spectacular and surprising result, from the point of view of the Standard Model of quantum theory.[22] Soon after that, tiny quantum-scale magnets in birds' eyes were found to guide birds, not physical electromagnetic fields but rather aesthetic (nonlocal) forms of those fields.[23]

How might ontology think nonlocality? The Copenhagen Interpretation of quantum theory spearheaded by Bohr holds that though quantum theory is a powerfully accurate heuristic tool, peering underneath this tool to see what kind of reality might underlie it would be absurd because quantum phenomena are "irreducibly inaccessible to us." Bohr argued that our measurement is "indivisible" with what is measured.[24] Yet the refusal to get ontological is already ontological: Newtonian atomism, with its granular view of matter, is left substantially alone. Things were less settled at Copenhagen than the victors' spin portrayed.[25] Bohm, Basil Hiley, Zeilinger, Antony Valentini, and others proceed along lines established by De Broglie: an "ontological interpretation" that takes Bohr's "indivisibility" to pertain to objects beyond (human) cognition.[26] Bohm postulated an "implicate order" in which particles are manifestations of some deeper process, like waves on the ocean.[27] Just as ocean waves subside, particles fold back into the implicate order. "Particles" are abstractions of a Leibnizian reality in which everything is enfolded in everything else.

The ontological interpretation is bad for holism as well as atomism. Holism requires some kind of top-level object consisting of parts that are separate from the whole and hence replaceable: another modulation of mechanism, holist protestations notwithstanding.[28] According to the Bohmian view, you aren't part of a larger whole. Everything is enfolded in everything as "flowing movement."[29] Unlike the Copenhagen Interpretation, the ontological interpretation is noncorrelationist: particles withdraw from one another, not because humans are observing them in certain ways, but because the implicate order is withdrawn from itself.

A hyperobject if ever there was one: an auto-affective ocean that lives between the size of an electron (10^{-17} cm) and the Planck length (10^{-33} cm). This whole might be strictly unanalyzable: the implicate order has an irreducible dark side because it's made of rotations within rotations, or as Harman puts it, "objects wrapped in objects wrapped in objects."[30]

Implication and explication suggest substances we think of as "matter" being enfolded and unfolded from something deeper. Even if it were the case that OOO should defer to physics, in the terms set by physics itself objects aren't made "of" any one thing in particular. Just as there is no top level, there may be no bottom level that is not a substantial, formed object. Electrons come and go, change into other particles, radiate energy. An electron is real. Yet in the act of becoming or unbecoming an electron, it's a statistical performance: "Quantum theory requires us to give up the idea that the electron, or any other object has, by itself, any intrinsic properties at all. Instead, each object should be regarded as something containing only incompletely defined potentialities that are developed when an object interacts with an appropriate system."[31] To argue thus approaches Harman's image of the withdrawn-ness of objects as a "subterranean creature."[32] Thus, the "something deeper" from which the electron unfolds is also withdrawn.

If they lack such a hidden essence, objects must be spatially external to one another like machine parts. A view such as this legitimates instrumentalization, which reduces objects to other objects. Objects would relate externally. Yet we can't predict the future state of reality even in principle, because we can't anticipate the position of every particle. It is impossible not only because this would take too long (it would) or break the speed of light, not only because of complementarity, but for a more fundamental reason, having nothing to do with epistemology or correlationism: there are no particles as such, no matter as such, only discretely quantized objects.[33] If this is the case at the most fine-grained level we currently know, then it will be much more so at higher scales, the scales on which evolution, biology, and ecology happen.

At the quantum level, genuine nonlocality operates: two entangled photons, two entangled electrons can indeed appear to influence one another at a distance. Einstein found precisely this aspect highly disturbing: he called it "spooky action at a distance."[34] The influence appears to be simultaneous: in other words, it could be faster than light. Since we now know that even a single photon obeys the speed of light, the supposed information transfer is indeed spooky. Something like telepathy or backward-in-time causation may be necessary to allow us to continue to cleave to the ontology of discrete particles.[35]

If there is indeed a physical basis for nonlocality—a subquantum level of which what appear to be two particles are simply the peaks of ripples—then this level is a hyperobject.[36] Below 10^{-17} cm, the size of an electron, there is as much a difference in size as one approaching the Planck length of 10^{-33} cm as there is between you and an electron. What might be down there? Is it really just nothing at all, just pure relationships? Such a hyperobject would be massively distributed "in" time and space in the most radical sense. Actually, "in" is not quite accurate. Since on this view time and space are only emergent properties of objects larger than some threshold size, the hypothetical subquantum hyperobject is "everywhere."[37] Yet I do not wish to suggest that true nonlocality applies to all hyperobjects. The action at a distance that hyperobjects manifest is nonlocal, but not in the quantum sense.

There are two ways to think about this more carefully, however. The first approach is to consider the way in which entities that are nowhere nearly as small as traditional quanta such as electrons seem to exhibit nonlocality. As we saw, nonlocal effects have now been observed in objects considerably larger than traditional quanta: buckyball-shaped fullerenes; certain configurations of carbon engineered by nanotechnology; and a tiny metal fork thirty microns long, placed in a state of quantum superposition and seen with the naked eye to "breathe," vibrating and not vibrating at the same time.[38] Photons entering the photosynthesizing molecules in a chloroplast go into superposition—such molecules are galaxy-scale objects relative to regular quanta.[39] Again, a bird detects the quantum signature of an electromagnetic wave, not the wave itself, by means of a quantum scale magnet in its eye. Birds perceive not some traditional material lump, but an aesthetic shape.

Quantum objects are massively distributed both in a conventional (yet still extraordinary) sense, and in a highly unconventional sense. First, the roughly conventional. On De Broglie's view a wave packet is a blob that contains something like a particle, distributed in the wave packet across a range of locations according to probability. The wave packet may be imagined as distributed across a vast area of spacetime. Some physicists use the Solar System as a good enough reference point: the elusive electron is bound to be found somewhere in there. This sounds like a joke but it isn't—it's how Bohm shows undergraduates how to solve for the location of a particle in his textbook on quantum theory.

And now for the unconventional explanation. To say the least, quantum nonlocality seriously forces us to rewrite our ideas of matter and of materialism. Nonlocality is precisely a theory of textuality at the quantum level, in which information is dispersed among particles seemingly occupying different regions of spacetime. If I say reality qua me and you and this essay doesn't really exist, am I a nihilistic postmodernist or a New Ager in academic drag? Yet my colleague in the physics building gets away with asserting that the universe must be a hologram projected from an inscribed surface inside a black hole—that the extent to which we exist is not unlike the extent to which the image on your credit card exists. Bohm uses the analogy of a hologram to describe the "immense ocean of cosmic energy" from which seeming particles are explicated.[40] Images "captured" with a lens conjure single, solid, independent-seeming things. A hologram can't be seen directly, but is a mesh of interference patterns created by light waves bouncing off the object and light waves passing through a beam splitter. When you pass light through the interference pattern, a three-dimensional rendering of the object appears in front of the pattern. Cut a little piece of hologram out, or shine light through a little piece of it (same thing), and you still see a (slightly more blurry) version of the whole object. Every piece of the hologram contains information about the whole.

The quantum real is a play of difference within which particle-like phenomena arise, just as for deconstruction language is a play of difference out of which meaning arises. A hologram is a form of writing.[41] A holographic universe explains nonlocality. Gravity wave detectors reveal suspiciously regular patterns emanating from the cosmic background radiation, as if at some level reality were pixelated—made of regular little "dots" of information: the regularity you'd expect if reality were indeed a projection of an actual hologram.[42] A holographic universe would be a hyperobject—massively distributed in time and space, exhibiting non-local effects that defied location and temporality, cuttable into many parts without losing coherence.

To those great Victorian period discoveries, then—evolution, capital, the unconscious—we must now add spacetime, ecological intercon-nection, and nonlocality. These discoveries all share something insofar as they humiliate the human, decisively decentering us from a place of pampered privilege in the scheme of things. Nonlocality is perhaps the most drastic of all of these, since it implies that the notion of being located at all is only epiphenomenal to a deeper, atemporal implicate order.

Let us now consider very large objects in this light. The intrinsic in-consistency in objects that nonlocality implies—the tiny fork can vibrate and not vibrate at once—will become very significant as we proceed with hyperobjects. Although this is not clear right now, by the end of this sec-tion it should become evident that hyperobjects are contradictory beasts. Moreover, the aesthetic-causal realm in which hyperobjects appear to operate is in some sense nonlocal and atemporal. Or at any rate, such gigantic scales are involved—or rather such knotty relationships between gigantic and intimate scales—that hyperobjects cannot be thought as occupying a series of now-points "in" time or space. They confound the social and psychic instruments we use to measure them—even digital devices have trouble. Global warming requires tremendous computing power to model in a realistic way.

Nonlocality means just that—there is no such thing, at a deep level, as the local. Locality is an abstraction. Metaphorically this applies to hyper-objects. The wet stuff falling on my head in Northern California in early 2011 could have been an effect of the tsunami churning up La Niña in the Pacific and dumping it on the land, La Niña being a manifestation of global warming in any case. The Japan earthquake of 2011 was also plausibly a manifestation of global warming, since changing tempera-tures in the ocean change the pressure on the Earth's crust. Heavy rain is simply a local manifestation of some vast entity that I'm unable directly to see. Thus, the right-wing talking heads are quite correct to be afraid of global warming. It means something ontologically scary about our world. It means that not only is everything interconnected—a fatal blow to individualists everywhere—but also that the "I refute it *thus*" stone-kicking that we've come to expect from reactionaries no longer works.[43] The "Well it's snowing in Boise, Idaho, so global warming is a crock" meme is a desperate attempt to put this ontological genie back in its bottle.

Stop the tape of evolution anywhere and you won't see it. Stand under a rain cloud and it's not global warming you'll feel. Cut your coat into a thousand pieces—you won't find capital in there. Now try pointing to the unconscious. Did you catch it? Hyperobjects compel us to think ecologically, and not the other way around. It's not as if some abstract environmental system made us think like this; rather, plutonium, global warming, pollution, and so on, gave rise to ecological thinking. To think otherwise is to confuse the map with the territory. For sure, the idea of hyperobjects arose because of quantum-theoretical thinking about the nuclei of atoms and electron orbits (nuclear bombs), and because of systems-theoretical approaches to emergent properties of massive amounts of weather data, and so on. Yet hyperobjects are not the data: they are hyperobjects.

When you feel raindrops, you are experiencing climate, in some sense. In particular you are experiencing the climate change known as global warming. But you are never directly experiencing global warming as such. Nowhere in the long list of catastrophic weather events—which will increase as global warming takes off—will you find global warming. But global warming is as real as this sentence. Not only that, it's viscous. It never stops sticking to you, no matter where you move on Earth. How can we account for this? By arguing that global warming, like all hyperobjects, is nonlocal: it's massively distributed in time and space. What does this mean? It means that my experience of the weather in the *hic et nunc* is a false immediacy. It's *never the case* that those raindrops only fall on my head! They are always a manifestation of global warming! In an age of ecological emergency—in an age in which hyperobjects start to oppress us with their terrifying strangeness—we will have acclimatize ourselves to the fact that locality is always a false immediacy. When you see a Magic Eye picture, you realize that all the little squiggles that you thought were individual squiggles are actually distributed pieces of a higher-dimensional object that seems to emerge when you do that crossing-your-eyes thing. In a Magic Eye picture, the cup or flower is distributed throughout the mesh of fuzzy little patches of the image. *The object is already there.* Before we look at it. Global warming is not a function of our measuring devices. Yet because it's distributed across the biosphere and beyond, it's very hard to see as a unique entity. And yet, there it is, raining on us, burning down on us, quaking the Earth, spawning gigantic hurricanes. Global warming is an object of which many things are distributed pieces: the raindrops falling on my head in Northern California. The tsunami that pours through the streets of Japanese towns. The increasing earthquake activity based on changing pressure on the ocean floor. Like the image in a Magic Eye picture, global warming is real, but it involves a massive, counterintuitive perspective shift to see it. Convincing some people of its existence is like convincing some two-dimensional Flatland people of the existence of apples, based on the appearance of a morphing circular shape in their world.

The book *Hiroshima* is a series of testimonies by people in the town when the bomb was dropped.[44] Each witness gives a unique account of the bomb. No single witness experiences the entire bomb. No witness was too close to the bomb: otherwise they would have been evaporated, or quickly incinerated, or blown to pieces. There is a core of human silence around which the witnesses give their testimony. Each testimony is a local manifestation (Bryant's term) of the bomb. Some witnesses assume that they are very close to a powerful conventional bomb, when they are relatively far away from the first nuclear bomb. Each story is told in a narrative present that is necessarily different from the moment at which the bomb hit. The constraints of human physicality and memory displace the bomb. It becomes distant and close at the same time and for the same reasons. Possibly the most uncanny aspect of the bomb is the energy flash that the witnesses experienced as a silent, sudden bathing of everything in light so intense that they couldn't quite see. Light ceases to be a neutral, transparent medium in which everything is illuminated, and becomes a potent force:

With the blood specimen in his left hand, walking in a kind of distraction he had felt all morning, probably because of the dream and his restless night, [Doctor Terufumi Sasaki] started along the main corridor on his way toward the stairs. He was one step beyond an open window when the light of the bomb was reflected, like a gigantic photographic flash, in the corridor. He ducked down on one knee and said to himself . . . "Sasaki, *gamare!* Be brave!" Just then (the building was 1,650 yards from the center), the blast ripped through the hospital. The glasses he was wearing flew off his face; the bottle of blood crashed against one wall; his Japanese slippers zipped out from under his feet—but otherwise, thanks to where he stood, he was untouched.[45]

The disorientation of scale—from "blood specimen" to "the blast ripp[ing] through the hospital"—and of physicality—from slippers to energy flash— is immense. Doctor Sasaki does not see the bomb directly: instead, he sees it "reflected . . . in the corridor." Like Steven Spielberg's version of J. G. Ballard's Jim, he sees the bomb as a photographic flash. The bomb is nonlocal, elsewhere, even as "the blast ripped through the hospital." As Jim says, "I learned a new word today. Atom bomb. It was like a white light in the sky. Like God taking a photograph."[46] The very pinnacle of modernity, encapsulated in Robert Oppenheimer's "I am become death, shatterer of worlds," is the arrival of what Heidegger would have called *the last god,* if he had been able to include nonhumans in his view.[47] Heidegger was unable to ascertain how this last god would manifest in the very core of technological enframing.[48] Like God taking a photograph, the nonhuman sees us, in the white light of its fireball, hotter than the sun. *Like* God, yet unlike a scholastic *causa sui* inhabiting a beyond: rather the prose reminds us that we are dealing with a physical entity. Yet this is a *weird* physical entity, with all the fateful force of that term. To what are we tuning when we attune to the hyperobject? Is this uncertainty not precisely *what* we are heeding? Isn't it the case that the effect delivered to us in the rain, the weird cyclone, the oil slick, is something uncanny?

The most poignant aspect of the stories is how they begin to mesh with the present time of narration. Each storyteller gradually brings her story up to date, slowly showing us how the bomb affected her entire life from that moment on. With increasing distance from the event of the explosion, the reality of the hyperobject looms ever larger. It is like the episode in Wordsworth's autobiographical poem *The Prelude,* in which the boy Wordsworth steals a boat.[49] As he rows away from a mountain, it seems for a while to loom ever larger in his field of vision, as if it were pursuing him, due to a strange parallax effect in which more of a suitably massive object is revealed as one goes farther away from it. This event is surely a good example of what the previous section calls *viscosity.* It is as if the mountain is stuck to Wordsworth, as if it won't let him go. Then the recounting of the episode in the long narrative of *The Prelude* shows how the mountain still haunts him. The moment was what Wordsworth calls a *spot of time,* a traumatic rupture in the continuity of his being, a wound around which his psyche secreted memories, fantasies, thoughts. The self, in this respect, is nothing more than the history of such wounds and the secretions we exuded to protect ourselves from them. Freud puts it this way: the ego is the "precipitate of abandoned object cathexes," like a mystic writing pad whose underlying wax is inscribed with every-thing that was ever drawn on it.[50] The ego is a poem about strangers: the blow of a hand, an abandonment, the hardness of a bed, the warmth of a teddy bear.

How much more is this the case with an object that leaves its alpha, beta, and gamma particle traces in your flesh, traces that alter your DNA for decades. This cannot be dismissed as merely a mental experience (though it is still an *aesthetic* one, in the strict sense that aesthetics has to do with the way one object impinges on another one), and similarly, we shouldn't dismiss Wordsworth's experience as merely mental. As we shall see in the section "Interobjectivity," this is far from a trivial matter of "mere" sensation, but has to do with causality as such. The parallax effect that spooks the young Wordsworth is far more true to something real than he supposed. In a sense, we can expect human egos to be pock-marked with the traces of hyperobjects. We are all burnt by ultraviolet rays. We all contain water in about the same ratio as Earth does, and salt water in the same ratio that the oceans do. We are poems about the hyperobject Earth.

It is clear that DNA has sometimes "learned" to cope with hyperobjects. *Extremophiles* such as the bacterium *Deinococcus radiodurans* suggest the possibility that life and its building blocks (amino acids) arose in conditions that would seem inhospitable to most contemporary lifeforms: on comets, on the surface of ancient Mars, in hot deep rocks, deep within ice, or in boiling undersea vents. *Deinococcus radiodurans* is a startling record of "abandoned object cathexes," encounters with extremes of heat, pressure, and radiation, and with genotoxic chemicals and dehydration. It is a poem about hyperobjects. For this reason, the bacterium is now being engineered to cope with human-made hyperobjects such as mercury spills.

What interests me here is not so much an answer to the question of exactly how lifeforms arose, but the fact that lifeforms themselves are poems about nonlife, in particular highly dangerous entities that could destroy life. Freud argued that the death drive was precisely the attempt to ward off death, to bind stimulation. I have argued that the death drive predates life as such, literally rather than merely figuratively as some psychoanalytic philosophers hold. RNA and the silicate replicators that it attached to in the preliving "RNA World" were molecules that were profoundly out of balance, resembling the liar paradox: "This sentence is false." Replication is just the attempt of such a molecule to "solve" the paradox inscribed within it, and thus to cancel out the disequilibrium, somewhat in the way that water "finds its own level."[51] Yet the very attempt to find a solution—to erase the stain of itself from existence—is what results in its continued existence as a copy of itself. In trying to cancel itself out, the replicator becomes beautifully defended against its environment. Our existence is due to more than a little bit of death, the headlong rush toward equilibrium.

As poems about the shocks that flesh is heir to, lifeforms incorporate and exclude deadly substances. Or better, lifeforms both include and exclude death, in the very same way that a poem is always talking about the paper it is written on and never talking about it. Thus, the Archean (ancient) Earth was awash with cyanide. Yet the very chemical reactions that cyanide induces that can kill lifeforms are also capable, for the very same reasons, of giving rise to complex carbon compounds, the basic elements of amino acids. In a further twist, it's possible that the plentiful cyanide on Earth resulted from reactions that happened when comets rushed through Earth's atmosphere, adding an extraterrestrial level of trauma, specifically *geotrauma*.[52] Certainly a trauma involving hyperobjects. Negarestani imagines the oil under our feet to be what I here call a hyperobject, "an omnipresent planetary entity": a vastly distributed agent with dark designs of its own, co-responsible for turning the surface into a desert, as if it were the prophet of some sinister mystical version of Islam.[53] Negarestani writes, "Petroleum poisons Capital with absolute madness," since it is not really on the side of humans, but is rather "an autonomous chemical weapon belonging to earth as . . . a sentient entity."[54] As one progresses deeper into *Cyclonopedia* (which is part novel, part nonfiction, and part philosophy, and is infused with a sinister intensity), Negarestani's delirious prose begins to look like the upsurge of oil itself, which he imagines as "the Nether Blob. An anorganically synthesized material seething up from the primal interstellar bacterial colonies existing in the bowels of the Earth (from Thomas Gold's theory of the Deep Hot Biosphere)."[55] Negarestani's text is a demonic parody of Nature writing, taking quite literally the idea that nonhumans are dictating the script.

Hiroshima and extremophiles and RNA tell us about the properties of art in general, and thus about causality. Art sends us information from another place. Snow falls in a poem, but it is not really falling.[56] Readers wonder about the intention of a ghostly author whom they think they see behind or within the poem.[57] Painters of paintings live in a society: perhaps the paintings are distorted records of the way that society organized its enjoyment—otherwise known as economics. Or maybe the music we are hearing tells us about the unconscious, coming from some place of archetypes or from the trauma of unspeakable secrets. Here is the poem. But the poem is not here.

Is the *beyond* that might explain the poem more real than the *here* of the poem? There is no way to tell. Like any stranger, the poem is caught between worlds, in an interstitial place that makes worlds as such seem flimsy and constructed—which, of course, they are. The viscous melting mirror takes Neo to a place in between worlds: the world of the Matrix and the world of the machines. The viscous coffee plops out of the cup in the Black Lodge in *Twin Peaks*. These zones are not really "between worlds," since there is nothing between which they exist. All of reality is a bardo, a "between" as Tibetan Buddhism puts it, or rather a series of bardos. Karma, namely the collected tendencies and habits that things run into, is what fuels the bardos. These bardos are simply the relationships between entities. Hyperobjects forces us to experience the bardos.

In some sense, our cognition is "an insect's waking dream."[58] Such is the force of the hyperobject evolution. In some sense, modernity is the story of how oil got into everything. Such is the force of the hyperobject oil. In some sense, cancer is the physical body's expression of radioactive materials. Such is the force of the hyperobject radiation. In some sense, everything changes. Such is the force of the hyperobject universe. Yet the converse is also true. From the standpoint of the end of the universe, everything is equally meaningless, smoothed out into maximum entropy. Yet this massive object is not more real than a safety pin or a snail shell. From the standpoint of radiation, soft tissues are invisible. Yet from my point of view, they are the painful seeping lesions on my back as I recover from sunstroke, glued by lymph to the pillow in a Maltese villa. From oil's point of view, my car is a shallow doll's house thimble. Yet from my point of view, oil makes America look the way it does: it covers the plains with highways while weeds grow through the rotting wood on a railway track. From evolution's point of view, I'm just an ephemeral expression of DNA. Yet from my point of view, I inhabit an extended phenotype that consists of computers, desks, lights, streets, children, and dinner plates.

When I think nonlocality in this way, I am not negating the specificity of things, evaporating them into the abstract mist of the general or the larger or the less local. Nonlocality is far weirder than that. When it comes to hyperobjects, nonlocality means that the general itself is compromised by the particular. When I look for the hyperobject oil, I don't find it. Oil just is droplets, flows, rivers, and slicks of oil. I do not find the object by looking *sub specie aeternitatis,* but by seeing things *sub specie majoris, sub specie inhumanae.* This brings us to our next section, in which we try to bring the hyperobject into an even sharper focus, by considering temporality.

Temporal Undulation

When you approach an object, more and more objects emerge. It's like being in a dream written by Zeno. Hyperobjects envelop us, yet they are so massively distributed in time that they seem to taper off, like a long street stretched into the distance. Time bends them and flattens them, the same way that an electromagnetic wave front shortens at its leading edge. Because we can't see to the end of them, hyperobjects are necessarily uncanny. Like the empty streets and open doorways in the paintings of Giorgio de Chirico, hyperobjects seem to beckon us further into themselves, making us realize that we're already lost inside them. The recognition of being caught in hyperobjects is precisely a feeling of strange familiarity and familiar strangeness. We already know the weather like the back of our hand. But this is weird weather, this global warming weather. We already know light. But this is weird light, this radiation. Bryant describes it thus:

> Hyperobjects are thus like our experience of a pool while swimming. Everywhere we are submersed within the pool, everywhere the cool water caresses our body as we move through it, yet we are nonetheless independent of the water. We produce effects in the water like diffraction patterns, causing it to ripple in particular ways, and it produces effects in us, causing our skin to get goosebumps.[1]

Space can no longer be construed as an absolute container, but rather should be thought of as a spacetime manifold that is radically *in* the universe, *of* it rather than ontologically outside it.

Das Rad (The Wheel) is a comical German cartoon about two rocks that witness the rise and fall of humans.[2] Time is sped up to accommodate the much vaster timescale of the rocks, who speak laconically about what seems to be going on around them. *Das Rad* exists in the context of human awareness of deep time and of the dangerous futures we have unleashed. Occasionally time slows to accommodate the temporal perspective, as when a little boy seemingly invents the wheel, to appropriately Straussian background music. Yet this invention is anticipated by one of the rocks themselves, who idly spins the wheel-rock— initially it's just a segment of his body—thus setting it up for the boy's inspection. Human technology, which Heidegger blames for its uncanny enframing of reality, is placed back into a larger contexture of equipment that includes rocks and their toys, in a flat ontology in which rocks and humans aren't all that different (Figure 5).

Felix Hess's *Air Pressure Fluctuations* is a sound art piece that employs a massively accelerated time, enabling us to hear sounds that are not usually accessible. Hess puts contact mikes on the window of his apartment in New York. They can record sounds for five days and nights. Then he speeds up the recording by 360 times. Traffic begins to sound like the tinkling of tiny insects. A slow, periodic hum begins to become audible. When I hear *Air Pressure Fluctuations,* I am hearing the standing wave caused by pressure changes in the air over the Atlantic Ocean. I am hearing the sound of the air over the Atlantic. A gigantic entity has been channeled into a sound recording audible to humans.[3]

Harman writes that, because objects withdraw irreducibly, you can't even get closer to objects.[4] This becomes clearer as we enter the ecological crisis—"Has it started yet? How far in are we?" This anxiety is a symptom of the emergence of hyperobjects. It's like trying to get closer to the moon by running toward it, all the while forgetting that you are on the surface of the earth. The more data we have about lifeforms, the more we realize we can *never* truly know them. This has partly to do with something strange that has happened to temporality. The ocean of

FIGURE 5. Tom Gauld, *Two Rocks Converse* (2010). This and the German cartoon *Das Rad* (*The Wheel*) comically show the temporal scale at which geological change occurs, and the ways in which this temporality intersects with human temporality, and indeed human agency. One of the rocks in *Das Rad* plays with something that a human child "discovers" as a wheel. Copyright Tom Gauld. Reproduced by permission.

floating temporality and spatiality wafts to and fro, "in front of things": not spatially in front, but ontologically in front, like the undulating red curtain of a theater.

The Florida Everglades have lasted for about five thousand years. Some call them *Nature* because that is what they are used to. But beyond this, they are a hyperobject, massively distributed in time and space in ways that baffle humans and make interacting with them fascinating, disturbing, problematic, and wondrous. Joel Trexler is an ecologist who's totally at home out on the Everglades. This at-homeness is palpable in the way he scoops up a carnivorous plant, bladderwort, or in his excitement about the gar, a living fossil: so many things that are hard to spectate or to photograph but are nevertheless compelling to think about. Trexler argues that it's possible to restore the Everglades to a condition they had fifty, one hundred, or one thousand years ago. There is no "pristine," no Nature, only history. Indeed, as Adorno puts it, Nature is simply reified history.[5]

I start the engine of my car. Liquefied dinosaur bones burst into flame. I walk up a chalky hill. Billions of ancient pulverized undersea creatures grip my shoes. I breathe. Bacterial pollution from some Archean cataclysm fills my alveoli—we call it *oxygen*. I type this sentence. Mitochondria, anaerobic bacteria hiding in my cells from the Oxygen Catastrophe, spur me with energy. They have their own DNA. I hammer a nail. In consistent layers of ore, bacteria deposited the iron in Earth's crust. I turn on the TV and see snow. A sliver of the snow is a trace of the Cosmic Microwave Background left over from the Big Bang. I walk on top of life-forms. The oxygen in our lungs is bacterial outgassing. Oil is the result of some dark, secret collusion between rocks and algae and plankton millions and millions of years in the past. When you look at oil you're looking at the past. Hyperobjects are time-stretched to such a vast extent that they become almost impossible to hold in mind.

I look at a temperature chart derived from the Godard Institute for Space Studies (Figure 1). It shows me one century of global warming, an upward zigzag. I read that 75 percent of global warming effects will persist until five hundred years from now. I try to imagine what life was like in 1513. Thirty thousand years from now, ocean currents will have absorbed more of the carbon compounds, but 25 percent will still hang around in the atmosphere. The half-life of plutonium-239 is 24,100 years. These periods are as long as all of visible human history thus far. The paintings in the Chauvet Cave in France date back thirty thousand years (Figure 6). But 7 percent of global warming effects will still be occurring one hundred thousand years from now as igneous rocks slowly absorb the last of the greenhouse gases.[6] I have decided to call these timescales the *horrifying*, the *terrifying*, and the *petrifying*. The last is particularly appropriate given that all that will remain of human beings in the flesh

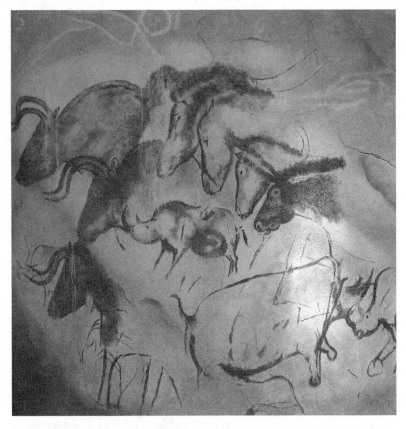

FIGURE 6. Replica of the paintings in the Chauvet Cave. It is difficult to project one's imagination back as far as this earliest known example of human art, as it also is to project one's imagination forwards to the end of the half-life of plutonium-239 (24, 100 years).

one hundred thousand years from now may indeed be fossils; and that the new "minerals" such as concrete, created with extreme rapidity by humans (we have doubled the number of such minerals on Earth), form built structures (skyscrapers, overpasses, garnets for lasers, graphene, bricks) that will indeed be a layer of geological strata at that point; not to mention the "mineraloids" such as glasses and ceramics, and materials such as plastics. The timescale is a Medusa that turns us to stone. We know this now, just as we know that we have changed the future fossils of Earth. The future hollows out the present.

These gigantic timescales are truly humiliating in the sense that they force us to realize how close to Earth we are. Infinity is far easier to cope with. Infinity brings to mind our cognitive powers, which is why for Kant the mathematical sublime is the realization that infinity is an uncountably vast magnitude beyond magnitude.[7] But hyperobjects are not forever. What they offer instead is *very large finitude.*[8] I can think infinity. But I can't count up to one hundred thousand. I have written one hundred thousand words, in fits and starts. But one hundred thousand years? It's unimaginably vast. Yet there it is, staring me in the face, as the hyperobject global warming. And I helped cause it. I am directly responsible for beings that far into the future, insofar as two things will be true simultaneously: no one then will meaningfully be related to me; and my smallest action now will affect that time in profound ways. A Styrofoam cup will outlive me by over four hundred years. The plastic bag in Ramin Bahrani's movie (in the voice of Werner Herzog) wishes to talk to the woman it knows as its maker, the woman who used it to carry her groceries: "If I could meet my maker, I would tell her just one thing: I wish that she had created me so that I could die."[9] To hear a plastic bag wish such a thing is profoundly different from thinking abstract infinity. There is a real sense in which it is far easier to conceive of "forever" than very large finitude. Forever makes you feel important. One hundred thousand years makes you wonder whether you can imagine one hundred thousand anything. It seems rather abstract to imagine that a book is one hundred thousand words long.

The philosophy of vast space was first opened up by Catholicism, which made it a sin not to suppose that God had created an infinite void.[10]

Along with the scholastic view of substances, Descartes inherited this void and Pascal wrote that its silence filled him with dread.[11] Vast non-human temporal and spatial magnitudes have been physically near humans since the Romantic period, when Mary Anning discovered the first dinosaur fossil (in 1811) and natural historians reckoned the age of Earth. Yet it was not until Einstein that space and time themselves were seen as emergent properties of objects. The Einsteinian view is what finally gave us the conceptual tools to conceptualize the scope of very large finitude.

Einstein's discovery of spacetime was the discovery of a hyperobject— the way in which mass as such grips space, distorts it from within, stretching space and time into whorls and vortices. For Einstein, entities—which may or may not include living observers—comprise indivisible "world tubes." By *world tube*, relativity theory means to include the apprehending aspect of an entity with its entitive aspect. A world tube is a hyperobject. That is, world tubes stretch and snap our ideas of what an object is in the first place. Each world tube encounters a fundamentally different universe depending on its mass and velocity. World tubes recede from other world tubes in an inescapable and irreducible way. There are two main reasons for this.

(1) Light rays bouncing off an object only exert an influence within what Hermann Minkowski (the mathematician who proved relativity theory geometrically) calls the *light cone*. There is an absolute past and an absolute future relative to any reference frame, a concept that approaches Derrida's idea of *l'avenir*.[12] Relativity limits prediction to the light cone. For every object in the universe there is a genuinely *future future* that is radically unknowable. There is a genuinely *elsewhere elsewhere* that is radically unknowable. Yet the future future and the elsewhere elsewhere exist. They are, in my terminology, strange strangers, knowable yet uncanny. We will reinvestigate this topic shortly.

(2) When we examine a world tube up close, it has all kinds of strange properties. Because time ripples and melts along its surface, sensual interactions between one tube and another are always melting and

dripping rather than being rigid and uniform. Thus, time or space aren't physically real; rather physical events are real and they contain time and space in their interior—an argument of Einstein's that Harman does in another way.[13] Only infinitesimally small areas of space-time may be regarded as Galilean—that is, as rigid and container-like.[14]

The Einsteinian object isn't a unity. Thus, "it is not possible in relativity to obtain a consistent definition of an extended rigid body, because this would imply signals faster than light."[15] That means the pencil you are holding in your fingers is only a rigid extended body on account of a false immediacy. Nothing in the universe apprehends the pencil like that, really. *Not even the pencil* apprehends itself like that. The physical universe consists of objects that are more like turbulence in a stream than (gooey or hard) extended bodies.[16] A "world tube," with its irreducible past and future, is a withdrawn object. Relativity guarantees that real objects will be forever withdrawn from any object that tries to access them, including those objects themselves. General relativity gives us the most obviously withdrawn object of all—the black hole.

Molten, Gaussian temporality ceases simply to be an analogy when you're thinking about some hyperobjects such as planets, which really do have time melting and rippling along their surfaces and out into space through their gravitational field. Of course relativity applies equally to a pencil or to your feet, it's just that the effects are negligible at small scales. But hyperobjects are long-lasting enough and huge enough for genuine relativistic effects to manifest.

The totality of the Einsteinian universe is like a stream filled with countless vortices of energy. It only makes a relative sense to differentiate one vortex from another, so that the significance of such an object changes depending on circumstances. This is much more strange than saying that you can read an object any way you like, that you can walk around a single, solid-seeming object and view it just how you like. Power is on the side of the object apprehended, not on the side of the apprehending thing (whether it's us or a pencil or a reverse thruster). What we have is the inverse of perspectivism, a world of compulsion, in which world tubes draw us into their gravity wells. Rippling with time, objects tease other objects into their sphere of influence, their "level," as Lingis puts it.[17] They exercise all kinds of imperatives on the sensitivities of apprehending objects, such as human nervous systems, antennae, and tape heads.

Spacetime turns from a grid-like box into what Einstein fantastically calls a "reference-mollusk." Reference mollusks exist precisely *because* of hyperobjects that emanate gravitational fields. In these fields geometry is not Euclidean.[18] In the absence of graphics software that could morph and stretch a grid to convey Gaussian, non-Euclidean coordinates, a squishy shellfish was the best Einstein could come up with. But in a sense the mollusk is just right. Time and space emerge from things, like the rippling flesh of a sea urchin or octopus. The flesh emerges from the gyrations of DNA and RNA molecules, struggling to solve their inherent inconsistency, and ending up repeating themselves in the process. Likewise time blossoms from what I shall call *the Rift* between the appearance and the essence of a thing.[19]

Thinking time this way is a profound post-Kantian shift, to which we are only beginning to catch up. It's a false cliché that we have grasped the meaning of relativity. Far from it. In our daily social and psychic practices, we are still Newtonians, still in awe of infinite space, and behind that in awe of the infinite God of infinite space. At most we see infinity and space as transcendental categories, as Kant does. Ironically, space and time are the two things that Kant allows most to be like "objects" in the OOO sense, autonomous quanta that can't be divided further. Kant's spuriously "Copernican" turn was more like a Ptolemaic counterrevolution, as Meillassoux has pointed out.[20] It's Einstein who continues the Copernican legacy, by showing how time and space emerge from objects, not from synthetic judgments that preunderstand being to be thus and so.

The undulating fronds of space and time float in front of objects. Some speculative realism maintains there is an abyss, an *Ungrund* (unground) deeper than thought, deeper than matter, a surging vortex of dynamism.[21] To understand hyperobjects, however, is to think *the abyss in front of things*. When I reach out to mop my sweating brow on a hot day, the California sun beating down through the magnifying lens of global warming, I plunge my hand into a fathomless abyss. When I pick a blackberry from a bush, I fall into an abyss of phenotypes, my very act of reaching being an expression of the genome that is not exclusively mine, or exclusively human, or even exclusively alive. In the following section on how hyperobjects are phased, we shall explore in more detail the abyss that floats in front of objects.

Hyperobjects are *Gaussian,* disturbingly squishy and mollusk-like. The undulations of the mollusk flesh of spacetime fail to drop to zero. Gravity waves from the "beginning of time" are right now passing through my body from the edge of the universe. It is as if we were inside a gigantic octopus. H. P. Lovecraft imagines the insane god Cthulhu this way.[22] Cthulhu inhabits a non-Euclidean city, just like Gaussian spacetime. By understanding hyperobjects, human thinking has summoned Cthulhu-like entities into social, psychic, and philosophical space. The contemporary philosophical obsession with the monstrous provides a refreshing exit from human-scale thoughts. It is extremely healthy to know not only that there are monstrous beings, but that there are beings that are not purely thinkable, whose being is not directly correlated with whatever thinking is. It's what Meillassoux calls *le grand dehors,* though the queer ecologist in me has a pang of dislike when I see this translated as "the great outdoors."[23] I fear another assault on the "introverted" and the "perverse." I am happier with the idea that this outdoors is already indoors, in the very failure of my thought to be the object that it is thinking.

Relativity is what guarantees that objects are never as they seem, and not because they are ideas in my head—but because they aren't. Large objects emit gravitational fields that bend light, giving rise to the red shift from distant stars that remained a mystery until Einstein proposed relativity theory.[24] Spacetime isn't an empty box, but rather an undulating force field that emanates from objects. Now the thing about undulating temporality is that it really is measurably obvious in hyperobjects, objects that are massive from a human standpoint. Clocks run slightly faster when you are inside a plane traversing the ocean at thirty-nine thousand feet, because the gravity well of Earth makes clocks run slower closer to its surface. An experiment in 2011 involving a number of very accurate gyroscopes confirmed the existence of a gigantic spacetime vortex around Earth.[25] Time ripples along the surfaces of things, causing them to bend. It gets better. If I am flying in a space shuttle above the plane, and somehow able to read the clock on the plane, I will be able to see it telling a different time again, due to the relative motion of the plane and the shuttle. This has nothing to do with idealism or correlationism. This relativity is hardwired into things themselves. Objects entangle one another in a crisscrossing mesh of spacetime fluctuations.

Once we become aware of it, undulating temporality corrodes the supposed fixity of smaller objects that lie around me. What is temporal sauce for the goose of hyperobjects is also sauce for the gander of a pencil twirled in my fingers. Tiny clocks on the twirling eraser at the far end of the pencil register a slightly different time than tiny clocks on the graphite tip that remains still, while tiny clocks on the tip of my nose . . . and so on. Of course, humans may not notice such things, but the electrons in humans notice them all the time. The very idea of spatial extension, fundamental to Cartesian ontology, comes into question. The notion of bland, consistent substance is not deep enough to account for hyper-objects. The very notion of a consistent substance is a species of acci-dent, no different from the regular candy sprinkles of color, shape, and so on. Salvador Dali's rather cheesy painting of melting clocks is just the way it is.

Hyperobjects end the idea that time and space are empty containers that entities sit in. Newton and the rest inherited this empty-vessel model basically intact as part of the legacy of Augustianian Neoplatonism. It is rather strange, on reflection. It is surely part of a general overreaction to Aristotle as Europe exited the Middle Ages, an overreaction that posited modernity as such. Ironically, modern science—I here use *modernity* and *modern* in the Latourian sense—continues to run with this Christian Neoplatonist meme.[26] It's not until 1900 that time and space become thinkable as effects of objects, rather than as absolute containers. So the speculative realism movement must not only address correlationism— the reduction of thinking to the human–world correlation—but also the long history of anti-Aristotelianism.

The Islamic world was spared the hobbling inheritance of a certain Platonism, since it was indebted to Aristotle, a proto-object-oriented thinker who held that the essence of a thing is in its form (morphē), not in some beyond. From this idea it becomes plausible to think the universe as finite. Consider ar-Razi's *Doubts against Galen* (that is, Galen, the Greek physician). Ar-Razi holds that the subgroup that posited infinite and eternal space and time was in error, though not because they were wrong to critique Galen and Aristotle. However, ar-Razi thinks the problem of the infinite in Aristotelian terms. Ar-Razi argues that all entities that are created are subject to corruption (that is, they degrade and are impermanent). Thus, the heavens, although we are told they are permanent, might simply consist of some very long-lasting substances that only appear to be eternal to our human eyes. If not, then you are claiming that they are uncreated, which is absurd. (Recall that this generation of Aristotelians thought what Ptolemy thought, namely that the stars were fixed to orbs of a glass-like substance. Ignore the wrongness of this supposition, because it's irrelevant.)

Now for the truly amazing part. Ar-Razi writes that gold, gems, and glass can disintegrate, but at much slower speeds than vegetables, fruits, and spices. So we can expect whatever the celestial sphere is made of to degrade over the course of thousands of years. Astronomical events take place on scales vastly larger even than the scales on which epochs between peoples happen. Think of a catastrophe such as a flood or a plague, ar-Razi says. Such events create ruptures between epochs so that the time of one entire people can pass to the time of another. How much would a ruby degrade between the time of Hipparchus and the time of Galen? So the degradation rate of a celestial body might be to that of a ruby as that of a ruby is to that of a bunch of herbs. Now think about spatial scales. If you were to add a mountain's worth of mass to the sun, you would not be able to detect it on Earth because the sun is so massive in the first place.[27] By thinking through Aristotle, ar-Razi discovered hyperobjects in the tenth century. It's time we made a return to Aristotle, who is weirder than we think.[28]

Since objects don't float in an infinite void, every entity has its own time, both in a physical and in a deep ontological sense. Minkowski's geometrical proof of relativity reveals something profound about this fact. Since the speed of light is an unbreakable limit, every event takes place within a light cone that specifies what counts as past and future. Within the light cone, events relative to the event in question can be specified as taking place in the past or in the present, here or elsewhere. But outside the light cone, differentiating between now and then becomes meaningless, as does differentiating between here and there. An event outside the light cone cannot be specified as happening at a certain place and at a certain time. I just can't tell whether it occurs in the "present" or the "past." Time as such, construed as a series of points that extends like Cartesian substances "into" the future "from" the past, is itself an aesthetic phenomenon, not a deep fact that underlies things.

Thus, like the *strange stranger*, there is a *future future*. There is a time that is beyond predictability, timing, or any ethical or political calculation. There is an *elsewhere elsewhere*. There is a place that is "nowhere" and yet real: not a Neoplatonic beyond, but a real entity in the real universe. We should then entertain the possibility that hyperobjects allow us to see that there is something *futural* about objects as such. If time is not a neutral container in which objects float, but is instead an emission of objects themselves, it is at least theoretically more plausible that an object could exert a backward causality on other entities, than if objects inhabit a time container that slopes in one particular direction. This wake of causality would appear to flow backward "into" the present. The strange strangeness of things is futural. Its shadow looms out of the future into the present, like the shadows of futurity that Shelley sees casting their flickering presence on the cave wall of poetry.[29]

Like all objects, hyperobjects compel us to handle them in certain ways. They forcefully exert what Lingis calls *the imperative*. But because of temporal foreshortening, hyperobjects are impossible to handle just right. This aporia gives rise to a dilemma: we have no time to learn fully about hyperobjects. But we have to handle them anyway. This handling causes ripples upon ripples. Entities that are massively distributed in time exert downward causal pressure on shorter-lived entities. Thus, one vivid effect of global warming has been phenological asynchrony: the way plant and animal life events have gone out of sync.[30] When the time that one entity emits intersects with the time another entity emits, we get an interference pattern, like the wavy lines in a painting by Bridget Riley or Yukultji Napangati, artists to whom this study shall return somewhat frequently, particularly in the following section. This interference pattern is known as *phasing*. Humans are caught in intersecting phases of time. It is to this that we now turn, since the massiveness of hyperobjects makes phasing vivid.

Phasing

When I look at *Untitled 2011* by the Aboriginal artist Yukultji Napangati, I am gripped immediately in the tractor beam of the painting, which seems to be gazing at me as much as or more than I am looking at it (Plate 1). A simple JPEG of the painting doesn't look like much. It's a largish square of thin brown waving lines, hand drawn. Yet as I approach it, it seems to surge toward me, locking onto my optic nerve and holding me in its force field. Napangati's painting strafes me with layer upon layer of interference patterns. Her work makes Bridget Riley's op art look simple by comparison, though I find both painters astonishing.

I don't experience Napangati's painting as a series of lines that I resolve into a whole. The whole painting leaps at me, as a unit. The painting is a slice of the Dreamtime, the Aboriginal hyperobject, and a map of desert sand hills where a small group of women gathered food and performed rituals. Even though *Untitled 2011* is a piece about a larger space, both cosmic and earthly, the painting is a quantum all to itself, not an incomplete part. In no sense do I assemble the painting. Nothing about the painting is passive, inert, waiting to be interpreted or completed. I find it impossible to leave the painting. Hairs standing up on my body, tears streaming down my face, slowly I tear myself away, only to return an hour later to be drenched in its resonance.

My sense of being "in" a time and of inhabiting a "place" depends on forms of regularity. The periodic rhythms of day and night, the sun "coming up"—only now I know that it doesn't really come up. It is now common knowledge that the moon's "phases" are just the relationship between the earth and the moon as they circumnavigate the sun. Hyperobjects seem to phase in and out of the human world. Hyperobjects are *phased*: they occupy a high-dimensional *phase space* that makes them impossible to see as a whole on a regular three-dimensional human-scale basis.

We can only see pieces of hyperobjects at a time. The reason why they appear nonlocal and temporally foreshortened is precisely because of this transdimensional quality. We only see pieces of them at once, like a tsunami or a case of radiation sickness. If an apple were to invade a two-dimensional world, first the stick people would see some dots as the bottom of the apple touched their universe, then a rapid succession of shapes that would appear like an expanding and contracting circular blob, diminishing to a tiny circle, possibly a point, and disappearing. What we experience as a lava-lamp fluidity—flowing and oozing metaphors abound in the new materialism—is precisely a symptom of our less than adequate perception of higher dimensions of structure, which is where the hyperobjects live.

That's why you can't see global warming. You would have to occupy some high-dimensional space to see it unfolding explicitly. Think of a daffodil. A daffodil flower is a three-dimensional map of an algorithm executed by DNA and RNA in the daffodil's genome. The tips of the crinkly stem show the latest state of the algorithm unfolding in three-dimensional phase space. The base of the flower is a plot of the beginnings of the flower algorithm. Your face is a map of everything that happened to it. Now think of global warming. We only see snapshots of what is actually a very complex plot of a super complex set of algorithms executing themselves in a high-dimensional phase space. When the weather falls on your head, you are experiencing a bad photocopy of a piece of that plot. What you once thought was real turns out to be a sensual representation, a thin slice of an image, a caricature of a piece of global climate. A process just is a real object, but one that occupies higher dimension than objects to which we are accustomed.

A phase space is the set of all the possible states of a system. Objects in phase space are intriguing and strange. If, for example, you plot the sum of weather events in phase space, you discover an attractor, a shape that looks like a folded figure *8* (Figure 7). Edward Lorenz discovered the first strange attractor (the Lorenz Attractor) in precisely this way. A high enough dimensional being could see global warming itself as a static object. What horrifyingly complex tentacles would such an entity have, this high-dimensional object we call global warming?

As it is, I only see brief patches of this gigantic object as it intersects with my world. The brief patch I call a *hurricane* destroys the infrastructure of New Orleans. The brief patch I call *drought* burns the plains of

FIGURE 7. Lorenz Attractor. The first strange attractor was this pattern made by weather events plotted in a suitably high dimensional space.

Russia and the midwestern United States to a crisp. The back of my neck
itches with yesterday's sunburn. Percy Shelley writes, "The awful shadow
of some unseen power / Floats through unseen among us."[1] Shelley was
writing about "intellectual beauty," but now the line resonates in a speculative realist universe, as does his poem *Mont Blanc,* which begins "The
everlasting universe of things / Flows through the mind . . . "[2] The mountain acts like a beacon in the poem, appearing, then disappearing, then
reappearing: "Mont Blanc yet gleams on high" (line 127). The mountain
comes in and out of phase.

Thinking things as Nature is thinking them as a more or less static,
or metastable, continuity bounded by time and space. The classic image
of Nature is the Romantic or picturesque painting of a landscape. There
it is, over yonder—on the wall in the gallery. And it has over-yonder-ness
encoded throughout it: look at those distant hills, that branch suggesting
that we follow the perspective lines toward the vanishing point, and so on.[3]

We can animate this picture and produce an oozing, flowing, lava-
lampy version of the same thing. We should be suspicious of these new
and improved versions of Nature, which simply turn the static picture
into a flowing picture. Something remains the same: the sense of time as
a container. The picture appears complex—cinematic, Deleuzian: it is
no accident that Deleuze theorizes cinema beautifully. But this cinematic
flow had already been anticipated in the Romantic period. In an age
before the silver screen huge swathes of blank verse narrating the flow
of the subject opened up an ideological space in which cinema could
appear. Wordsworth is the first cinematic artist. The theorists of this
process relationism—Whitehead, Deleuze—conceive time as the liquid
in which the image melts and flows. This flowing aesthetic in contemporary thought manifests precisely to the extent that it has enabled us
to track hyperobjects. Think of the movie *Manufactured Landscapes,* a
study of the photographer Edward Burtynsky.[4] The camera traces processes of production, the piling of e-waste, and so on. The pathos of that
incredible opening shot, tracking through an outlandishly large Chinese
factory, is precisely the pathos of a gaze floating through time—we have
no idea when the shot will finish, and, concurrently, just how enormous
the factory is. A process is simply an object seen from a standpoint that

is 1 + *n* dimensions lower than that object's dimensionality. As Burtynsky keeps including more and more in each shot, the movie includes more and more of how industrial "functioning" is just a small, normalized region of a much larger space of *mal-functioning*: I hyphenate the word to suggest that this space concerns a kind of dark or weird functioning, in which every movement, even "correct" functioning, becomes visible as a distortion or "mistake." Such is the disturbing quality of the ecological vision, not some holistic oneness.

Process philosophy helps us to visualize how high-dimensional entities execute. Thus, a slightly upgraded way of seeing hyperobjects would be the *plot* or *graph*. From cinematic aesthetics we can proceed to plots and maps of algorithms that execute in phase space. Enormously powerful processors can do this now when they map climate. The arithmetical calculations, called floating-point operations ("flops") that climate mapping requires are measured in petaflops, namely one million billion per second (10^{15}). The graphics that draws attractors is not for providing an incidental visual aid, but is instead the scientific work as such. Now what the software is seeing really does exit from the world of the aesthetic container and aesthetic distance, since we're no longer dealing with time or space as containers, but including time and space as dimensions of the high-dimensional phase space. Time is now radically inside objects, rippling through them as I argued a while back. And space is inside objects, differentiating their parts from one another. The trouble is that we cannot help but fail to see such high-dimensional entities when they are plotted in this way. Software "sees" them for us, then we see data or slices of that phase space, rendered in some way to make it usable.

Thinking hyperobjects as transdimensional real things is valuable. Global warming is not simply a mathematical abstraction that doesn't really pertain to this world. Hyperobjects don't inhabit some conceptual beyond in our heads or out there. They are real objects that affect other objects. Indeed the philosophical view behind thinking that objects are one thing and relations (which is what we're really talking about when we talk about math or transcendence) are another positively inhibits our transition to an ecological age, even as it poses sophisticated theories of emergence or process.

Phasing means to approach, then diminish, from a certain fullness. Jimi Hendrix–style guitar phasing seems to whoosh toward one's hearing and away from it, as the phaser pedal restricts, then unrestricts, the harmonic range of the sound. Hyperobjects seem to come and go, but this coming and going is a function of our limited human access to them. What we experience as the slow periodic recurrence of a celestial event such as an eclipse or a comet is a continuous entity whose imprint simply shows up in our social or cognitive space for a while. On this view, then, what is called *weather* is as antiquated as the idea that the phases of the waxing and waning moon are in the moon itself, rather than in the relationship between the moon and Earth. Rather, weather is a sensual impression of climate that happens to both humans and the nonhuman entities they concern themselves with: cows, flood barriers, tundra, umbrellas, and so on. The rain gauge buried in my garden selects a small sample of this hyperobject for my inspection, a tube of water a couple of inches high. Likewise, the contracting and expanding mercury in the thermometer in the hallway tells me about temperature fluctuations inside the house, while sensors in my car tell me about a sliver of climate while I'm driving. My attention span focuses on global warming for a few seconds each day before returning to other matters. A series of government regulations addresses one aspect of climate change (extinction), while ignoring others, such as runaway fossil fuel consumption. A human perception of a hyperobject is akin to the sectioning technique in architectural drawing. Since hyperobjects occupy a higher-dimensional phase space than we can experience directly, we can only experience somewhat constrained slices of them at any one time. The hyperobject global warming churns away, emitting ghosts of itself for my perusal. This horrible colossus is not capable of being visualized by humans. I can picture a Lorenz Attractor, somewhat roughly. But picturing the gigantic system of which Lorenz Attractors themselves are little footprints is daunting to say the least.

Napangati's *Untitled 2011* is a phase of Dreamtime, a phasing painting whose waves undulate like Hendrix's guitar. The painting itself forces me to see higher and higher dimensions of itself, as if layers of phase space were being superimposed on other layers. These layers appear deep, as if

I could reach my arms into them. They float in front of the picture surface. They move. The painting holds me, spellbound. The painting looks like a map or a plot in phase space, which is just what it is, in one sense: a map of how women walked across some sand hills. Yet what appears to be a map turns out to be a weapon. The painting emits spacetime, emits an aesthetic field. The painting is a unit, a quantum that executes a function. It is a device, not just a map but also a tool, like a shaman's rattle or a computer algorithm. The function of the painting seems to be to imprint me with the bright red shadow of a hyperobject, the Australian Outback, the Dreamtime, the long history of the Pintupi Nine, the Lost Tribe, some of the last Neolithic humans on Earth. We shall see when it comes to talking about art in the time of hyperobjects just how significant it is that Napangati somehow manages to combine *map* and *device*.

What is significant here is that we are dealing with the inverse of a view that says that mathematizable entities underlie other entities. On the view this book is advocating, the object subtends the mathematizable forms. In other words, number is really computability: *one* means *countably one*. This doesn't mean that I am supplementing "hard" math with something warm and fuzzy, a language that Heidegger himself, and more so his apologists, sometimes slips into. This defensive thinking won't do: it's precisely what has confined all the humanities to a smaller and smaller island of human meaning for the last two centuries. The Great Acceleration demands that we get our act together on that score.

The mathematical entity is the paraphrase—the mathematical entity is the "warm and fuzzy" one, on the hither side of human meaning. A hyperobject exists for us as a map in a high-dimensional phase space, because it is impossible for us to grasp as a whole with our senses. But this means the opposite of a Platonism that says that mathematical relationships underlie things. It only means that the mathematical as such just is *mathēsis*, which is a Greek term that comes close to the Tibetan *gom*, the term for meditation. *Gom* and *mathēsis* both mean something like "getting used to," "growing accustomed."[5] Mathematics in this sense, beyond number, is the way the mind acclimatizes itself to reality. The Lorenz Attractor is a way for us to breathe the rarefied conceptual oxygen of a higher-dimensional being, the climate. The climate is not a

"space" or an "environment," just a *higher-dimensional object* that we don't
see directly. When it rains on my head, climate is raining. The biosphere
is raining. But what I feel are raindrops, and gaps between raindrops,
as I showed in "A Quake in Being." Indeed, Kant's example of the withdrawal of the in-itself is the humble raindrop. When I feel them, I am
always feeling my human translation of them into wet, cold, small things
pattering on my raincoat. The raindrop itself is radically withdrawn.[6]

The gaps I perceive between moments at which my mind is aware
of the hyperobject and moments at which it isn't, do not inhere in the
hyperobject itself. This is not simply a matter of my "subjective" awareness versus an "objective" world. The same can be said of physical objects
that are lower-dimensional than the hyperobject in question. The gaps
a town experiences between being strafed by one set of tornadoes and
another set does not mark a gap of nothingness between two hyperobjects, or even within one hyperobject. Global warming doesn't go
golfing at the weekend. The gaps and ruptures are simply the *invisible
presence* of the hyperobject itself, which looms around us constantly. On
this view, hyperobjects are disturbing clowns in an Expressionist painting, clowns who cover every available surface of the painting, leering into
our world relentlessly. The notion of "background" and its "foreground"
are only phases of an object that doesn't "go anywhere" at all, at least not
on a human- or town-sized scale.

The psychotic intensity of Expressionist painting, poetry, and music
thus expresses something about the hyperobject much more effectively
than a cool mathematical diagram of phasing flows. The diagram is the
caricature, not the leering clowns. A claustrophobic universe unveils itself
to us, crammed with things: radiation, solar flares, interstellar dust, lamp-
posts, and lice. Expressionism abolishes the play between background
and foreground. Objects thrust themselves towards us in a cramped or
claustrophobic pictorial space. The sensation of *world*, on this view, is
the false consciousness of gaps and backgrounds between and behind
things. In this way hyperobjects bring about *the end of the world*, as I
shall argue in part 2.

When a sound phases, now thicker, now narrower, another wave is
intersecting with a series of sound waves. At a lower level, a beat happens

when one wave cancels out part of another wave. For a beat to exist, there must be $1 + n$ waves that intersect. Phasing happens because one object translates another one. This is a feature of how objects affect one another in general, and we should explore this a little before accounting more fully for how hyperobjects are phased.

An MP3 sample compresses a sound wave in a "lossy" way by cutting some of it out. The preferred sampling rate for music recording is now 44,000 cycles per second, so there are 44,001 holes in between and on either side of one second of sound. (Now they know how many holes it takes to fill the Albert Hall.)[7] Likewise, a JPEG is a lossy, compressed sample of an image, and when you make a copy of a JPEG, the copy has more holes in it than the original, so each JPEG copy becomes increasingly degraded. When a JPEG is made, optically sensitive electronics on a chip are bombarded with photons, some of which are translated into visible information in pixels on a screen. A series of tools executes a function, withdrawn into the background against the image that results. When we scrutinize the whole system, we find a bunch of gadgets that work on one another, transducing and otherwise altering inscription events such as photons or sound waves into electronic signals or electrochemical ones.

A hyperobject passes through a thousand sieves, emerging as translated information at the other end of the mesh. Thick raindrops tell me of the coming storm, which flashes lightning in an unusual way that is an index of global warming. Phasing is an *indexical sign* of an object that is massively distributed in a phase space that is higher dimensional than the equipment (our ears, the top of my head, a weather vane) used to detect it. An index is a sign that is directly a part of what it indicates. In the mesh of interconnectivity, the sieve through which hyperobjects pass, smaller things become indexes of the hyperobjects inside which they exist. A flock of birds stays on the lake for a curiously long period. Frogs huddle for warmth and moisture on a wet doorstep.

What we are dealing with, with the phenomenon of phasing, is an indexical sign that is a *metonymy* for the hyperobject. Metonymy is the mereological figure, the figure that deals with parts and wholes and relationships. What we encounter when we study hyperobjects is a strange

mereology in which parts do not disappear into wholes.[8] Quite the reverse. Indeed, what we seem to have is what in Lacanian terminology is
called a *not-all* set. Objects seem to contain more than themselves. A
flock of birds on a lake is a unique entity, yet it is also part of a series
of hyperobjects: the biosphere, evolution, global warming. There is an
inevitable dislocation between the hyperobject and its indexical signs.
Otherwise, what's the fuss all about? Gaia will eliminate its pathogens
and get on with the business of being itself. But an object is and is not
itself, at the same time, because it has parts that cannot be wholly sub-
sumed into it. Otherwise phasing, and the beats and more generally the
indexical signs that are aspects of interactions between things, would fail
to occur. A phasing object is a sign of a rupture at the heart of being.

This rupture is not a physically definable place, like a crack or a seam.
It cannot be physically located "in" space or time, since space and time
are precisely on "this" side of it. Hyperobjects are big enough relative
to us that they cause us to become aware of the rupture, which following
Heidegger I have begun to call *the Rift*. The Rift exists at an *ontological*
intersection, not a physical one. The intersection is between a thing and
its appearance-for another thing, or things. Thus, the mesh of relations
is on one side of the Rift, the hither side, while what I call the strange
stranger is on the yonder side—again, not spatially but ontologically.

Now because of the strange mereology we have spoken of, one of
these "other things" can be the very object in question! An object can be
a member of itself, thus giving rise to set theoretical paradoxes that
plagued Russell. If a set can be a member of itself, then one can imagine
a set of sets that are not members of themselves. In order to cope with
such paradoxes we can do one of two things. One is to forget everything
we have just found out about hyperobjects. The other is to allow for the
existence of contradictory entities. It is the second path that we shall take
in this book. The path has been well established by the logician Graham
Priest, in a number of groundbreaking books and essays.[9]

Russell's set paradox is the stepchild of something like mathematical
hyperobjects, the transfinite sets discovered by Georg Cantor. Think of
a line. Now split the line into two by cutting out the middle third por-
tion. You now have two lines separated by a gap. Now repeat the process

with the two lines. Continue ad infinitum: you have a Cantor Set, an entity that contains infinity points, and infinity no-points: an outrageous double infinity, as if we could suddenly see that some infinities were larger than others. Infinity stops being a vague abstraction and starts to become very precise. We can do calculations with it. We can, as Blake wrote, hold infinity in the palm of our hand.[10] A two-dimensional Cantor Set known as a *Sierpinski Carpet* forms the aerial of a cell phone, because electromagnetic waves are fractal and contain infinitesimal copies of themselves: more wave is sampled by a fractal aerial than by a simple one. If it is the case that an entity has more parts than it can encompass in a whole, then objects are transfinite in some sense, fractals that contain more of themselves than they let on on the outside.

Objects, then, are like Doctor Who's Tardis, a time-traveling spaceship that is bigger on the inside than it is on the outside. The Tardis has a "chameleon circuit" that enables it to enter into phase with other objects in its vicinity: sadly for the Doctor, this chameleon circuit is stuck as a 1960s police telephone box. The uncanny grinding, roaring sound of the Tardis as it appears and disappears, coming in and out of phase with specific regions of spacetime is a good image of the phasing of the hyperobject. But the image of the time tunnel that frames each episode of *Doctor Who* does not underlie things. Rather, it is the mesh that exists on the hither side of the Rift between an entity and its appearance-for: an abyss that floats in front of things. The abyss does not underlie things, but rather allows things to coexist: it is the nonspatial "betweenness" of things. Whenever I put my hand into the toaster oven I am thrusting part of my body into an abyss.

The abyss opens up in the interaction of any two or more objects. Indeed, since objects are inherently inconsistent (a fact to which we shall return), an abyss opens up simply because of *the Rift*, the fact that an object can "interact with itself" because it is a spacing and a timing, not a given, objectified entity. We have seen already how at the quantum level systems seem to auto-affect, looping around on themselves. Phasing is evidence of some interaction between things, or *between a thing*, if that is not too paradoxical a thing to say at this point (reminiscent of the joke, "What is the difference between a duck? One of its legs is both the same.") Entities seem to come and go, swaying to and fro in the breeze of some carrier wave, now faint, now strong. An object *times* another one, in a transitive sense. The moon times the earth. The sun times the earth another way. The seasons are the way the earth's orbit translates the sun. The daylight and the night time the house, with its sunny and shady sides. A blinking turn signal puts my car, the road, and other cars into phase with one another. Electromagnetic waves put water into different phases (for example, a liquid or gas). The smoothness of phase transition is a smoothness-for me, not for the electrons in the H_2O that jump, or don't jump, from one orbit to another. Phasing is an aesthetic event, a sensual entity-for some other entity or more.

The abyss is not an empty container, but rather a surging crowd of beings, like the fanciful representation of hyperspace in the *Doctor Who* credits, repeated in *Star Wars* episode 4 when the *Millennium Falcon* flies faster than light.[11] The "hyperness" of the hyperobject is precisely the abyssal quality that I sense when I become aware that a flock of birds on the lake is resting there because of global warming. The abyss is vivid and it lies on "this" side of things. We have already seen that, as the right-hand wing mirrors of American cars say, objects in mirror are closer than they appear.

Interobjectivity

In a gigantic bamboo forest on Qi Lai Mountain in central Taiwan, it is as if one is surrounded by a theater of air, leaves, and stalks. The bamboo sways, sometimes violently, sometimes delicately, to the wind that rushes through it. Each gust causes a cascade of bamboo clicks to sound in front, to the right, to the left, and behind. A ridiculously complex assemblage of high-pitched frequencies floats, resembling something between percussion and a hand stirring a bowlful of pebbles or small crystals. The wind is heard *in* the bamboo. The bamboo forest is a gigantic wind chime, modulating the wind into bambooese. The bamboo forest ruthlessly bamboo-morphizes the wind, translating its pressure into movement and sound. It is an abyss of bamboo-wind.

The abyss in front of things is *interobjective*. It floats among objects, "between" them; though this between is not "in" spacetime—it *is* spacetime. On this view, what is called *intersubjectivity*—a shared space in which human meaning resonates—is a small region of a much larger interobjective configuration space. Hyperobjects disclose *interobjectivity*. The phenomenon we call intersubjectivity is just a local, anthropocentric instance of a much more widespread phenomenon, namely interobjectivity. Please don't think that I mean something prior to or underneath or behind intersubjectivity. Think of intersubjectivity as a particular instance of interobjectivity with which humans are familiar. In other words, "intersubjectivity" is really human interobjectivity with lines drawn around it to exclude nonhumans. This seems particularly clear in deconstructive critiques of intersubjectivity: they often rely on the ways in which intersubjectivity as a concept excludes the media that organize and transmit human information, such as classrooms, cell phones, and markets. Or paper and ink and writing. Or two photocopiers or video monitors, as in the art of Steve Calvert, in which various devices provide feedback to one another in a way similar to what happens when you point a TV camera at a TV monitor (Figure 8). The wiring in my house is an interobjective system. Objects such as light bulbs, a microwave oven, wire, fuses, three computers, solar panels, and plugs are distributed so that energy flows among them as evenly and as equally as possible. If they were arranged differently—if the circuitry were put in series rather than in parallel—then they would perform very differently: some items would not operate at all, and some would be at a much higher risk of bursting

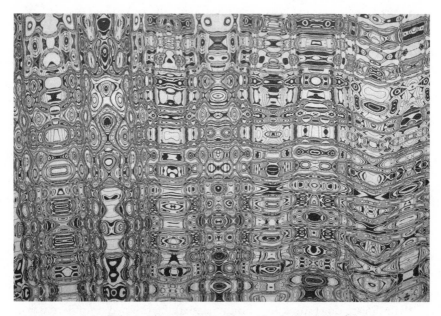

FIGURE 8. Steve Calvert, *Electromagnetic Life 3*, video feedback. Feedback loops occur when enough of one entity resonates with enough of another. In the terms this book uses, the system is *interobjective*. Intersubjectivity can be considered a small region of a larger interobjective possibility space. Reproduced by permission.

into flame. Likewise, the houses in my street form an interobjective system with the street itself and vehicles, stray dogs, and bouncing basketballs. We may scale up like this as far as we like. We will find that all entities whatsoever are interconnected in an interobjective system that elsewhere I call *the mesh*.[1]

A mesh consists of relationships between crisscrossing strands of metal and gaps between the strands. Meshes are potent metaphors for the strange interconnectedness of things, an interconnectedness that does not allow for perfect, lossless transmission of information, but is instead full of gaps and absences. When an object is born it is instantly enmeshed into a relationship with other objects in the mesh. Heidegger calls this mesh the *contexture of equipment*, a term that has roughly the same metaphorical provenance.[2] Ontologically speaking (from the standpoint of OOO), the mesh does not subtend things, but rather it floats "on top of" them, "in front of" things.[3]

A mesh consists of links, and also of gaps between links. These links and gaps are what enable causality to happen, when we think causality in an expanded way, to include what I have been calling *translation*. An MP3 is a highly perforated version of a sound, a JPEG is a highly perforated version of a picture. The meshwork that each object demonstrates is common to less perforated sets of links, and less regular ones too. It is precisely the gaps between and within things that enable entities to grip them, like the synchromesh in the manual transmission system of a car. *Mesh* means the threads and the holes between the threads.[4]

This fact profoundly affects our understanding of causality. It is the causal dimension in which things are able to happen, and not happen. To be born and to die, as well as to persist, is for the mesh to undergo some distortion that might be felt throughout the mesh if the instruments were sensitive enough. Gravity wave detectors in Illinois are now able to detect the waves emitted by objects from the beginning of the known universe.[5] The information received so far is strangely periodic, as if pixilated: just like the regular sequence of holes in an industrially produced mesh. Happily, *mesh* has etymological associations both with *mass* and with *mask*: that is, the heft of a thing, and its illusory qualities (qualities that, as I argue briefly here, have a causal reach).[6]

Authors of integral studies in the vein of Ken Wilber have coined the term *interobjectivity* to refer to systems of related objects, as opposed to systems of related subjects.[7] To use the term in this way is to cause nothing whatsoever to change. On the view I expound here, by contrast, what is called *subject* and what is called *mind* just are interobjective effects, emergent properties of relationships between enmeshed objects. Some neurons are wired together in a brain, and the brain sits in the skull of a lifeform that is sitting at this computer, typing these words. Mind is not "in" the brain but rather, to use the Heideggerian term, "thrown" into the interobjective space consisting of a banker's lamp, skull, computer, and keyboard, as well as fingers, neurons, and Mahler's seventh symphony playing on iTunes, Michael Tilson Thomas conducting the San Francisco Symphony Orchestra, a pair of eyes, a medium sized wooden Danish dining chair covered with black velvet, the muscular system, and so on.[8]

The view that mind is interobjective is shared by enactive theories of intelligence that have arisen from "connectionist" thinking in artificial intelligence. On this view, if you walk and quack like a mind, then you are one. This means that your mind is an effect-for some "observer." It is not "in" anything and it is not prior to objects but is rather an aftereffect of them. To assert that mind is interobjective is to accede to the basic argument in Alan Turing's seminal essay "Computing Machinery and Intelligence." A human and a computer running some software are hidden from view. They feed an observer answers to questions posed by the observer. If the observer reckons that the answers come from a person, then they come from a person.[9] Such a form of personhood is quite attenuated: it means that in effect, *I am not a nonperson,* since no distinction can be made between the answers given by a machine and answers given by a person. Personhood then is also an effect in the mesh—it may look solid from a distance, but as we approach it we find that it is full of holes. If we think consciousness is an emergent property of certain kinds of neural organization, we end up with Sorites paradoxes: What constitutes a heap? Or to put it another way, exactly where does consciousness begin to emerge from nonconsciousness?

What is called *consciousness* is an aesthetic effect: it is consciousness-for. Yet this does not make it unreal. When I walk gingerly over some sharp rocks, what looks like intelligence to a passing balloonist with a pair of binoculars might simply be my trying not to fall. The same applies to an ant walking over a scattering of sand grains.[10] Intelligence need not be thought of as having a picture of reality in the mind, but as an interaction between all kinds of entities that is somewhat "in the eye of the beholder"—including, of course, myself, who feels quite clever stumbling over the glacier, until my reflection causes me to topple sideways into the freezing water. My body, the glacier, the freezing water, my brain, and my boots form an interobjective system, a little eddy of metastability in the mesh. But it's hyperobjects that give us the most vivid glimpse of interobjectivity. Since we only see their shadow, we easily see the "surface" on which their shadow falls as part of a system that they corral into being. We see a host of interacting indexical signs.

On this view, a brain in a bucket, a favorite object of the philosopher of mind, might indeed be a mind system: bucket plus water plus brain plus wiring. But it's likely that it would be a very different mind than the same brain in a swimming pool full of jelly, or a brain in a skull in a living, breathing body. Now since hyperobjects are by definition the largest, longest-lasting objects we know; and since they strafe and penetrate the physical body at every available opportunity, like some demonic version of the Force (from *Star Wars*); is it not highly likely that the way our minds are is to some extent, perhaps a large extent, influenced by hyperobjects? So that when we think the hyperobject, we are in some sense thinking the conditions of possibility for the human mind? That thinking the hyperobject is thus thinking, in Marxist terms, the *base* of the mind, and not simply the (ideological, cultural) superstructure? This would mean that an account of hyperobjects was among other things an account of the fabric of the human mind. My thinking is thus a mental translation of the hyperobject—of climate, biosphere, evolution—not just figuratively, but literally. Some speculative realist philosophy has indeed pushed thinking to recognize its physical roots in this rather disturbing manner, most notably the work of Iain Hamilton Grant.[11]

Interobjectivity provides a space that is ontologically "in front of" objects, in which phenomena such as what is called *mind* can happen. The massiveness and distribution of hyperobjects simply force us to take note of this fact. Hyperobjects provide great examples of interobjectivity—namely, the way in which nothing is ever experienced directly, but only as mediated through other entities in some shared sensual space. We never hear the wind in itself, argues Heidegger, only the wind in the door, the wind in the trees.[12] This means that for every interobjective system, there is at least one entity that is withdrawn. We see the footprint of a dinosaur left in some ancient rock that was once a pool of mud (Figure 9). The dinosaur's reality exists interobjectively: there is some form of shared space between the rock, ourselves, and the dinosaur, even though the dinosaur isn't there directly. The print of a dinosaur's foot in the mud is seen as a foot-shaped hole in a rock by humans sixty-five million years later. There is some sensuous connection, then, between the dinosaur, the rock, and the human, despite their vastly differing timescales.

Now, when we return in our mind's eye to the time of the dinosaur herself, we discover something very strange. All we find there is another

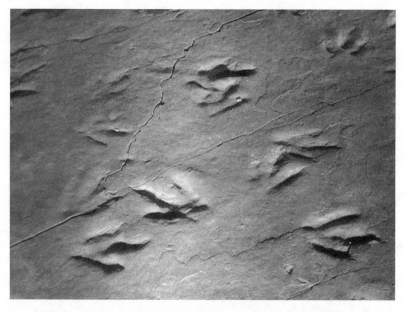

FIGURE 9. Dinosaur footprints at Dinosaur State Park and Arboretum, Rocky Hill, Connecticut. An interobjective system consisting (at least) of a dinosaur, mud, a human photographer, and electromagnetic waves. Photograph by Daderot.

region of interobjective space in which impressions of the dinosaur are transmitted—tooth marks in some hapless prey, the frozen stare of the dinosaur as she looks at her next victim, the smooth, scaly feel of her skin. The dinosaur leaves a footprint in some mud. The footprint is not the dinosaur. A fly lands on the dinosaur's left eyelid. The fly's apprehension of the dinosaur's eyelid is not the dinosaur. The dinosaur blinks. Her blink is not the dinosaur. The dinosaur's pea-sized brain registers the fly's feet. The registration is not the dinosaur, and so on. More dinosaur prints, even when the dinosaur is alive. Even the dinosaur doesn't know herself entirely, but only in a rough translation that samples and edits her being. A mosquito or an asteroid has their own unique sample of dinosaur-ness, and these samples are not dinosaurs. Why?

Because there is a real dinosaur, withdrawn even from herself. The real dinosaur is a *mystery,* yet not nebulous—just this dinosaur, this actual one, she who stepped in the mud. *Mystery* comes from the Greek *muein* (to close). The dinosaur is closed off, secret, unspeakable—even to herself. Whatever happens concerning her—the gyrations of her tiny mind, the imprint of the foot, the delicate tracery of the fly, my thinking about dinosaurs—occurs in an interobjective space that is ontologically in front of this mystery realm. Evolution and geological time are simply large enough beings to make this interobjective space visible.

An ancient bamboo forest on Qi Lai Mountain is a hyperobject. Watching a movie of the forest, you hear and see the wind in the bamboo, the bamboo stems clicking one another. What you are also seeing is a QuickTime movie, which samples visual images and sound at a certain rate, translating them into a more-or-less perforated version of themselves. What you are watching is my hand, moving slightly as the muscles in my right forearm fail to maintain stillness. What you are watching are photons from the sun, reflecting from quanta in the chloroplasts that make the bamboo green. What you are watching are chloroplasts, bacteria hiding from the environmental cataclysm they created, the cataclysm called oxygen, two and a half billion years ago. The sum total of all the sampling events by which an object inscribes itself on other objects is a history, in both senses of that wonderfully ambivalent Greek term—since "history" can mean both events and recording.

Hyperobjects have a history of their own, not simply insofar as they interact with humans.

This history is strictly *the time of hyperobjects*. Raindrops splatter on the ground in western California. They record the history of La Niña, a massive weather system in the Pacific. In particular, they record how the Japanese tsunami scooped up some of La Niña and dumped it on trees and hills and other objects in the object called the United States. La Niña itself is the footprint of a hyperobject called *global warming*. Another footprint may well have been the Japanese earthquake itself, since the changing oceanic temperature may have changed the pressure on Earth's crust, resulting in an earthquake. The quake destroyed four nuclear reactors. Quanta from these reactors, known as alpha, beta, and gamma particles, inscribe themselves in soft tissue around the world. We are living textbooks on global warming and nuclear materials, crisscrossed with interobjective calligraphy.

A dinosaur footprint in fossilized mud is not a dinosaur. Rather, the footprint is a trace of the hyperobject evolution that joins me, the dinosaur, and the mud together, along with my intentional act of holding them in mind. There is a gigantic smudge in the Cosmic Microwave Background, which to some astrophysicists now tells of a bubble universe that collided with our own.[13] Hyperobjects leave footprints everywhere, like the invisible goddess Astraea, the goddess of justice, "forever departing from this world."[14] Yet however useful it is, there is something disturbing about this vision, something slightly uncanny that has forced many philosophers to (1) rigorously separate the causal level from the aesthetic realm, and (2) regard the aesthetic realm as a domain of evil.

There is something even more startling about the footprints of hyperobjects. These footprints are *signs of causality*, and *of* here is both subjective and objective genitive. Causality and the aesthetic, the realm of signs and significance and sensation, are one and the same. Hyperobjects are so big that they compel us toward this counterintuitive view. Interobjectivity eliminates the difference between *cause* and *sign*. Let's pause and consider just how remarkable this is.

To do so, it would be most illuminating to take a short detour through an area that seems tangential: cognition and consciousness. One benefit of the detour is that it will allow us to discern why the view of interobjectivity is so surprising: it has to do with the long history of correlationism—the restriction of thinking to the human–world correlation—resulting in phenomena such as the pure relationism of structuralist accounts of linguistics and anthropology (and so on), and the cybernetics of Spencer-Brown.

With its interest in how firing neurons can give rise to mind, neuroscience has an inkling of the magical quality of bringing signs and causality together, when it thinks the systems theory of Luhmann and, behind it, the Mark of Spencer-Brown's *Laws of Form*.[15] What the perspective of hyperobjects adds to this theory is exactly what deconstruction adds to structuralist theories of relational meaning. Or possibly what deconstruction *takes away*: for every system of meaning, there must be some opacity for which the system cannot account, which it must include–exclude in order to be itself. Here is the substantial difference between Spencer-Brown's Mark and Jacques Derrida's contemporaneous *re-mark*, a sign that is also not a sign, just a smudge or a blot, or simply the inscribable surface on which the mark is written.[16] In this case, it is the seeming weirdness of deconstruction's observation that is more demystifying than the relationism that it deconstructs.

Every interobjective space implies at least one more object in the vicinity: let us call this the $1 + n$. Writing depends on $1 + n$ entities: paper, ink, letters, conventions. The human anthropomorphizes the cup and the cup cup-omorphizes the human, and so on. In this process there are always $1 + n$ objects that are excluded. Returning to the question of consciousness, we can see how interobjectivity does work very similarly to deconstruction's discovery of the re-mark. Deconstruction may simply be the tip of a larger iceberg altogether. "Mind" emerges from interactions between neurons and other objects precisely because those interactions themselves are always-already aesthetic–causal. The magic of systems thinking evaporates in the face of a deeper magic, the magic of real objects that subtend the object system, objects that emit time, space, and causality. Hyperobjects simply enable us to see what is generally the case:

(1) Protagoras notwithstanding, objects are not made-to-measure for humans.

(2) Objects do not occur "in" time and space, but rather emit spacetime.

(3) Causality does not churn underneath objects like a machine in the basement, but rather floats in front of them.

(4) The causal dimension, in which things like explosions are taken to happen, is also the aesthetic dimension, in which things like *Nude Descending a Staircase* are taken to happen.

Thus, the idea that causality is the machinery in the basement and the aesthetic is the candy on top—the Scylla and Charybdis against which medium-sized objects, such as global warming, a dinosaur, and a droplet of soy sauce, have been ground to a pulp by eliminative materialism—is now obsolete. We have hyperobjects to thank for its obsolescence.

Now we are in a position to reach quite a stunning conclusion about the nature of temporality when it comes to thinking hyperobjects. As was just noted, the apparent traces of hyperobjects appear as indexical signs, like the footprints of an invisible person walking across the sand: Astraea, "constantly departing from the world."[17] From this we can draw a conclusion that startlingly strikes against the metaphysics of presence (the idea that time is a succession of now points, that *being present* is being real, and so on). Instead, we discover that the "present moment" is a shifting, ambiguous stage set, like the beach washed by the tide and imprinted by the footsteps of Astraea. The appearance of things, the indexical signs on the seashore, is the *past* of a hyperobject. What we commonly take to lie underneath a present thing, its past state, is its appearance-for some entity (a rain gauge, a sensor, a philosopher). Its causal traces float in front of it, in the realm of appearance, the aesthetic dimension.

Think of a city. A city contains all kinds of paths and streets that one might have no idea of on a day-to-day basis. Yet even more so, you could live in a city such as London for fifty years and never fully grasp it in its scintillating, oppressive, joyful London-ness. The streets and parks of London, the people who live there, the trucks that drive through its streets, constitute London but are not reducible to it. London is not a whole that is greater than the sum of its parts. Nor is London reducible to those parts. London can't be "undermined" downward or upward. Likewise, London isn't just an effect of my mind, a human construct—

think of the pigeons in Trafalgar Square. Nor is London something that only exists when I walk through the Victoria Line tunnel to the Tate Gallery at Pimlico Underground Station, or when I think about London, or write this sentence about London. London can't be "overmined" into an aftereffect of some (human) process such as thinking or driving or essay writing. To this extent writing about music really is like dancing about architecture—and a good thing too. Everything is like that.

The streets beneath the streets, the Roman Wall, the boarded-up houses, the unexploded bombs, are records of everything that happened to London. London's history is its form. Form is memory. We make a weird return to Aristotle, who specified that the form of a thing is its essence and that matter ("material cause") is a perspective trick, a backward glance at the object—quarry, sand, crushed dinosaur bones—that were appropriated to form the object in question. London is a photograph of its past. When you walk through the streets (it seems corny to put it this way, but it's not really) you are walking through history. The dirt on a building is part of the building's form, which John Ruskin called *the stain of time*.[18] Just as a hard drive is a surface on which data is inscribed, so London is a series of surfaces on which causality has been inscribed. There is no difference between causality and aesthetic appearance *(aisthēsis)*.

Appearance is the past. *Essence is the future.* The strange strangeness of a hyperobject, its invisibility—it's the future, somehow beamed into the "present." The futurality is what is meant by the term *attractor,* as in the Lorenz Attractor, an entity occupying a high-dimensional phase space that traces weather patterns. It is hard to think an attractor as the precise opposite of a telos, a destiny or destination or end. But this is exactly what an attractor is. An attractor does not pull things toward it through time. In this sense, *attractor* is a misleading term. Rather, the attractor radiates temporality from the future into the present. An attractor is the *future future* of a hyperobject, in the terms outlined in the section on undulating temporality. The future future lies ontologically "underneath" the past! Any local manifestation of an attractor is simply an old photograph, an appearance-for that exists in an interobjective space. Even more astonishing than the fact that appearance is the past, essence is the future.

What we need, then, is not only *ecology without Nature,* for which I have argued. We also need, as I shall argue later in this study, *ecology without matter.* And just to cap it all, we need *ecology without the present.* Indeed, one could successfully argue that it's the *presentism* of contemporary environmentalisms that put them on the wrong side of history. This presentism manifests in a wide variety of ways. Consider the rhetoric of immediacy common to what I have called *ecomimesis*: stop thinking, go out into Nature, turn off your irony. Presentism also manifests in the injunction to stop thinking and *do something,* the paradoxical form taken by the contemporary beautiful soul, a defining, overarching subject position of modernity that has been with us since the late eighteenth century.[19] All too often the siren song of the beautiful soul these days comes in the form of a call to act, *now*! In this sense it appears to be its opposite. Consider a brief example from a Twitter exchange I had recently, based on a comment I had read there: "Michael Moore is self-serving because his movies have not created real, substantial social change. The point is to *change* things, *now.*" It sounds awfully like the Nature injunction: "The point is to stop thinking, stop reflecting, go *out* and *act.*" For this reason, I grow a little queasy when I read Brassier's translation of Quentin Meillassoux's speculative realist *cri de guerre*: "the great outdoors."[20]

The cynical ideological distance typical of modernity is maintained by these injunctions to act, which induce the guilt that cripples genuine action—which of course includes reflection and art. But more important for our purposes, hyperobjects themselves prevent us from being presentist. The present is precisely nowhere to be found in the yawning Rift opening between the future and past, essence and appearance. We simply make it however big we want, and this product of our imagination is a fetish, a fiction: one second, one hour, one day, a century—even a millennium or a geological period. The overbearing metaphysics of presence inscribed into every timekeeping device (especially the digital ones) is, I suppose (without much evidence), responsible in some measure for the psychic distress of modern humans. There is a very simple explanation for this distress: there is no present, yet the clock screams that you must change your focus *now* and have that meeting, pull that face on the chat show, sign the divorce paper, buy the product.

Please don't think that this is Luddite primitivism. It is only an observation based on some quite graphic experiences of different kinds of temporality. It is difficult to believe, naturally, when one is immersed in a vast ocean of presentist metaphysics inscribed into every device about one's person. My solution to presentism is not a quasi-Buddhist "living in the now" popular with forms of Nature mysticism. Nonhuman sentient beings are admired (or pitied) for living in this "now." In admiring (or pitying) them thus, we only see them as instruments of our technological era, extensions of the ticking clocks of metaphysical presence. This is not a progressive ecological strategy. Like Nature, like matter, the present has not served ecology well.

I shall not advocate presentism to fight presentism. Rather I am suggesting aikido—an *exaggeration* of the lack of a true now. What is called *nowness* in Buddhist contemplative theory is not a point or even a bubble, no matter how wide, but a fluid, uncanny washing back and forth like a current and an undertow. There is a Rift between essence and appearance, the slide between future and past.[21] The exaggeration of the Rift of no present is given to us by hyperobjects.

The present does not truly exist. We experience a crisscrossing set of force fields, the aesthetic–causal fields emanated by a host of objects. Anyone familiar with relativity theory will find this idea reasonably intuitive. What is called the *present* is simply a reification, an arbitrary boundary drawn around things by a particular entity—a state, philosophical view, government, family, electron, black hole. Time is not a series of now-points (Aristotle himself refuted this idea) but rather a sickening surge, like crosstown traffic, or an ocean with many currents; or "a river without banks," like the title of a painting by Marc Chagall.[22] Time is a flurry of spells and counterspells cast by objects themselves. Past and future do not intersect in the usually visualized way, as (say) the left-hand and right-hand sides of a cursor blinking on a screen. What we have instead is a nonspatial rift between past and future that corresponds to the Rift between appearance and essence. Between these two fundamental forces, the present is *nowhere*: objects are *never present*. The present is not even a small sliver, like the cursor—a now-point. Nor is the present a bubble whose far side is the past and whose near side is the future (or however one wants to imagine it). Currently, hyperobjects are so large, compared with humans, that the way in which essence is the future and appearance is the past simply become far more vivid than when we consider a pea or a tomcat. Let us consider a brief example.

When the little boy Jim in the movie *Empire of the Sun* sees the energy flash of the first nuclear bomb, he says that it is "like God taking a photograph."[23] We might at first consider this phrase to be a judgment, a demonic repetition of medieval eschatology. But a photograph is not the essence of a thing: the world remains, the future now disclosed to be on *this* side, the hither side of things, by the shocking appearance of the energy flash of a hyperobject. The future is the world after the bomb, this world, the Great Acceleration. God's photograph does not bring about an apocalypse in the sense of a total dissolution of things, but rather it brings about the end of the world as a horizon or limit that exists "over there," over yonder, like Nature, or indeed, like God.

A strange beingness is injected back into the coexistence of things on Earth. The injection needles are every gamma, beta, and alpha particle that radiates from the exploding bomb. The cataclysm closes the beyond as either a place of meaning or a void of no-meaning, cut off from this "mere" Earth. A hyperobject literally photographs us, casting uncanny shadows on the walls of Hiroshima, engraving our flesh with light. Simplistic presence and simplistic absence are what evaporate, along with the lifeforms. The unknown soul of things, the essence, remains on the hither side of the flash, which is why there are at least two movies that talk about hyperobjects in terms of "the day after."[24] By no means should we be happy that we exploded a nuclear bomb that day. It is more like this: the cataclysm was such that it forced us to see. Hyperobjects bring about the end of modernity.

Futurality is reinscribed into the present, ending the metaphysics of presence: not through some neat philosophical footwork, but because the very large finitude of hyperobjects forces humans to coexist with a strange future, a future "without us." (Recall that plutonium and global warming have amortization rates of 24,100 and 100,000 years respectively.) Thanks to hyperobjects, the idea that events are tending toward the future, drawn by some ineluctable telos, is discovered decisively to be a human reification of aesthetic–causal appearance-for. It is the *-for* that indicates that we are already in an interobjective space when it comes to thinking this way, a space demarcated by entities that subtend the interobjective space.

Hyperobjects are simply vast enough to force us to this conclusion. Nonhuman beings strike a devastating blow against teleology, a blow detected by Darwin and celebrated by Marx, who wrote Darwin a fan letter for his opposition to teleology.[25] The end of teleology is *the end of the world*. This end is precisely not an instant vaporization, but rather a lingering coexistence with strange strangers. For the end of the world is the end of endings, the end of telos, and the beginning of an uncertain, hesitating futurality. It is appropriate then that we leave part 1 of this book in this way, glimpsing the end of the world that constitutes the beginning of part 2. It is to the "reaction shot" that we must now turn, since the first part of the book has done something like an adequate job of shocking us, a faint echo of the shocking power of hyperobjects themselves. What reality is it that humans now inhabit? How should they dispose themselves toward the entities they have discovered?

FIGURE 10. Judy Natal, *Future Perfect: Steam Portrait #28.* The uncanny nothingness of the cloud forces the viewer into a disturbing intimacy with the clothed figure. Part of Natal's *Future Perfect* series, this image dramatizes the way the environment encroaches on human social, psychic, and philosophical space. Copyright Judy Natal 2012, www.judynatal.com. Reproduced by permission.

PART II
The Time of Hyperobjects

Polla ta deina k'ouden anthrōpou deinoteron pelei

—SOPHOCLES

The End of the World

You are walking out of the supermarket. As you approach your car, a stranger calls out, "Hey! Funny weather today!" With a due sense of caution—is she a global warming denier or not?—you reply yes. There is a slight hesitation. Is it because she is thinking of saying something about global warming? In any case, the hesitation induced you to think of it. Congratulations: you are living proof that you have entered the time of hyperobjects. Why? You can no longer have a routine conversation about the weather with a stranger. The presence of global warming looms into the conversation like a shadow, introducing strange gaps. Or global warming is spoken or—either way the reality is strange.

A hyperobject has ruined the weather conversation, which functions as part of a neutral screen that enables us to have a human drama in the foreground. In an age of global warming, there is no background, and thus there is no foreground. It is the end of the world, since worlds depend on backgrounds and foregrounds. *World* is a fragile aesthetic effect around whose corners we are beginning to see. True planetary awareness is the creeping realization not that "We Are the World," but that we aren't.

Why? Because *world* and its cognates—*environment, Nature*—are ironically more objectified than the kinds of "object" I am talking about in this study. *World* is more or less a container in which objectified things float or stand. It doesn't matter very much whether the movie within the context of *world* is an old-fashioned Aristotelian movie of substances decorated with accidents; or whether the movie is a more avant-garde Deleuzian one of flows and intensities. *World* as the background of events is an objectification of a hyperobject: the biosphere, climate, evolution, capitalism (yes, perhaps economic relations compose hyperobjects). So when climate starts to rain on our head, we have no idea what is happening. It is easy to practice denial in such a cognitive space: to set up, for example, "debates" in which different "sides" on global warming are presented. This taking of "sides" correlates all meaning and agency to the human realm, while in reality it isn't a question of sides, but of real entities and human reactions to them. Environmentalism seems to be talking about something that can't be seen or touched. So in turn environmentalism ups the ante and preaches the coming apocalypse. This constant attempt to shock and dismay inspires even more defiance on the opposite side of the "debate."

Both sides are fixated on *world,* just as both sides of the atheism debate are currently fixated on a *vorhanden* ("present at hand"), objectively present God. As irritating for New Atheists such as Richard Dawkins to hear that atheism is just another form of belief, it nevertheless is—or at any rate, it holds exactly the same *belief about belief* as the fundamentalists. Belief is a token, a mental object that you grip as hard as possible, like your wallet or car keys. In exactly the same way, it is annoying for environmentalists to talk about ecology without Nature. The argument is heard as nihilism or postmodernism. But really it is environmentalism that is nihilist and postmodernist, just as fundamentalism's belief about belief marks it as a form of ontotheological nihilism. The ultimate environmentalist argument would be to drop the concepts *Nature* and *world,* to cease identifying with them, to swear allegiance to coexistence with nonhumans without a world, without some nihilistic Noah's Ark.

In any weather conversation, one of you is going to mention global warming at some point. Or you both decide not to mention it but it looms over the conversation like a dark cloud, brooding off the edge of an ellipsis.[1] This failure of the normal rhetorical routine, these remnants of shattered conversation lying around like broken hammers (they must take place everywhere), is a symptom of a much larger and deeper ontological shift in human awareness. And in turn, this is a symptom of a profound upgrade of our ontological tools. As anyone who has waited while the little rainbow circle goes around and around on a Mac, these upgrades are not necessarily pleasant. It is very much the job of philosophers and other humanities scholars to attune ourselves to the upgrading process and to help explain it.

What is the upgrading process? In a word, the notion that we are living "in" a world—one that we can call Nature—no longer applies in any meaningful sense, except as nostalgia or in the temporarily useful local language of pleas and petitions. We don't want a certain species to be farmed to extinction, so we use the language of Nature to convince a legislative body. We have a general feeling of ennui and malaise and create nostalgic visions of hobbit-like worlds to inhabit. These syndromes have been going on now since the Industrial Revolution began to take effect.

As a consequence of that revolution, however, something far bigger and more threatening is now looming on our horizon—looming so as to abolish our horizon, or any horizon. Global warming has performed a radical shift in the status of the weather. Why? Because *the world* as such—not just a specific idea of world but *world* in its entirety—has evaporated. Or rather, we are realizing that we never had it in the first place.

We could explain this in terms of the good old-fashioned Aristotelian view of substance and accidents. For Aristotle, a realist, there are *substances* that happen to have various qualities or *accidents* that are not intrinsic to their substantiality. In section Epsilon 2 of the *Metaphysics* Aristotle outlines the differences between substances and accidents. What climate change has done is shift the weather from accidental to substantial. Aristotle writes, "Suppose, for instance, that in the season of the Cynosure [the Dog Days of summer] arctic cold were to prevail, this we would regard as an accident, whereas, if there were a sweltering heatwave, we would not. And this is because the latter, unlike the former, is always or for the most part the case."[2] But these sorts of violent changes are exactly what global warming predicts. So every accident of the weather becomes a potential symptom of a substance, global warming. All of a sudden this wet stuff falling on my head is a mere feature of some much more sinister phenomenon that I can't see with my naked human eyes. I need terabytes of RAM to model it in real time (this has been available for about ten years).

There is an even spookier problem arising from Aristotle's arctic summer idea. If those arctic summers continue, and if we can model them as symptoms of global warming, then there *never was* a genuine, meaningful (for us humans) sweltering summer, just a long period of sweltering that seemed real because it kept on repeating for, say, two or three millennia. Global warming plays a very mean trick. It reveals that what we took to be a reliable world was actually just a habitual pattern—a collusion between forces such as sunshine and moisture and humans expecting such things at certain regular intervals and giving them names, such as Dog Days. We took weather to be real. But in an age of global warming we see it as an accident, a simulation of something darker, more withdrawn—climate. As Harman argues, *world* is always presence-at-hand—a mere caricature of some real object.[3]

Now let's think the evaporation of *world* from the point of view of *foreground* and *background*. A weather conversation provides a nice background to our daily affairs, nice to the extent that we don't pay too much attention to it. Precisely for it to be a background, it has to operate in our peripheral vision. Thus, the conversation about the weather with a stranger is a safe way to acknowledge our coexistence in social space. It's "phatic," according to Roman Jakobson's six-part model of communication; that is, it draws attention to the material medium in which the communication is occurring.[4] Likewise, the weather as such is a background phenomenon. It might loom distressingly into the foreground as a tornado or as a drought, but most often those are temporary affairs—there is a larger temporal backdrop against which they seem to occur as isolated incidents.

Now what happens when global warming enters the scene? The background ceases to be a background, because we have started to observe it. Strange weather patterns and carbon emissions caused scientists to start monitoring things that at first only appeared locally significant. That's the old definition of climate: there's the climate in Peru, the climate on Long Island, and so on. But climate in general, climate as the totality of derivatives of weather events—in much the same way as inertia is a derivative of velocity—is a beast newly recognized via the collaboration of weather, scientists, satellites, government agencies, and other entities. This beast includes the sun, since it's infrared heat from the sun that is trapped by the greenhouse effect of gases such as CO_2. So global warming is a colossal entity that includes entities that exist way beyond Earth's atmosphere, and yet it affects us intimately, right here and now. Global warming covers the entire surface of Earth, and 75 percent of it extends five hundred years into the future. Remember what life was like in the early 1500s?

Global warming is really here—even more spookily, it was already here, already influencing the supposedly real wet stuff falling on my head and the warm golden stuff burning my face at the beach. That wet stuff and that golden stuff, which we call weather, turns out to have been a false immediacy, an ontic pseudo-reality that can't stand up against the looming presence of an invisible yet far more real global climate. Weather, that handy backdrop for human lifeworlds, has ceased to exist, and along with it, the cozy concept of *lifeworld* itself. *Lifeworld* was just a story we were telling ourselves on the inside of a vast, massively distributed hyperobject called climate, a story about how different groups were partitioned according to different horizons—concepts now revealed as ontic prejudices smuggled into the realm of ontology. Global warming is a big problem, because along with melting glaciers it has melted our ideas of *world* and *worlding*. Thus, the tools that humanists have at their disposal for talking about the ecological emergency are now revealed, by global warming itself, to be as useless as the proverbial chocolate teapot. It is rather like the idea of using an antique (or better, antiqued) Christmas ornament as a weapon.

The spooky thing is, we discover global warming precisely when it's already here. It is like realizing that for some time you had been conducting your business in the expanding sphere of a slow-motion nuclear bomb. You have a few seconds for amazement as the fantasy that you inhabited a neat, seamless little world melts away. All those apocalyptic narratives of doom about the "end of the world" are, from this point of view, part of the problem, not part of the solution. By postponing doom into some hypothetical future, these narratives inoculate us against the very real object that has intruded into ecological, social, and psychic space. As we shall see, the hyperobject spells doom now, not at some future date. (*Doom* will assume a special technical meaning in this study in the "Hypocrisies" section.)

If there is no background—no neutral, peripheral stage set of weather, but rather a very visible, highly monitored, publicly debated climate— then there is no foreground. Foregrounds need backgrounds to exist. So the strange effect of dragging weather phenomena into the fore- ground as part of our awareness of global warming has been the gradual realization that there is no foreground! The idea that we are embedded in a phenomenological lifeworld, tucked up like little hobbits into the safety of our burrow, has been exposed as a fiction. The specialness we granted ourselves as unravelers of cosmic meaning, exemplified in the uniqueness of Heideggerian Dasein, falls apart since there is no meaningfulness possible in a world without a foreground–background distinction. Worlds need horizons and horizons need backgrounds, which need foregrounds. When we can see everywhere (when I can use Google Earth to see the fish in my mom's pond in her garden in London), the world—as a significant, bounded, horizoning entity—disappears. We have no world because the objects that functioned as invisible scenery have dissolved.[5]

World is an aesthetic effect based on a blurriness and aesthetic dis- tance. This blurriness derives from ignorance concerning objects. Only in ignorance can objects act like blank screens for the projection of meaning. "Red sky at night, shepherd's delight" is a charming old saw that evokes days when shepherds lived in worlds bounded by horizons on which things such as red sunsets occurred. The sun goes down, the sun comes up—of course now we know it doesn't: Galileo and Coperni- cus tore holes in that notion of *world*. Likewise, as soon as humans know about climate, weather becomes a flimsy, superficial appearance that is a mere local representation of some much larger phenomenon that is strictly invisible. You can't see or smell climate. Given our brains' processing power, we can't even really think about it all that concretely. At the very least, *world* means significantly less than it used to—it doesn't mean "sig- nificant for humans" or even "significant for conscious entities."

A simple experiment demonstrates plainly that *world* is an aesthetic phenomenon. I call it *The Lord of the Rings* vs. the Ball Popper Test. For this experiment you will need a copy of *The Two Towers,* the second part of director Peter Jackson's *Lord of the Rings* trilogy.[6] You will also require a Playskool Busy Ball Popper, made by Hasbro. Now play the scene that I consider to be the absolute nadir of horror, when Frodo, captured by Faramir, is staggering around the bombed-out city Osgiliath when a Nazgul (a ringwraith) attacks on a "fell beast," a terrifying winged dragon-like creature.

Switch on the Ball Popper. You will notice the inane tunes that the Popper plays instantly undermine the coherence of Peter Jackson's narrative world.

The idea of *world* depends on all kinds of mood lighting and mood music, aesthetic effects that by definition contain a kernel of sheer ridiculous meaninglessness. It's the job of serious Wagnerian worlding to erase the trace of this meaninglessness. Jackson's trilogy surely is Wagnerian, a total work of art *(Gesamtkunstwerk)* in which elves, dwarves, and men have their own languages, their own tools, their own architecture, done to fascist excess as if they were different sports teams. But it's easy to recover the trace of meaninglessness from this seamless world— absurdly easy, as the toy experiment proves. In effect, this stupid kids' toy "translated" the movie, clashing with it and altering it in its own limited and unique way.

Objections to wind farms and solar arrays are often based on arguments that they "spoil the view."[7] The aesthetics of Nature truly impedes ecology, and a good argument for why ecology must be without Nature. How come a wind turbine is less beautiful than an oil pipe? How come it "spoils the view" any more than pipes and roads? You could see turbines as environmental art. Wind chimes play in the wind; some environmental sculptures sway and rock in the breeze. Wind farms have a slightly frightening size and magnificence. One could easily read them as embodying the aesthetics of the sublime (rather than the beautiful). But it's an ethical sublime, one that says, "We humans choose not to use carbon"—a choice visible in gigantic turbines. Perhaps it's this very visibility of choice that makes wind farms disturbing: visible choice, rather than secret pipes, running under an apparently undisturbed "landscape" (a word for a painting, not actual trees and water). As a poster in the office of Mulder in the television series *The X-Files* says, "The Truth Is Out There." Ideology is not just in your head. It's in the shape of a Coke bottle. It's in the way some things appear "natural"—rolling hills and greenery—as if the Industrial Revolution had never occurred, and moreover, as if agriculture was Nature. The "landscape" look of agriculture is the original "greenwashing." Objectors to wind farms are not saying "Save the environment!" but "Leave our dreams undisturbed!" *World* is an aesthetic construct that depends on things like underground oil and gas pipes. A profound political act would be to choose another aesthetic construct, one that doesn't require smoothness and distance and coolness. *World* is by no means doing what it should to help ecological criticism. Indeed, the more data we have, the less it signifies a coherent world.

World is a function of a very long-lasting and complex set of social forms that we could roughly call the logistics of agriculture. New Zealand is an astonishing place where there are fifteen sheep for every human, a hyperbolic blowup of the English Lake District. It was deliberately manufactured that way. *World* is not just an idea in your head. It's in the way the fields roll toward a horizon, on top of which a red setting sun augurs peace and contentment. It's in the smooth, lawn-like texture of sheep-nibbled grass: "First the labourers are driven from the land, and then the sheep arrive."[8] Wind farms are an eyesore on this aestheticized landscape. Agriculture, in this view, is an ancient technological *world-picture*, to use Heidegger's terms: a form of framing that turns reality into so much stuff on tap *(Bestand)*.[9] Agriculture is a major contributor to global warming, not just because of flatulent cows, but because of the enormous technical machinery that goes into creating the agricultural stage set, the *world*. Perhaps the solution to this is suggested by the kinds of "perverse" technologies developed by pot farmers: to create intensive growth in a small space. Just as the porn industry accelerated the development of the Internet, so the drug industry might be our ecological savior. Stranger things have happened. Preserving the agricultural world picture just as it is, however, has already become a costly disaster.

To return to an example close to New Zealand's heart, *The Lord of the Rings* presents an agricultural landscape that never explains itself. Sure, the Rangers such as Aragorn protect it. But how does it work? For whom and with whom is the growing and the harvesting and the selling done? Hobbiton is constructed to induce nostalgia for a suburban future that thinks itself as a Georgic idyll. To do so requires all kinds of lighting, rendering, and mood music—it also requires the threats of Mordor and orcs that make us care about bland suburbia. Just changing the Wagnerian music would destroy its delicate "balance."

Village Homes is a world-like real illusion that rests in the northwest area of Davis, California. Each street is named after a place or person in *The Lord of the Rings*: Evenstar Lane, Bombadil Lane. The streets are concentric yet nontopologically equivalent, so there is a real feeling of being lost in there. There are vineyards and pomegranate trees. There is a village-green-like space with an amphitheater built into the grass. There is a children's day care called Rivendell. It is all very beautiful; it's very well done. There is already a nostalgia for the present there, not simply for Tolkien, but for an ecological vision of the 1970s when Village Homes was designed. There is one slight problem: you have to have an awful lot of money to live there. And there is a rule that you have to work in the collective allotments. As a friend quipped, "One homeowner's association to rule them all."

There are many reasons why, even if *world* were a valid concept altogether, it shouldn't be used as the basis for ethics. Consider only this: witch ducking stools constitute a world just as much as hammers. There was a wonderful world of witch ducking in the Middle Ages in which witches were "discovered" by drowning them, strapped to an apparatus that submerged them in the local stream: if the supposed witch didn't drown, she was a witch—and should thus be burned at the stake. Witch ducking stools constituted a world for their users in every meaningful sense. There is a world of Nazi regalia. Just because the Nazis had a world, doesn't mean we should preserve it. So the argument that "It's good because it constitutes a world" is flimsy at best. The reason not to interfere with the environment because it's interfering with someone's or something's world is nowhere near a good enough reason. It might even have pernicious consequences. *World* and *worlding* are a dangerously weak link in the series of late-Heideggerian concepts.[10] It is as if humans are losing both their world and their idea of *world* (including the idea that they ever had a world) at one and the same time, a disorienting fact. In this historical moment, working to transcend our notion of *world* is important. Like a mannerist painting that stretches the rules of classicism to a breaking point, global warming has stretched our *world* to breaking point. Human beings lack a world for a very good reason: because *no entity at all* has a world, or as Harman puts it, "There is no such thing as a 'horizon.'"[11] The "world" as the significant totality of what is the case is strictly unimaginable, and for a good reason: it doesn't exist.

What is left if we aren't the world? Intimacy. We have lost the world but gained a soul—the entities that coexist with us obtrude on our awareness with greater and greater urgency. Three cheers for the so-called *end of the world*, then, since this moment is the beginning of history, the end of the human dream that reality is significant for them alone. We now have the prospect of forging new alliances between humans and non-humans alike, now that we have stepped out of the cocoon of *world*.

About six minutes into Pierre Boulez's piece *Répons*, the percussive instruments come in. They surround the smoother instruments (brass, strings), which are playing in a square in the center of the concert hall. The percussive instruments (piano, dulcimer, harp, and so on) are processed through various delays and filters. The sound of their entry is now evocative of speculative realism: the sound of a vaster world bursting into the human, or the reverse, the sound of a trapdoor opening in a plane, or the plane itself disappearing so we find ourselves in the wide blue sky. A terrifying, wonderful sound, the Kantian sublime of inner freedom giving way to a speculative sublime of disturbing intimacy. The sound of the *end of the world* but not an apocalypse, not a predictable conclusion. The sound of something beginning, the sound of discovering yourself *inside of something*. Boulez himself probably thought *Répons* was about the sound of modern human technology, *Gesellschaft* (modern "society") impinging on *Gemeinschaft* (the "organic community"), and so forth. Or the idea of a dialogue between equal partners, a dialectical play between the organic and electronic. The piece is much more that that. It's the sound of real entities appearing to humans. But as I've been arguing, real nonhuman entities appear to humans at first as blips on their monitors. But they are not those blips. The sound of a higher-dimensional configuration space impinging on extreme Western music (total serialism). The sound of hyperobjects. The sound of a nonmusic. Listen to the very end: the sound echoes and reverberates, repeating glissandos; then, suddenly, it's over. No fade out. Robert Cahen captures it well in his deceptively simple film of *Répons,* visualizing the "human sounds" as a traditional orchestral ensemble juxtaposed with revolving and panning shots of trees, and the percussive sounds as humans mediated by *a luminous ocean.*[12] When the percussive instruments enter, the camera on the orchestra pans back to reveal them surrounding the other players, and we see the studio lighting rig, as if the structures that hold the fragile fiction of *world* together have evaporated. Just as most of Earth's surface is water, the sonic space is surrounded by the chilling, sparkling sounds of piano, harp, and glockenspiel.

Instead of trying constantly to tweak an illusion, thinking and art and political practice should simply relate directly to nonhumans. We will never "get it right" completely. But trying to come up with the best world is just inhibiting ecological progress. Art and architecture in the time of hyperobjects must (automatically) directly include hyperobjects, even when they try to ignore them. Consider the contemporary urge to maximize throughput: to get dirty air flowing with air conditioners. Air conditioning is now the benchmark of comfort; young Singaporeans are starting to sweat out of doors, habituated to the homogeneous thermal comfort of modern buildings.[13] Such architecture and design is predicated on the notion of "away." But there is no "away" after the end of the world. It would make more sense to design in a dark ecological way, admitting our coexistence with toxic substances we have created and exploited. Thus, in 2002 the architectural firm R&Sie designed *Dusty Relief,* an electrostatic building in Bangkok that would collect the dirt around it, rather than try to shuffle it somewhere else (Figures 11 and 12).[14] Eventually the building would be coated with a gigantic fur coat of dirt.[15]

Such new ideas are counterintuitive from the standpoint of regular post-1970s environmentalism. Process relationism has been the presiding deity of this thinking, insofar as it thinks flows are better than solids. But thinking this way on a planetary scale becomes absurd. Why is it better to stir the shit around inside the toilet bowl faster and faster rather than just leaving it there? Monitoring, regulating, and controlling flows: Is ecological ethics and politics just this? Regulating flows and sending them where you think they need to go is not relating to nonhumans. Regulation of flows is just a contemporary mode of window dressing of the substances of ontotheological nihilism, the becomings and processes with which Nietzsche wanted to undermine philosophy.

FIGURE 11. New Territories/R&Sie, *Dusty Relief* (2002). By François Roche, Stephanie Lavaux, and Jean Navarro. Contemporary architecture and design is thinking beyond models based on vectors and flow. When one considers Earth or the biosphere as a whole, pushing pollution "somewhere else" is only redistributing it, sweeping it under the carpet. Reproduced by permission.

The common name for managing and regulating flows is *sustainability*. But what exactly is being sustained? "Sustainable capitalism" might be one of those contradictions in terms along the lines of "military intelligence."[16] Capital must keep on producing more of itself in order to continue to be itself. This strange paradox is fundamentally, structurally imbalanced. Consider the most basic process of capitalism: the turning of raw materials into products. Now for a capitalist, the raw materials are not strictly natural. They simply exist prior to whatever labor process the capitalist is going to exert on them. Surely here we see the problem. Whatever exists prior to the specific labor process is a lump that only achieves definition as valuable product once the labor has been exerted on it.

FIGURE 12. New Territories/R&Sie, *Dusty Relief* (2002). By François Roche, Stephanie Lavaux, and Jean Navarro. An electrostatic building attracts pollution rather than redistributing it. The proposed building is an art gallery, speaking to ways in which care for hyperobjects is now redefining the aesthetic. Reproduced by permission.

What capitalism makes is some kind of stuff called capital. The very definition of "raw materials" in economic theory is simply "the stuff that comes in through the factory door." Again, it doesn't matter what it is. It could be sharks or steel bolts. At either end of the process we have featureless chunks of stuff—one of those featureless chunks being human labor. The point is to convert the stuff that comes in to money. Industrial capitalism is philosophy incarnate in stocks, girders, and human sweat. What philosophy? If you want a "realism of the remainder," just look around you. "Realism of the remainder" means that yes, for sure, there is something real outside of our access to it—but we can only classify it as an inert resistance to our probing, a *grey goo,* to adapt a term suggested by thinking about nanotechnology—tiny machines eating everything until reality becomes said goo.

It's no wonder that industrial capitalism has turned the Earth into a dangerous desert. It doesn't really care what comes through the factory door, just as long as it generates more capital. Do we want to sustain a world based on a philosophy of grey goo? (Again, the term that some futurologists use to describe the nightmare of nanoscale robots mashing everything up into a colorless morass.) Nature is the featureless remainder at either end of the process of production. Either it's exploitable stuff, or value-added stuff. Whatever it is, it's basically featureless, abstract, grey. It has nothing to do with nematode worms and orangutans, organic chemicals in comets and rock strata. You can scour the earth, from a mountaintop to the Marianas Trench. You will never find Nature. It's an empty category looking for something to fill it.

Rather than only evaporating everything into a sublime ether (Marx via *Macbeth*: "All that is solid melts into air"), capitalism also requires and keeps firm long-term inertial structures such as families, as Fernand Braudel explored.[17] The Koch brothers and GE are two contemporary examples. One part of capital, itself a hyperobject, is its relentless revolutionizing of its mode of production. But the other part is tremendous inertia. And the tremendous inertia happens to be on the side of the modern. That is, the political ontology in which there is an "away." But there is no "away" in the time of hyperobjects.

Capitalism did away with feudal and prefeudal myths such as the divine hierarchy of classes of people. In so doing, however, it substituted a giant myth of its own: Nature. Nature is precisely the lump that exists prior to the capitalist labor process. Heidegger has the best term for it: *Bestand* (standing reserve). *Bestand* means "stuff," as in the ad from the 1990s, "Drink Pepsi: Get Stuff." There is an ontology implicit in capitalist production: materialism as defined by Aristotle. This specific form of materialism is not fascinated with material objects in all their manifold specificity. It's just stuff. This viewpoint is the basis of Aristotle's problem with materialism. Have you ever seen or handled matter? Have you ever held a piece of "stuff"? To be sure one has seen plenty of objects: Santa Claus in a department store, snowflakes, photographs of atoms. But have I ever seen matter or stuff as such? Aristotle says it's a bit like searching through a zoo to find the "animal" rather than the various species such as monkeys and mynah birds.[18] Marx says exactly the same thing regarding capital.[19] As Nature goes, so goes matter. The two most progressive physical theories of our age, ecology and quantum theory, need have nothing to do with it.

What is *Bestand*? *Bestand* is stockpiling. Row upon row of big box houses waiting to be inhabited. Terabyte after terabyte of memory waiting to be filled. Stockpiling is the art of the zeugma—the yoking of things you hear in phrases such as "wave upon wave" or "bumper to bumper." Stockpiling is the dominant mode of social existence. Giant parking lots empty of cars, huge tables in restaurants across which you can't hold hands, vast empty lawns. Nature is stockpiling. Range upon range of mountains, receding into the distance. Rocky Flats nuclear bomb trigger factory was sited precisely to evoke this mountainous stockpile. The eerie strangeness of this fact confronts us with the ways in which we still believe that Nature is "over there"—that it exists apart from technology, apart from history. Far from it. Nature is the stockpile of stockpiles.

What exactly are we sustaining when we talk about sustainability? An intrinsically out-of-control system that sucks in grey goo at one end and pushes out grey value at the other. It's Natural goo, Natural value. Result? Mountain ranges of inertia, piling higher every year, while humans boil away in the agony of uncertainty. Look at *Manufactured Landscapes,* the ocean of telephone dials, dials as far as the eye can see, somewhere in China.[20] Or consider the gigantic billowing waves of plastic cups created by Tara Donovan in *Untitled (Plastic Cups)* (2006; Figure 13). In massive piles, the cups reveal properties hidden from the view of a person who uses a single cup at a time, a viscous (in my terms) malleability. In Donovan's title, "cups" are in parentheses, the "untitled" outside parenthesis, as if to highlight the way the cups are "saying" something beyond their human use: something unspeakable for a human. The title of no-title places the work both inside and outside human social and philosophical space, like a garbage dump, an idea the gigantic pile surely evokes.

Societies embody philosophies. What we have in modernity is considerably worse than just instrumentality. Here we must depart from Heidegger. What's worse is the location of essence in some *beyond,* away from any specific existence. To this extent, capitalism is itself Heideggerian!

FIGURE 13. Tara Donovan, *Untitled (Plastic Cups)* (2006), plastic cups, dimensions variable. A billowing cloud of plastic made of mundane cups. Donovan plays with the disorienting way in which the human ability to calculate scale evokes strange entities that exist as much as a single plastic cup, but that occupy a dimension that is less available (or wholly unavailable) to mundane human perception. Photograph by Ellen Labenski. Copyright Tara Donovan, courtesy of Pace Gallery. Reproduced by permission.

Whether we call it scientism, deconstruction, relationism, or good-old-fashioned Platonic forms, there is no essence in what exists. Either the beyond is itself nonexistent (as in deconstruction or nihilism), or it's some kind of real away from "here." The problem, then, is not essentialism but *this very notion of a beyond.* This beyond is what Tara Donovan's work destroys.

Tony Hayward was the CEO of BP at the time of the Deepwater Horizon oil pipe explosion, and his callousness made international headlines. Hayward said that the Gulf of Mexico was a huge body of water, and that the spill was tiny by comparison. Nature would absorb the industrial accident. I don't want to quibble about the difference in size between the Gulf and the spill, as if an even larger spill would somehow have gotten it into Hayward's thick head that it was bad news. I simply want to point out the metaphysics involved in Hayward's assertion, which we could call capitalist essentialism. The essence of reality is capital and Nature. Both exist in an ethereal beyond. Over here, where we live, is an oil spill. But don't worry. The beyond will take care of it.

Meanwhile, despite Nature, despite grey goo, real things writhe and smack into one another. Some leap out because industry malfunctions, or functions only too well. Oil bursts out of its ancient sinkhole and floods the Gulf of Mexico. Gamma rays shoot out of plutonium for twenty-four thousand years. Hurricanes congeal out of massive storm systems, fed by the heat from the burning of fossil fuels. The ocean of telephone dials mounts ever higher. Paradoxically, capitalism has unleashed myriad *objects* upon us, in their manifold horror and sparkling splendor. Two hundred years of idealism, two hundred years of seeing humans at the center of existence, and now the objects take revenge, terrifyingly huge, ancient, long-lived, threateningly minute, invading every cell in our body. When we flush the toilet, we imagine that the U-bend takes the waste away into some ontologically alien realm.[21] Ecology is now beginning to tell us about something very different: a flattened world without ontological U-bends. A world in which there is no "away." Marx was partly wrong, then, when in *The Communist Manifesto* he claimed that in capitalism all that is solid melts into air. He didn't see how a hypersolidity oozes back into the emptied-out space of capitalism. This oozing real can no longer be ignored, so that even when the spill is supposedly "gone and forgotten," there it is, mile upon mile of strands of oil just below the surface, square mile upon square mile of ooze floating at the bottom of the ocean.[22] It can't be gone and forgotten—even ABC News knows that now.

When I hear the word "sustainability" I reach for my sunscreen.

The deep reason for why sustainability fails as a concept has to do with how we are not living in a *world*. It is thus time to question the very term *ecology*, since ecology is the thinking of home, and hence world (*oikos* plus *logos*). In a reality without a home, without world, what this study calls *objects* are what constitute reality. Objects are unique. Objects can't be reduced to smaller objects or dissolved upward into larger ones. Objects are withdrawn from one another and from themselves. Objects are Tardis-like, larger on the inside than they are on the outside. Objects are uncanny. Objects compose an untotalizable nonwhole set that defies holism and reductionism. There is thus no top object that gives all objects value and meaning, and no bottom object to which they can be reduced. If there is no top object and no bottom object, it means that we have a very strange situation in which there are more parts than there are wholes.[23] This makes holism of any kind totally impossible.

Even if you bracket off a vast amount of reality, you will find that *there is no top and bottom object in the small section you've demarcated*. Even if you select only a sector of reality to study somewhere in the middle, like they do in ecological science (the *mesocosm*), you will also find no top or bottom object, even as it pertains to that sector alone. It's like a magnet. If you cut it, the two halves still have a north and a south pole. There is no such thing as "half" a magnet versus a "whole" one.

Why is holism such a bad idea? Surely there could be other possible holisms that adopt some version of both–and thinking so that neither the parts nor the whole—whatever the whole might be—are greater. Perhaps the parts are not necessarily lesser than the whole but exist in some both–and synergistic fashion; you could have—simultaneously— "withdrawn" objects and something else (just to satisfy our modern need for things that aren't static, let's say an open-ended, possibly always-expanding, something else).

First, we must walk through some semirelated points about this line of questioning. It sounds like good value to have "both–and" rather than "either–or," to our somewhat consumerist minds ("buy one get one free"). But I'm afraid this is a case of either–or: holism or not. The parts are *not* replaceable components of the whole. The more we open up the Russian doll of an object, the more objects we find inside. Far more than the first object in the series, because *all the relations between the objects and within them also count as objects*. It's what Lacanians call a not-all set. Objects in this sense are fundamentally not subject to phallogocentric rule. (Commercial break: If you're having trouble with "object" at this point, why not try another term, such as "entity"?) What we encounter in OOO, which I have been expounding in these last couple of pages, is a Badiou-like set theory in which any number of affiliations between objects can be drawn. The contents of these sorts of sets are bigger than the container.

Sometimes children's books explore deep ontological issues. The title of *A House Is a House for Me* couldn't be better for a book about ecology (see my observation above about *oikos* and *logos*). The text is a wonderfully jumbly plethora of objects:

Cartons are houses for crackers.
Castles are houses for kings.
The more that I think about houses,
The more things are houses for things.[24]

Home, *oikos*, is unstable. Who knows where it stops and starts? The poem presents us with an increasingly dizzying array of objects. They can act as homes for other objects. And of course, in turn, these homes can find themselves on the inside of other "homes."

"Home" is purely "sensual": it has to do with how an object finds itself inevitably on the inside of some other object. The instability of *oikos*, and thus of ecology itself, has to do with this feature of objects. A "house" is the way an object experiences the entity in whose interior it finds itself. So then these sorts of things are also houses:

A mirror's a house for reflections . . .
A throat is a house for a hum . . .
   . . .
A book is a house for a story.
A rose is a house for a smell.
My head is a house for a secret,
A secret I never will tell.
A flower's at home in a garden.
A donkey's at home in a stall.
Each creature that's known has a house of its own
And the earth is a house for us all.[25]

The time of hyperobjects is the time during which we discover ourselves on the inside of some big objects (bigger than us, that is): Earth, global warming, evolution. Again, that's what the *eco* in *ecology* originally means: *oikos,* home. The last two lines of *A House Is a House for Me* make this very clear.

To display the poem's effortless brio, a lot of silly, fun "houses" are presented in the penultimate section as we hurry toward the conclusion, which then sets the record straight by talking about a "real" house, the Earth. But this is not the case. OOO doesn't claim that any object is "more real" than any other. But it does discount some objects, which it calls *sensual objects.* What is a sensual object? *A sensual object is an appearance-for another object.* The table-for my pencil is a sensual object. The table-for my eyes is a sensual object. The table-for my dinner is a sensual object. Sensual objects are wonderfully, disturbingly entangled in one another. *This is where causality happens,* not in some mechanical basement. This is where the magical illusion of appearance happens. *A mirror's a house for reflections.* Yes, *the mesh* (the interrelatedness of everything) is a sensual object! Strange strangers are the real objects! Some very important entities that environmentalism thinks of as real, such as *Nature,* are also sensual objects. They appear "as" what they are *for an experiencer or user or apprehender.* They are manifestations of what Harman calls the *as-structure.*[26] They are as-structured even though they appear to be some deep background to (human) events.

This confusion of sensual and real, in the terms of *A House Is House for Me*, is like thinking that bread *really is* a house for jam, and jam alone. Rather than simply an idea that occurs to me, and perhaps to the jam, when it finds itself slathered in there. Marmalade wants in on the bread? Too bad, marmalade is an artificial, unnatural parasite! Peanut butter? Illegal alien! Only jam is "natural," such that bread is only made-for-jam. See the problem with *Nature*? In OOO-ese, *reification* is precisely *the reduction of a real object to its sensual appearance-for another object*. Reification is the reduction of one entity to another's *fantasy* about it.

Nature is a reification in this sense. That's why we need *ecology without Nature*. Maybe if we turn Nature into something more fluid, it would work. *Emergence* is also a sensual object. And thus it's in danger of doing the work of reifying—strangely enough, given its reputation as an un-reified, flowy thing, despite its popularity as a replacement for terms such as *nature*. Emergence is always *emergence-for*. Yet there is a deeper way to think emergence. *Physis, emergence, sway, the way a flower unfurls, seeming, upsurge of Being*, are some of the terms Heidegger uses to characterize what he considers to be the primary notion of the ancient Greek philosophers. There is an appearing-to, an emerging-for, going on. Being is not separated from seeming, at the most fundamental stage of Heidegger's account. And so there is no reason why a poem can't be construed as a physical object in as rich a sense as you like. It's only counterintuitive if you think that entities come with two floors: basement mechanics and a pretty living room on top. But for OOO, Heidegger's terms for being are simply elaborations on the *as-structure*. Whether you call it *emergence* or *appearance*, what we are talking about is a *sensual object*.

Thinking on a planetary scale means waking up inside an object, or rather a series of "objects wrapped in objects": Earth, the biosphere, climate, global warming.[27] Ecological being-with does not mean dusting some corner of an object so one doesn't feel too dirty. Ecological being-with has to do with acknowledging a radical uniqueness and withdrawal of things, not some vague sludge of *apeiron* (using Anaximander's term for "the limitless"). A circle, not an endless line, is a better emblem for the constraint, yet openness, of things.[28] Indeed, the vague sludge is precisely the problem of pollution. Process relationism is simply the last philosophical reflex of the modernity that creates the sludge. We need a philosophy of sparkling unicities; quantized units that are irreducible to their parts or to some larger whole; sharp, specific units that are not dependent on an observer to make them real.

These are considerations concerning the normative value of different ontologies. But there is a deeper reason why hyperobjects are best seen not as processes, but as real entities in their own right. Seen from a suitably high dimension, a process just is a static object. I would appear like a strange worm with a cradle at one end and a grave at the other, in the eyes of a four-dimensional being. This is not to see things *sub specie aeternitatis,* but as I argued previously, *sub specie majoris:* from a slightly higher-dimensional perspective. Processes are sophisticated from a lower-dimensional viewpoint. If we truly want to transcend anthropocentrism, this might not be the way to go. To think some things as processes is ironically to reify them as much as the enemy of the process philosopher supposedly sees things as static lumps. As static lumps go, Lorenz Attractors are pretty cool. Processes are equally reifications of real entities. A process is a sensual translation, a parody of a higher-dimensional object by a lower-dimensional being. A hyperobject is like a city—indeed a city such as London could provide a good example of a hyperobject. Cities and hyperobjects are full of strange streets, abandoned entrances, cul-de-sacs, and hidden interstitial regions.

The Nuclear Guardianship movement advocates an approach to nuclear materials that is strikingly similar to the way in which the electrostatic building simply accumulates dirt without shunting it under the rug.[29] There is no *away* to which we can meaningfully sweep the radioactive dust. Nowhere is far enough or long-lasting enough. What must happen instead is that we must care consciously for nuclear materials, which means keeping them above ground in monitored retrievable storage until they are no longer radioactive. Remember that the half-life of plutonium-239 is 24,100 years. That's almost as long into the future as the Chauvet Cave paintings are in our past. The future of plutonium exerts a causal influence on the present, casting its shadow backward through time. All kinds of options are no longer thinkable without a deliberate concealment of the reality of radioactive objects. Far, far more effort must be put into monitored retrievable storage than Thomas Sebeok's disturbing idea of an "atomic priesthood" that enforces ignorance about the hyperobject in question.[30] The documentary *Into Eternity* explores the immense challenge that the now immense heap of nuclear materials on Earth pose to thinking and to democracy.[31] The film is narrated for a far future addressee, displacing the spurious now, which we habitually think as a point or a small, rigid bubble.

Guardianship, care—to *curate* is to care for. We are the curators of a gigantic museum of non-art in which we have found ourselves, a spontaneous museum of hyperobjects. The very nature of democracy and society—Whom does it contain? Only humans? Whom, if any, can it exclude?—is thrown into question. The atomic priesthood would prevent others from knowing the truth.[32] The attempt to care for hyperobjects and for their distant future guardians will strikingly change how humans think about themselves and their relationships with nonhumans. This change will be a symptom of a gradually emerging ecological theory and practice that includes social policy, ethics, spirituality, and art, as well as science. Humans become, in Heidegger's words, the guardians of futurality, "the stillness of the passing of the last god."[33] Nuclear Guardianship has suggested encasing plutonium in gold, that precious object of global reverence and lust, rather than sweeping it away out of view. Encased in gold, which has the advantage of absorbing gamma rays, plutonium could become an object of contemplation. Set free from use, plutonium becomes a member of a democracy expanded beyond the human. Nature as such is a byproduct of automation. By embracing the hyperobjects that loom into our social space, and dropping Nature, *world,* and so on, we have a chance to create more democratic modes of coexistence between humans and with nonhumans. But these modes are not discernible within traditional Western parameters, since future generations—and further futures than that, are now included on "this" side of any ethical or political decision.[34]

Nuclear Guardianship sees nuclear materials as a unit: a hyperobject. This vision summons into human fields of thinking and action something that is already there. The summoning is to nuclear materials to join humans in social space, rather than remain on the outside. Or better, it's an acknowledgment by humans that nuclear materials are already occupying social space. It's an intrinsically scary thought. But wishing not to think it is just postponing the inevitable. To wish this thought away is tantamount to the cleanup operations that simply sweep the contaminated dust, garbage, and equipment away to some less politically powerful constituency. As a member of society, nuclear materials are a unit, a quantum that is not reducible to its parts or reducible upward into some greater whole. Nuclear materials constitute a unicity: *finitude* means just this. Nuclear materials may present us with a very large finitude, but not an infinitude. They simply explode what we mean by finitude. They are not objective lumps limited in time and space, but unique beings.[35] They have everything that Heidegger argues is unique to Dasein.

Hyperobjects are *futural,* as the section "Interobjectivity" demonstrated. They scoop out the objectified now of the present moment into a shifting uncertainty. Hyperobjects loom into human time like the lengthening shadow of a tree across the garden lawn in the bright sunshine of an ending afternoon. The end of the world is not a sudden punctuation point, but rather it is a matter of deep time. Twenty-four thousand years into the future, no one will be meaningfully related to me. Yet everything will be influenced by the tiniest decisions I make right now.[36] Inside the hyperobject nuclear radiation, I am like a prisoner, and a future person is like another prisoner. We are kept strictly apart, yet I guess his existence. There is a rumor going around the prison. If I make a deal with the police and pin the blame for my crime on the other prisoner, and he says nothing, I can go free and he receives a longer sentence. However, if I say nothing and he says nothing together, we both get a minor sentence. Yet if we both betray the other, we receive an even longer sentence. I can never be sure what the other will do. It would be optimal if I emphasize my self-interest above all other considerations. Yet it would be best if I act with a regard to the well-being of the other prisoner.

This is the Prisoner's Dilemma. In 1984 Derek Parfit published the groundbreaking *Reasons and Persons,* a book that exploded long-held prejudices about utility and ethics from within utilitarianism itself. Parfit showed that no self-interest ethical theory, no matter how modified,

can succeed against such dilemmas.[37] Specifically Parfit has in mind
hyperobjects, things such as pollution and nuclear radiation that will
be around long after anyone meaningfully related to me exists. Since in
turn my every smallest action affects the future at such a range, it is as if
with every action I am making a move in a massive highly iterated Prisoner's Dilemma game. We might as well rename it Jonah's Dilemma or
the Dilemma of the Interior of a Hyperobject. Default capitalist economics is rational choice theory, which is deeply a self-interest theory. Yet the
Prisoner's Dilemma indicates we're profoundly social beings. Even self-
interest accounts for the other somehow.

Parfit subjects an astonishing array of self-interest theories (variously
modified to include relatives, friends, neighbors, descendants, and so
on) to numerous tests based on the Prisoner's Dilemma. The Prisoner's
Dilemma encourages one to think about how change begins: one thinks
of the other, one brings the other into decisions that are supposedly about
one's self-interest. To this extent the Prisoner's Dilemma is formally collectivist even though it lacks a positive collectivist or socialist content.
The kinds of compromise necessitated by the Prisoner's Dilemma may
strike ideological purists as weak. It is precisely this *weakness* that makes
the so-called compromises workable and just. Imagine a future self with
interests so different from one's own that to some extent she or he constitutes a different self: not your reincarnation or someone else—you yourself. This person in the future is like the prisoner being interrogated in
the other room. The future self is thus unimaginably distant in one sense,
and yet hyperobjects have brought her into the adjoining prison cell. She
is strange yet intimate. The best course of action is to act with regard
to her. This radical letting go of what constitutes a self has become necessary because of hyperobjects. The *weakness* of this ethical position is
determined by the radical withdrawal of the future being: I can never
fully experience, explain, or otherwise account for her, him, or it. The
end of the world is a time of weakness.

The ethics that can handle hyperobjects is directed toward the unknown and unknowable future, the future that Jacques Derrida calls
l'avenir.[38] Not the future we can predict and manage, but an unknowable
future, a genuinely *future future.* In the present moment, we must develop

an ethics that addresses what Derrida calls *l'arrivant,* the absolutely un-expected and unexpectable arrival, or what I call the *strange stranger,* the stranger whose strangeness is forever strange—it cannot be tamed or rationalized away. This stranger is not so unfamiliar: uncanny *familiar-ity* is one of the strange stranger's traits. Only consider anyone who has a long-term partner: the person they wake up with every day is the strangest person they know. The future future and the strange stranger are the weird and unpredictable entities that honest ecological thinking compels us to think about. When we can see that far into the future and that far around Earth, a curious blindness afflicts us, a blindness far more mysterious than simple lack of sight, since we can precisely see so much more than ever. This blindness is a symptom of an already-existing intimacy with all lifeforms, knowledge of which is now thrust on us whether we like it or not.

Parfit's assault on utilitarian self-interest takes us to the point at which we realize that we are not separate from our world. Humans must learn to care for fatal substances that will outlast them and their descendants beyond any meaningful limit of self-interest. What we need is an ethics of the other, an ethics based on the proximity of the stranger. The deci-sion in the 1990s, rapidly overturned, to squirrel plutonium away into knives and forks and other domestic objects appears monstrous, and so would any attempt to "work" it into something convenient. Hyperobjects insist that we care for them in the open. "Out of sight, out of mind" is strictly untenable. There is no "away" to throw plutonium in. We are stuck with it, in the same way as we are stuck with our biological bod-ies. Plutonium finds itself in the position of the "neighbor" in Abrahamic religions—that awkward condition of being alien and intimate at the very same time.

The enormity of very large finitude hollows out my decisions from the inside. Now every time I so much as change a confounded light bulb, I have to think about global warming. It is the end of the world, because I can see past the lip of the horizon of human worlding. Global warm-ing reaches into "my world" and forces me to use LEDs instead of bulbs with filaments. This aspect of the Heideggerian legacy begins to teeter under the weight of the hyperobject. The normative defense of worlds looks wrongheaded.[39] The ethical and political choices become much clearer and less divisive if we begin to think of pollution and global warming and radiation as effects of hyperobjects rather than as flows or processes that can be managed. These flows are often eventually shunted into some less powerful group's backyard. The Native American tribe must deal with the radioactive waste. The African American family must deal with the toxic chemical runoff. The Nigerian village must deal with the oil slick. Rob Nixon calls this the *slow violence* of ecological oppression.[40] It is helpful to think of global warming as something like an ultra slow motion nuclear bomb. The incremental effects are almost invisible, until an island disappears underwater. Poor people—who include most of us on Earth at this point—perceive the ecological emergency not as degrading an aesthetic picture such as *world* but as an accumulation of violence that nibbles at them directly.

Without a world, there are simply a number of unique beings (farmers, dogs, irises, pencils, LEDs, and so on) to whom I owe an obligation through the simple fact that existence is coexistence. I don't have to run through my worlding checklist to ensure that the nonhuman in question counts as something I could care for. "If you answered mostly (A), then you have a world. If you answered mostly (B), then you are poor in world (German, *weltarm*). If you answered mostly (C), then you have no world whatsoever." What remains without a world is intimacy. Levinas touches on it in his ethics of alterity, although he is incorrect to make this otherness as vague as the "rustling" of blank existence, the "there is" *(il y a)*.[41] The other is fully here, before I am, as Levinas argues. But the other has paws and sharp surfaces, the other is decorated with leaves, the other shines with starlight. Kafka writes:

> At first glance it looks like a flat star-shaped spool for thread, and indeed it does seem to have thread wound upon it; to be sure, they are only old, broken-off bits of thread, knotted and tangled together, of the most varied sorts and colors. But it is not only a spool, for a small wooden crossbar sticks out of the middle of the star, and another small rod is joined to that at a right angle. By means of this latter rod on one side and one of the points of the star on the other, the whole thing can stand upright as if on two legs.[42]

"The idea that he is likely to survive me I find almost painful."[43] Kafka's
Odradek resembles the hyperobject in this respect. Indeed we have let
him into our home somehow, like mercury and microwaves, like the
ultraviolet rays of the sun. Odradek is what confronts us at the end of the
world, not with a shout but with a breathless voice "like the rustling of
fallen leaves."[44] Things appear in their disturbing *weakness* and *lameness,*
technical terms describing the human attunement to hyperobjects that I
have begun to elucidate.

Without a world, there is no Nature. Without a world, there is no life.
What exists outside the charmed circles of Nature and life is a *charnel
ground,* a place of life and death, of death-in-life and life-in-death, an
undead place of zombies, viroids, junk DNA, ghosts, silicates, cyanide,
radiation, demonic forces, and pollution. My resistance to ecological
awareness is a resistance to the charnel ground. It is the calling of the
shaman to enter the charnel ground and to try to stay there, to pitch a
tent there and live there, for as long as possible. Since there are no charnel grounds to speak of in the West, the best analogy, used by some
Tibetan Buddhists (from whom the image derives), is the emergency
room of a busy hospital. People are dying everywhere. There is blood
and noise, equipment rushing around, screams. When the charm of
world is dispelled, we find ourselves in the emergency room of ecological
coexistence.

In the charnel ground, worlds can never take root. Charnel grounds
are too vivid for that. Any soft focusing begins to look like violence.
Haunting a charnel ground is a much better analogy for ecological coexistence than inhabiting a world. There is something immensely soothing about charnel grounds. It is what is soothing about Buddhism's First
Noble Truth, the truth of suffering. Traditionally, Buddhism recognizes
three types of suffering. There is the pain of pain, as when you hit your
thumb with a hammer, and then you close your whole hand in the door
as you rush into the car to get to the doctor's because of your thumb.
Then there is the pain of alteration, in which you experience first pleasure, then pain when pleasure evaporates. Then there is "all-pervasive
pain," which Chögyam Trungpa beautifully describes as a "fundamental creepy quality" akin to Heidegger's description of Angst.[45] It is this

quality that comes close to the notion of *world*. All-pervasive pain has to do with the fixation and confusion that constitute the Six Realms of Existence (traditionally, animals, humans, gods, jealous gods, hungry ghosts, and hell). In paintings of the Wheel of Life, the Six Realms are held in the jaws of Yama, the Lord of Death.

It is this outermost perspective of the jaws of death that provides an entry point into the charnel ground. To a Buddhist, ecophenomenological arguments that base ethics on our embeddedness in a lifeworld begin to look like a perverse aestheticization, celebrations of confusion and suffering for confusion's and suffering's sake. It doesn't really matter what is on the TV (murder, addiction, fear, lust). Each realm of existence is just a TV show taking up "space" in the wider space of the charnel ground of reality, "the desert of the real."[46] Trebbe Johnson and others have established the practice of Global Earth Exchanges, actions of finding, then giving something beautiful in a "wounded place," such as a toxic dump or a nuclear power facility.[47] Or consider Buddhist practitioners of tonglen: "sending and taking," a meditation practice in which one breathes out compassion for the other, while breathing in her or his suffering. Tonglen is now used in the context of polluted places. Consider Chöd, the esoteric ritual of visualizing cutting oneself up as a feast for the demons, another practice that has been taken on with reference to ecological catastrophes. Or consider the activities of Zen priests at the Rocky Flats nuclear bomb trigger factory, such as walking meditation.

Our actions build up a karmic pattern that looks from a reified distance like a realm such as hell or heaven. But beyond the violence that we do, it's the distance that reifies the pattern into a *world picture* that needs to be shattered. Whether it's Hobbiton, or the jungles of *Avatar,* or the National Parks and conservation areas over yonder on the hither side of the screen (though possibly behind the windshield of an SUV), or the fields and irrigation channels on the hither side of the wilderness—it's all a world picture. I'm not saying we need to uproot the trees—I'm saying that we need to smash the aestheticization: in case of ecological emergency, break glass.

Our increasing knowledge of global warming ends all kinds of ideas, but it creates other ones. The essence of these new ideas is the notion of coexistence—that is after all what ecology profoundly means. We co-exist with human lifeforms, nonhuman lifeforms, and non-lifeforms, on the insides of a series of gigantic entities with whom we also coexist: the ecosystem, biosphere, climate, planet, Solar System. A multiple series of nested Russian dolls. Whales within whales within whales.

Consider the hypothetical planet Tyche, far out in the Oort Cloud beyond Pluto. We can't see it directly but we can detect evidence of its possible existence. Planets are hyperobjects in most senses. They have Gaussian geometry and measurable spacetime distortion because they are so massive. They affect everything that exists on and in them. They're "everywhere and nowhere" up close *(viscosity)*. (Point to Earth right now—you have a number of options of where to point.) They are really old and really huge compared with humans. And there's something disturbing about the existence of a planet that far away, perhaps not even of "our" solar system originally, yet close enough to be uncanny (a very large finitude). And it's unseen except for its hypothetical influence on objects such as comets: "The awful shadow of some unseen power," in Shelley's words. Tyche is a good name. It means *contingency* in Greek, so it's the speculative realism planet par excellence. ("Luck" and "chance" are rather tame alternative translations. *Tyche* is what happens to you in a tragedy if your name is Oedipus.) And for now, what could be more obviously withdrawn?

The historic moment at which hyperobjects become visible by humans has arrived. This visibility changes everything. Humans enter a new age of sincerity, which contains an intrinsic irony that is beyond the aestheticized, slightly plastic irony of the postmodern age. What do I mean?

This is a momentous era, at which we achieve what has sometimes been called *ecological awareness*. Ecological awareness is a detailed and increasing sense, in science and outside of it, of the innumerable interrelationships among lifeforms and between life and non-life. Now this awareness has some very strange properties. First of all, the awareness ends the idea that we are living in an environment! This is so bizarre that we should dwell on it a little. What it means is that the more we know about the interconnection, the more it becomes impossible to posit some entity existing beyond or behind the interrelated beings. When we look for the environment, what we find are discrete lifeforms, non-life, and their relationships. But no matter how hard we look, we won't find a container in which they all fit; in particular we won't find an umbrella that unifies them, such as *world,* environment, ecosystem, or even, astonishingly, Earth.

What we discover instead is an open-ended mesh that consists of grass, iron ore, Popsicles, sunlight, the galaxy Sagittarius, and mushroom spores. Earth exists, no doubt, but not as some special enormous bowl that contains all the "ecological" objects. Earth is one object coexisting with mice, sugar, elephants, and Turin. Of course there are many scenarios in which if Earth ceased to exist, Turin and mice would be in trouble. But if the mice were shot into space aboard a friendly extraterrestrial freighter, Earth wouldn't be the cause of their death. Even Turin might be rebuilt, brick by brick, on some other world.

Suddenly we discover the second astonishing thing. Mice are surely mice no matter what we call them. But mice remain mice as long as they survive to pass on their genome—it's what neo-Darwinism calls *satisficing.* Satisficing is a performative standard for existing. And there is no mouse-flavored DNA. There isn't even any DNA-flavored DNA—it's a palimpsest of mutations, viral code insertions, and so on. There isn't even any life-flavored life. DNA requires ribosomes and ribosomes require DNA, so to break the vicious cycle, there must have been an RNA world of RNA attached to a nonorganic replicator, such as a silicate crystal. So there is a mouse—this is not a nominalist nor is it an idealist argument. But the mouse is a non-mouse, or what I call a *strange stranger.*[48] Even more weirdly: this is why the mouse is real. The fact that wherever we look, we can't find a mouse, is the very reason why she exists! Now we can say this about everything in the universe. But one of the most obvious things we can say this about is a hyperobject. Hyperobjects are so huge and so long-lasting, compared with humans, that they obviously seem both vivid and slightly unreal, *for exactly the same reasons.*

Hyperobjects such as global warming and nuclear radiation surround us, not some abstract entity such as Nature or environment or *world.* Our reality has become more real, in the sense of more vivid and intense, and yet it has also become less knowable as some one-sided, facile thing—

again, for exactly the same reasons. In Berkeley, California, in early 2011, radiation levels in water spiked 181 times higher than normal because of the Sendai reactor meltdowns. We know this. We know we are bathed in alpha, beta, and gamma rays emanating from the dust particles that now span the globe. These particles coexist with us. They are not part of some enormous bowl called Nature; they are beings like us, strange strangers.

Should we stop drinking water? Should we stop drinking cow's milk because cows eat grass, which drinks rainwater? The more we know, the harder it is to make a one-sided decision about anything. As we enter the time of hyperobjects, Nature disappears and all the modern certainties that seemed to accompany it. What remains is a vastly more complex situation that is uncanny and intimate at the same time.

There is no exit from this situation. Thus the time of hyperobjects is a time of sincerity: a time in which it is impossible to achieve a final distance toward the world. But for this very reason, it is also a time of irony. We realize that nonhuman entities exist that are incomparably more vast and powerful than we are, and that our reality is caught in them. What things are and how they seem, and how we know them, is full of gaps, yet vividly real. Real entities contain time and space, exhibiting nonlocal effects and other interobjective phenomena, writing us into their histories. Astonishingly, then, the mesh of interconnection is secondary to the strange stranger. The mesh is an emergent property of the things that coexist, and not the other way around. For the modernist mind, accustomed to systems and structures, this is an astounding, shocking discovery. The more maps we make, the more real things tear through them. Nonhuman entities emerge through our mapping, then they destroy them.

Coexistence is in our face: it *is* our face. We are made of nonhuman and nonsentient and nonliving entities. It's not a cozy situation: it's a spooky, uncanny situation. We find ourselves in what robotics and CGI designers call *the uncanny valley* (Figure 14). It's a commonly known phenomenon in CGI design that if you build figures that look too much like humans, you are at risk of crossing a threshold and falling into the uncanny valley (Plate 2). In the uncanny valley, beings are strangely familiar and familiarly strange. The valley seems to explain racism quite well, because the dehumanization suffered by victims of racism makes them more uncanny to the racist than, say, a dog or a faceless robot. Hitler was very fond of his dog Blondi and yet dehumanized Jews and others. That's the trouble with some kinds of environmentalist language: they skip blithely over the uncanny valley to shake hands with beings on the other side. But, as I'm going to argue, there is only another side if you are holding on to some fictional idea of humanness, an idea that ecological awareness actually refutes. The uncanny valley, in other words, is only a valley if you already have some quite racist assumptions about lifeforms.

With ecological awareness there is no "healthy person" on the other side of the valley. Everything in your world starts to slip into the uncanny

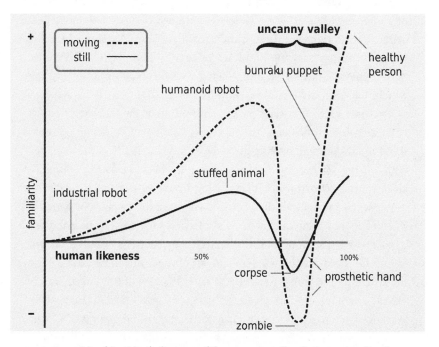

FIGURE 14. Masahiro Mori's diagram of the uncanny valley. Intimacy implies the grotesque. Since ecological awareness consists in a greater intimacy with a greater number of beings than modernity is capable of thinking, humans must pass through the uncanny valley as they begin to engage these beings. For reasons given in the book, this valley might be infinite in extent.

valley, whose sides are infinite and slick. It's more like an uncanny charnel ground, an ER full of living and dying and dead and newly born people, some of whom are humans, some of whom aren't, some of whom are living, some of whom aren't. Everything in your world starts to slip into this charnel ground situation, *including your world.*

Isn't it strange that we can admire comets, black holes, and suns—entities that would destroy us if they came within a few miles of us—and we can't get a handle on global warming? Isn't global climate now in the uncanny valley? Doesn't this have something to do with art? Because when you look at the stars and imagine life on other planets, you are looking through the spherical glass screen of the atmosphere at objects that appear to be behind that glass screen—for all the developments since Ptolemy, in other words, you still imagine that we exist on the inside of some pristine glass sphere. The experience of cosmic wonder is an aesthetic experience, a three-dimensional surround version of looking at a picturesque painting in an art gallery. So Jane Taylor's Romantic-period poem "The Star" is about seeing stars through the atmosphere, in which they seem to "Twinkle, twinkle."

Two and a half thousand people showed up at the University of Arizona in Tucson for a series of talks on cosmology.[49] Evidently there is a thirst for thinking about the universe as a whole. Why is the same fascination not there for global warming? It's because of the oppressive claustrophobic horror of actually being inside it. You can spectate "the universe" as an ersatz aesthetic object: you have the distance provided by the biosphere itself, which acts as a spherical cinema screen. Habit tells us that what's displayed on that screen (like projections in a planetarium) is infinite, distant—the whole Kantian sublime. But inside the belly of the whale that is global warming, it's oppressive and hot and there's no "away" anymore. And it's profoundly regressing: a toxic intrauterine experience, on top of which we must assume responsibility for it. And what neonatal or prenatal infant should be responsible for her mother's existence? Global warming is in the uncanny valley, as far as hyperobjects go. Maybe a black hole, despite its terrifying horror, is so far away and so wondrous and so fatal (we would simply cease to exist anywhere near it) that we marvel at it, rather than try to avoid thinking about it or feel grief about it. The much smaller, much more immediately dangerous hole that we're in (inside the hyperobject global warming) is profoundly disturbing, especially because we created it.

Now the trouble with global warming is that it's right here. It's not behind a glass screen. It *is* that glass screen, but it's as if the glass screen starts to extrude itself toward you in a highly uncanny, scary way that violates the normal aesthetic propriety, which we know about from philosophers such as Kant—the propriety in which there should be a Goldilocks distance between you and the art object, not too close, not too far away. Global warming plays a very mean trick. It comes very, very close, crashing onto our beaches and forcing us to have cabinet meetings underwater to draw attention to our plight, and yet withdrawing from our grasp in the very same gesture, so that we can only represent it by using computers with tremendous processing speed.[50] The whale that Jonah is inside is a higher-dimensional being than ourselves, like two-dimensional stick people relative to a three-dimensional apple. We see that we are *weak,* in the precise sense that our discourse and maps and plans regarding things are not those things. There is an irreducible gap.

Spookily, the picture frame starts to melt and extrude itself toward us, it starts to burn our clothing. This is not what we paid twelve bucks to see when we entered the art gallery. Human art, in the face of this melting glass screen, is in no sense public relations. It has to actually *be* a science, part of science, part of cognitively mapping this thing. Art has to be part of the glass itself because everything inside the biosphere is touched by global warming.

Hypocrisies

A small boy runs in front of an oncoming truck. You watch in horror as you realize the truck can't slow down in time. You think you should save the boy, but you are unsure. Still, the moment compels you to act: you rush into the street and grab the boy, yanking him out of the way just in time. As the truck bears down on you both, you manage to half stumble, half jump clear. The boy is safe.

You have no idea why you just did what you did. You just did it. It seemed like the right thing to do. A certain immediacy was involved, but you feel strange. You had no good reason to save the boy.

I walk down the same street two weeks later. Not having learned his lesson, the same small boy runs out in front of an oncoming truck. I think I should save him, but I'm not sure. I hesitate. I do a quick moral calculation. I believe that ethical action is based on utility, and existing as such is a good, so I think I should save the boy. Or the boy is related to me: he is my cousin, or he is my doctor's niece's school friend. In any case, I decide to save the boy: too late, the boy is dead.

Two weeks after that, in exactly the same spot (people wonder why accidents happen there for years afterward), another small child, a girl, runs out in front of another truck. A stranger is walking down the street. She thinks she should save the girl, but she is unsure. She does a quick series of calculations. Is the truck going so fast that it won't be able to slow down in time? Perhaps it can slow down. Does the truck have sufficient momentum that even if it slowed down, it would still plough into the girl? Is the friction of the road surface enough to weaken the truck's inertia and bring it to a halt even though it would continue to slide toward the girl even if the driver jammed on the breaks, all things being equal? The stranger decides that the truck will inevitably hit the girl, and she is correct: the truck did just hit the girl, killing her instantly.

It would be easy to confuse your actions—you are the one who just saves the boy, without a well-formed reason—for an irrationalist "just do it" attitude, an anti-intellectual or pseudo-Zen valuation of immediacy over reflection, doing versus thinking. But you are very intelligent. You know that all the reasons in the world are not enough of a reason to love. You just save the boy, but in doing so you experience an extraordinary feeling of uncanniness. A variation of the Talking Heads' song "Once in a Lifetime" springs to mind: "This is not my beautiful boy, / This is not my beautiful street, / This is not my beautiful action."[1]

Isn't this precisely the situation we are in when confronted with hyperobjects? When it comes to global warming, finding a good reason for tackling it may be one of the greatest factors inhibiting actually doing anything about it. There are just not enough reasons. Global warming is what some philosophers have called a *wicked problem*: this is a problem that one can understand perfectly, but for which there is no rational solution.[2] Global warming has now been labeled a *super wicked problem*: a wicked problem for which time is running out, for which there is no central authority, where those seeking the solution to it are also creating it, and where policies discount the future irrationally.[3]

Utilitarianism is deeply flawed when it comes to working with hyperobjects. The simple reason why is that hyperobjects are profoundly futural. No self-interest theory of ethical action whatsoever, no matter how extended or modified, is going to work when it comes to an object that lasts for a hundred thousand years. There is a radical asymmetry between the urgency and the passion and the horror that we feel when confronted with a hyperobject that could profoundly alter life on Earth, and the sense of cognitive weirdness and irony that we feel for exactly the same reason. The asymmetry is very refreshing, really. Hyperobjects reduce conservatism (what does it ever conserve?) to a vague abstraction, the sliver of the tip of an iceberg of false immediacy. But hyperobjects make hypocrites of us all.

The weirdness and irony derive from the fact that, to adapt a telling idea of Søren Kierkegaard's, "Inside the hyperobject we are always in the wrong."[4] Doing nothing evidently won't do at all. Drive a Prius? Why not (I do)? But it won't solve the problem in the long run. Sit around criticizing Prius drivers? Won't help at all. Form a people's army and seize control of the state? Will the new society have the time and resources to tackle global warming? Solar panels? They take a lot of energy to make. Nuclear power? Fukushima and Chernobyl, anyone? Stop burning all fossil fuels now? Are we ready for such a colossal transition? Every position is "wrong": every position, including and especially the know-it-all cynicism that thinks that it knows better than anything else.

The "insideness" is not (simply) a physical location. Even if you go to Mars, you have the same problem; in fact, it's magnified since you must create a biosphere from scratch. No, this "within" the hyperobject has to do with the way in which the hyperobject distorts my idea of time. Recall the three timescales of global warming: the horrifying, the terrifying, and the petrifying—five hundred, thirty thousand, and one hundred thousand years respectively. These *very large finitudes* collapse my clichéd ideas of time from within. It isn't that hyperobjects are special beings, like an angel or a demon or a god, sent to slap my objectification of reality upside the head by hurtling me into contact with a transcendental beyond. Far from it. Hyperobjects are real things, really existing, in this physical realm. And what they perform is far subtler and more effective than an angel or a god, or a traditional Heideggerian, for whom the human is the only shepherd of being, the most uncanny of the uncanny things on Earth. Five hundred years is a "real" timescale, in the sense that it has been measured using scientific instruments to a certain degree of precision. Three hundred and fifty parts per million is a "real" number, real in the sense that it fits the reified view of particles occupying points in an objective space and time. In this case, 350ppm is the upper bound of particles of carbon compounds in air that provides for a relatively recognizable Earth for the foreseeable future. (Earth is currently exceeding 400ppm.)

These numbers, these reified timescales, eat away at my reification from within. Like aikido masters, they use my energy against itself. I become convinced of the uncanny futurality of nonhumans, not through some religious conversion, but through reification itself. It "sticks" much better that way. I have not been converted to the belief in a nonobjectified beyond, but rather my prejudices have collapsed from within, through their very objectification. Is it possible, to lapse into Heideggerese, that hyperobjects are indeed the "last god" that appears in our world to save us from our technological manipulation? That, precisely as Heidegger argues, the cure for nihilism comes from within nihilism itself, from within the reified hyperobjects we have in part created through that very technology, whose measurements are products of the very latest, fastest, most complex performances of that same technology (complexity theory, mapping climate using supercomputers, and particle accelerators, for example)? This would indeed be a case of being healed by the spear that smote you (as in Wagner's *Parsifal*).[5]

Think of the weight of the sheer numbers with which global warming is thrust on us: like something from a book of records, global warming is spectated as the biggest, the most, the hugest. This "number crunching" stance toward global warming is far from simply "scientific" or "informational," which is not to say that this is merely a matter of "culture" or "worldview." Indeed, it directly embodies a philosophical stance that gave rise to global warming in the first place. Earth and actually existing beings that live here are bathed in a giant sea of numbers. Yet from within the nihilism of this phenomenon, which is what Heidegger calls *the gigantic*—the rise of sheer quantity—emerges the "other beginning" of history, not its end.[6] The ontological, not to mention the psychic and social, economy of such an arrangement is startling. I need no special props, no deus ex machina. I don't need the apocalypse—indeed, as we saw in the previous section, such thoughts inhibit intimacy with the strange strangeness of nonhumans. The trivially mathematized fact of hyperobjects' longevity is all the help I need. It is simply a matter of getting used to this mathematical fact—*getting used to* is a fair translation of the Greek *mathēsis*.

Derek Parfit's main reason for writing *Reasons and Persons*, as I showed in the previous section, was the existence of phenomena such as nuclear radiation and pollution: hyperobjects. What to do about them? Since no one meaningfully related to me will be living 24,100 years from now (the half-life of plutonium), my cognitive, ethical, and political dispositions toward plutonium must transcend my self-interest, however widely defined. Moreover, hyperobjects last so long that utilitarian concepts such as the social discount rate, a sliding scale for determining the value of future people for present actions, cannot be ethically or even meaningfully applied to them.[7] Hyperobjects compel us to adopt attitudes for which humans are not well prepared in an age of advanced consumer capitalism.

There is a further problem with timescales concerning global warming—there are lots of them. We are dealing with an object that is not only massively distributed, but that also has different amortization rates for different parts of itself. Hyperobjects are messages in bottles from the future: they do not quite exist in a present, since they scoop the standard reference points from the idea of present time. In order to cope with them, we require theories of ethics that are based on scales and scopes that hugely transcend normative self-interest theories, even when we modify self-interest by many orders of magnitude to include several generations down the line or all existing lifeforms on Earth.

Yet in transcending self-interest theories we need not throw the baby of intimacy out with the bathwater of self. Indeed, dropping self-interest theories involves us in what Parfit himself refers to as a more intimate contact with other lifeforms and future selves. In a moving passage in the middle of *Reasons and Persons,* a passage that is startlingly personal compared with the blisteringly rational mode of Oxbridge utilitarianism that his work exemplifies, Parfit writes:

Is the truth [of no-self] depressing? Some may find it so. But I find it liberating, and consoling. When I believed that my existence was [a "deep further fact, distinct from physical and psychological continuity, and a fact that must be all-or-nothing"], I seemed imprisoned in myself. My life seemed like a glass tunnel, through which I was moving faster every year, and at the end of which there was darkness. When I changed my view, the walls of my glass tunnel disappeared. I now live in the open air. There is still a difference between my life and the lives of other people. But that difference is less. Other people are closer. I am less concerned about the rest of my own life, and more concerned about the lives of others.[8]

Parfit's words themselves exemplify the intimacy and openness to the future that a no-self view bestows. On this view, "self" is reduced to mere physical and psychological continuity.

The no-self view is not a faceless, dehumanized abstraction, but a radical encounter with intimacy. What best explains ecological awareness is a sense of intimacy, not a sense of belonging to something bigger: a sense of being close, even too close, to other lifeforms, of having them under one's skin. Hyperobjects force us into an intimacy with our own death (because they are toxic), with others (because everyone is affected by them), and with the future (because they are massively distributed in time). Attuning ourselves to the intimacy that hyperobjects demand is not easy. Yet intimacy and the no-self view come together in ecological awareness. The proximity of an alien presence that is also our innermost essence is very much its structure of feeling.

Consider symbiosis, as explored by Lynn Margulis and others. One feature of symbiosis is endosymbiosis, the fact that lifeforms do not simply live alongside us: they are within us, so much so that on many levels the host–parasite distinction collapses. Our mitochondria are symbionts hiding from their own catastrophe, the environmental disaster called oxygen. Many cell walls are double, hinting at some ancient symbiotic coupling. To a great extent others are us: or as the poet Rimbaud put it, "Je est un autre."[9] On a nonphenomenological level (that is, one not dependent on experience), a level an extraterrestrial with a microscope could validate, we are strangers to ourselves. That is how close the other is. Ecology is about intimacy.

As well as being about mind-bending time- and spatial scales, hyperobjects do something still more disturbing to our conceptual frames of reference. Hyperobjects undermine normative ideas of what an "object" is in the first place. This sudden turnaround has an uncanny effect. Knowledge about radiation makes us question commonsensical ideas about the utility and benefits of the sun. Unlike sunlight we cannot directly see radiation. Yet it affects us far more intensely than visible light. Knowledge about ozone depletion, global warming, and radiation have turned ordinary reality into a dangerous place that Ulrich Beck calls "risk society," a place in which government policy now involves the distribution of risk across populations, often unevenly.[10] In the long run, no one is exempt from risk. Once we become aware of the long-term effects of hyperobjects, we cannot abolish this awareness, and so it corrodes our ability to make firm decisions in the present.[11]

The fact that we need devices such as computers and Geiger counters to see hyperobjects, objects that will define our future, is humbling in the same way Copernicus and Galileo brought humans down to Earth by insisting that the universe was not rotating around us.[12] In their era, "common sense" told people that the sun revolved around the earth once a day. Common sense also assured people that weird old ladies who proffered herbal remedies and failed to drown when thrown in water should be burnt, because they were witches. Common sense has a lot to answer for.

The problem of human society, wrote Jacques Lacan, is what to do with one's shit. Putting it this way is rather anthropocentric: many nonhumans also appear concerned about what to do with their waste.[13] Hyperobjects present us with the same problem, hugely amplified. A Styrofoam cup will take about five hundred years to biodegrade. Even the massive density of the exponentially increasing human population itself could be seen as a hyperobject created by leaps in agricultural technology and logistics since the eighteenth-century Agricultural Revolution, and even more so since 1945. What should we do about substances that will be around many centuries after our culture has either radically changed or disappeared entirely? The problem goes beyond how to dispose of human-sized things, like the stuff that gets flushed down a toilet. What should we do about substances on whose inside we find ourselves?

So what is it indeed like, inside the hyperobject, in which we are always in the wrong? Let us consider Lingis's reworking of Kantian ethics. Lingis does this by situating the transcendental a priori in what he calls the *level* generated by an object, its physical grip on me, a grip that sends *directives* to me. Here is Lingis's own example, which is compelling in an ecological way. You are walking through a sequoia forest in Northern California. The gigantic trees surround you with their ancient forms. Vast networks of lichen spread themselves around the branches. You smell smoke, and look in the direction of the smell, to see the glowing tip of a cigarette butt like a bright orange bead in the ferny undergrowth. You leap over toward the ferns, parting them with your foot, and stamp on the cigarette, before pouring water from your water bottle over the area to ensure that no fire can start again.

It's significant that Lingis chose the burning cigarette.[14] Not only does the ecological emergency confront us with countless moments such as this—you leave your house and realize you left the lights on, or you stop at a carwash and wonder whether you should turn the engine off and swelter in the drought outside, without air conditioning. Ecological issues more deeply present us with very pure versions of Lingis's *levels* and *directives*. Nonhumans, argues Lingis, tell us how to dispose ourselves toward them.[15] A hammer "wants" to be held in a certain way. A forest path issues directives to my body to walk at a particular pace, listen for animals, avoid obstacles. A cigarette butt demands that I put it out. These *directives* grip me already, before I can reflect (rationally or not) on the right course of action. The Kantian notion of synthetic judgments presupposes the levels. The directives issue from entities that establish zones of aesthetic causality in which I find myself caught (the levels). These directives ground the categorical imperative, not some decision in a void. We find ourselves thinking belatedly of how to dispose ourselves toward things.

Why do I step up to stamp out the burning cigarette? From this point of view, free will is overrated.[16] We are seduced and induced by leaves, tennis rackets, gas pedals, and passersby. I do not find myself in a (single, solid) *world,* but rather in a shifting set of zones emitted by specific objects. The hyperobject must also emit zones that gather us in like the tractor beam that locks onto the *Millennium Falcon* in *Star Wars.* I shall use the term *zone* rather than *level* from now on, since to my ear *zone* eliminates a sense of flatness and structure. In this notion of the emergence of time and space from an object we can begin to understand the term *zone. Zone* can mean *belt,* something that winds around something else. We talk of temperate zones and war zones. A zone is a place where events are happening: the zone winds around, it radiates heat, bullets fly, armies are defeated.

What action is taking place? "Not something that just is what it is, here and now, without mystery, but something like a quest . . . a tone on its way calling forth echoes and responses . . . water seeking its liquidity in the sunlight rippling across the cypresses in the back of the garden."[17] If, as suggested earlier, there is no functional difference between substance and accidence, if there is no difference between perceiving and doing, if there is no real difference between sentience and non-sentience, then causality itself is a strange, ultimately nonlocal aesthetic phenomenon. A phenomenon, moreover, that emanates from objects themselves, wavering in front of them like the astonishingly beautiful real illusion conjured in this quotation. The sentence does what it says, casting a compelling, mysterious spell, the spell of causality, like a demonic force field. Yet if we knew it as simply an illusion, it would cease to waver. It would not be an illusion at all. We would be in the real of noncontradiction. Since it is *like* an illusion, however, we can never be sure: "What constitutes pretense is that, in the end, you don't know whether it's pretense or not."[18]

A zone is not entirely a matter of "free will." Objects are far more threateningly autonomous, and sensually autonomous, than the Kantian version of autonomy. Objects are, in a sense, like the *temporary autonomous zone* celebrated by Hakim Bey.[19] The birth of a fresh object is a "political" interruption, a revolution that changes all the other objects, no matter how slightly.[20] A zone is not studiously decided on by committee before it goes into action. Irreducibly, *it is already happening*. We find ourselves in it, all of a sudden, in the late afternoon as the shadows lengthen around a city square, giving rise to an uncanny sensation of having been here before.

In the basement of the Chernobyl reactor, there is a gigantic "elephant's foot" of corium, a radioactive mash of metals and glass from the core. It cannot be seen directly, unless one wants to die quickly. The first attempt to photograph it with a camera on wheels was a failure, because the camera was destroyed by the emissions from this object. Eventually it had to be photographed in a mirror with the camera around the

PLATE 1. Yukultji Napangati, *Untitled* (2011). The painting as agential entity, holding the viewer in a series of crisscrossing interference patterns. Copyright Yukultji Napangati, licensed by Aboriginal Artist Agency. Reproduced by permission.

PLATE 2. Judy Natal, *Uncanny Valley ,The Juggler*. Taken at the MIT Robotics Institute, this image questions the difference between a human and an android. How and when would one know that the figure is not human? The Turing Test imposes a minimal criterion for being human: it is simply a matter of a certain negative performance. I perform in such a way that you cannot dismiss me as a nonhuman. Copyright Judy Natal 2012, www.judynatal.com. Reproduced by permission.

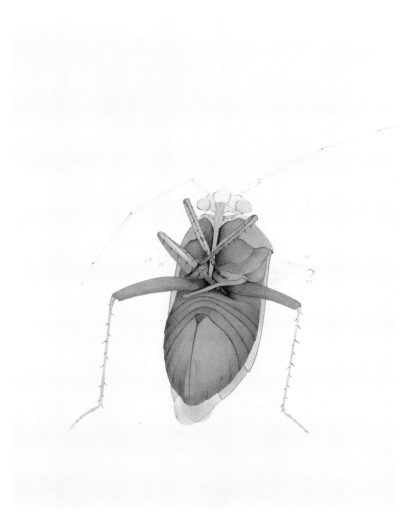

PLATE 3. Cornelia Hesse Honegger, *Soft Bug from Pripyat, Ukraine* (1990), watercolor. "Right side middle leg is short with no foot but two claws" (Honegger's note). Painstaking paintings of the mutagenic effects of radioactive materials reinvent the tradition of natural-historical art. Honegger's work exemplifies a care for the lifeform in question, and an acknowledgment of thinkable entities (high-frequency electromagnetic quanta) only visible at a human scale in their effects on others. Copyright Cornelia Hesse Honneger. Reproduced by permission.

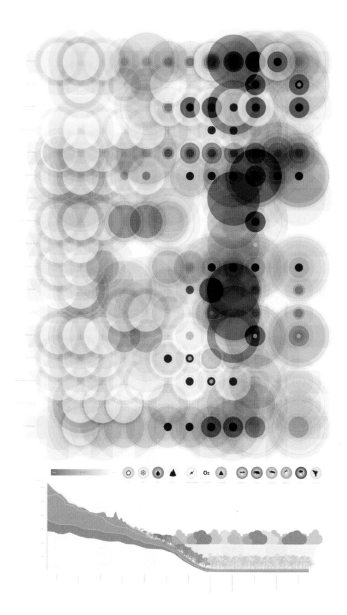

PLATE 4. Marije de Haas, *Wellness over Time, a Visual Diary of the Cape Farewell Andes Expedition* (2009), inkjet print on paper. De Haas was part of the Cape Farewell tours (which began in the Arctic). This work is a diagram of affective and physical responses to the tour, modeled after the original isothermal drawings of Humboldt, early nineteenth-century documents detailing how ecosystems change at different altitudes. Copyright Marije de Haas. Reproduced by permission.

PLATE 5. Chris Wainwright, *Red Ice 3* (2009), color type C print on aluminum. Iceberg as strange stranger, flooded by radiation. Hyperobjects are thinkable but not exhausted by (human) calculation. Art that evokes hyperobjects must therefore deal with their necessarily uncanny intimacy and strangeness. Copyright Chris Wainwright. Reproduced by permission.

PLATE 6. Comora Tolliver, *Pod* (2007), exterior environment detail, mylar, acrylic paint, and other media. When we try to visualize the environment, we encounter entities that are distorted (anamorphic) and spectral (physical yet suffused with nothingness). To see the environment as Nature is to skip over this necessary step of facing horror and fear. Copyright Comora Tolliver. Reproduced by permission.

PLATE 7. Marina Zurkow, frame from *Mesocosm* (*Wink, TX*) (2012). The animation formed part of Zurkow's *Necrocracy* installation at DiverseWorks, Houston, March 16–April 21, 2012. A mesocosm is a unit of ecological scientific measurement. Human attention is outscaled by an algorithm (the software art) that executes, as the environment does, in a much larger temporality. In Zurkow's animation, plastic bags, a train, and spectral clouds of oil coexist with butterflies and grasses. Copyright Marina Zurkow. Image courtesy of the artist and bitforms gallery. Reproduced by permission.

PLATE 8. Marina Zurkow, frame from *Elixir* II (2009). Human cognition has made available a reality that is not simply abstract and computational, but phenomenologically rich and disturbing. In particular, large-scale entities hollow out the (human) present as if the human is now adrift on a sea of nothingness, a nothingness that affects what happens "inside" human (social, psychic, philosophical) space (the interior of the decanters in Zurkow's animation). Copyright Marina Zurkow. Image courtesy of the artist and bitforms gallery. Reproduced by permission.

corner. Objects emit zones. Wherever I find myself, a zone is already happening, an autonomous zone, like a pair of carefully tuned sine waves that fills a house with a crisscrossing field of interference patterns (a brief description of La Monte Young and Marian Zazeela's Dream House in New York). Eliane Radigue's astonishingly layered ARP synthesizer tones fill a church with resonances whose lowest frequencies are felt physically as much as heard. A dissonance at that sonic depth results in the body being physically shaken, literalizing what Adorno says about how art shudders and shatters the subject.[21] The music is not "about" the environment: it *is* an environment. *Biogenesis* is simply a recording of Radigue's heartbeat, alongside which the sound of the heartbeat of the baby in her uterus begins to be heard.[22] Played through speakers capable of transmitting the bass frequencies, such as the ones used at the *33 1/3* exhibition at the San Francisco Museum of Modern Art in 2003, *Biogenesis* reaches into the listener's body. Coexistence is forced on us, whether we like it or not. With their vibrant lines, the paintings of Riley and Napangati emit zones that grip me in their wake, unleashing powers on my optic nerve. A human ethical or political decision is made caught in the force fields of intermeshed zones. There is no way to find oneself already having achieved a transcendental purchase on the zone. Kantian synthetic judgment a priori, in which I have decided what an object is, what object-ness is, is possible (if at all) only because I have already found myself strafed by the zones that objects emit. The simplest cigarette butt or a child running into the street reduces every ethical or political stance to the status of hypocrisy. It is the hyperobject that forces us to sense this hypocrisy most exquisitely. Hyperobjects are simply so large and so long lasting that the zones that cascade from them are rich and intense enough for us to become aware of them; and to become aware of the irreducible gap between zone and object, which Kant calls the gap between the phenomenon and thing.

Because of this gap, I am far from saying that we immediately encounter situations in which we know exactly what to do, as if everything were mechanically automated. Rather, my sense of distance and irony, my hesitation, becomes more pronounced when I find myself latched onto a zone. It is the ontological priority of the zone that accounts fully for the feeling of strangeness and belatedness in my decisions about the object that emits it. It is simply impossible to come up with the right reason for why I put the cigarette out in the sequoia forest. Indeed, if I try to generate a reason, I find myself watching the cigarette burn the undergrowth—I have already made a decision not to put out the cigarette. The zone has already grasped me in its beams. This does not mean that I know exactly how to dispose myself relative to the zone. Far from it: it means that I have no idea, or that I can feel the irreducible dissonance between my idea and the zone.

On what scale am I engaging the zone? Why do I put out the cigarette? Is it because I am concerned about the environment in general? Or this tree in particular? This forest? Is it because I understand global warming, and I see the cigarette as an indexical a sign of human ignorance, a small piece of a gigantic puzzle? Again, the zone is not a region of direct experience, but a shifting, illusory field of irony and weirdness. This is not Nature. This is Heidegger's *thrownness,* inverted.[23] I do not find myself in any old place, a projection of my Dasein's unique uncanniness. *Everything is doing that.* The uncertainty and hesitation are not just in my Dasein, but in the tree, the rock, the cigarette butt glowing in the ferns. My sincerity, my sensitivity to my phenomenological enmeshment in zones, is the very thing that prevents me from grasping the zone as solid and predictable.

This doesn't mean that I am irrevocably caught in a world of prejudices, and that this is a good thing—a common view in ecophenomenology. It means that I am caught in confusion and error and suffering, and that this is a good thing. Embeddedness in a world, as I have argued earlier, is no basis for ecological praxis and thinking. What the zones mean is just the opposite. It means that no matter what my prejudices are, no matter what "world" I feel embedded in, the zones burn through them. Some kind of nonconceptuality burns through my prejudice, which is exactly what hyperobjects, with their obvious futurality, surely do. Hyperobjects are genuinely apocalyptic (from the Greek term *apocaluptō*) in the sense that they *lift the veil* of prejudice—but in so doing they do not catapult us into a beyond. Rather they fix us more firmly to the spot, which is no longer an embeddedness in a world.

The existence of zones emitted by objects is the physical reason for Kantian beauty. Kantian beauty is a nonconceptual object-like entity that seems to float "between" me and the object. Kant reads it as a reflection of my a priori synthetic judgment. But in order for this aesthetic experience to arise, there must be a zone. The zone vibrates from an object and burns through my conceptual overlay, haunting me with its strange strangeness. The zone turns my beliefs and reifications to ash. In the case of hyperobjects, this happens even if I am thickheadedly not well attuned to zones. Hyperobjects are simply too vast to be ignored.

Thus, we are no longer left with a choice between a transcendental aesthetics that guarantees the freedom of positing in an act of synthetic judgment a priori (as Kant suggests), and a substantialist aesthetics that crushes me with the weight of its awesome authority (as proposed by Edmund Burke). The political implications of each aesthetic philosophy are quite evident—we should without doubt choose the Kantian option. Burke's theory represents the aesthetics of the Bush administration and their "Shock and Awe" tactics against Baghdad in the Second Iraq War. But now we have a good, realist reason to accept a Kantian aesthetic theory, not grounded in some transcendental beyond, but right here, before I think about it—in the zone. The zone is nonconceptual but not a blank nothing, not a Hegelian A = A of immediacy. The zone is unspeakable precisely because it is "in my face." I don't reach out to touch it—rather the object sends it to me.

Zones are real but they are not objectively "there," since that would mean that they were metaphysically present, and the hyperobject poses a serious and physical challenge to the metaphysics of presence. There are problems with thinking this nonobjectification. How is it possible to imagine entities that flicker and shimmer rather than remain obdurately "there"—a flickering and shimmering that post-Humean, post-Kantian thought and science necessitates? Yet hyperobjects seem to help us visualize this shimmering quite efficiently. Ontotheology wants to convince me that I must construe things as *real* by thinking of them as objectively present and "there" (*vorhanden*, using Heidegger's term).[24] But the hyperobject prevents me from objectifying it as "real" in this way—although it is of course real, without doubt; it seems to assail me like a nightmare or a threatening circus clown. It is never *vorhanden,* as it's always disappearing behind the rain cloud, the sunburn, the pile of garbage. The feeling of being inside a hyperobject contains a necessary element of *unreality*—yet this is a symptom of its reality!

"Anything you can do, I can do meta." Isn't this the maxim of modernity? For two hundred years, performing intelligence has been about saying something like "I am smarter than you to the extent that I can see around mere objects, or through your 'naïve' attitude." *Being right* in philosophy has most often been a case of *going meta. Monty Python*'s "Argument" sketch almost perfectly embodies it.[25] A man walks into a faceless bureaucratic office building that seems designed to dispense government aid of various kinds. At first he enters a room in which someone hurls insults at him. When he tells the insulter that "I came here for an argument," that man apologizes: "Oh, I'm sorry, this is abuse. Arguments are next door." Next door, the man encounters another bureaucrat, who refuses to engage with him. When the man announces that he is here for an argument, the bureaucrat argues the toss with him about whether or not he is here for an argument: immediately *he goes meta.*

If you've ever been in this type of argument, you'll know how intense it can get. Going meta is a great way to sneer at someone. You remove the rug from underneath the other's feet. Their mere immediacy is always false. It's the deep structure, the numinous background, the possibility of the possibility of the horizon of the event, that is more real, better, or just more rhetorically effective, than anything else. In this mode, the egg of potentiality comes before the chicken of the actual. This mode is exactly what *Monty Python* exploits, in particular in the "Argument" sketch. Much of their humor is based on this meta syndrome, which tells us something about how dominant it was in the age of British imperialism, both in its fully erect and collapsing phases.

The syndrome of going meta is repeated in countless different philosophical modes. I'm not sure which part came first, the thinking or the acting out, but this meta syndrome seems strangely parallel with the basic ontology of modern life. Such is the syndrome deeply responsible for the beautiful soul condition from which we mock anyone who dares to actually do something—the condition Lacan noted when he claimed

"Les non-dupes errent" ("Those who [assume they] are not duped are making a mistake"; it is also a pun on "The name of the father," "Le nom du père," and "The No of the father," "Le non du père").[26] Those who sit up high on the mountain looking down at us poor saps beneath, because they think they can see through everything, are the most deluded of all. Since, as I've argued, the beautiful soul is the mode of consumerism—the default subjective framework since 1800—we can expect the meta syndrome to be pervasive in culture.[27]

Hyperobjects end the world, and they end the transcendental a priori that jumps out of the world to decide its reality. They do so not by dint of clever arguments, nor by remaining mute and impenetrable. There is a rhetorical mode of hyperobjects, since all objects are a form of *delivery*, as we shall see. Hyperobjects don't smack us upside the head or hit us like Doctor Johnson's boot, refuting Berkeley with the nonargument of an aggressive kick. They are not prereflective, if by that we mean they supply some immediate hotline to truth. Indeed, if the rhetorical delivery has a name, it would need to include something like an inducement to reflection. Aristotle's *Rhetoric* is a profoundly original meditation on human affect—rhetoric is as much the art of listening as it is the art of speaking. But to what are we listening when we attune to the hyperobject? Is this uncertainty not precisely *what* we are hearing? Doesn't the affect delivered to us in the rain, or through the weird cyclone or the oil slick, reveal something uncanny? If it has a name, it is *weirdness*. Perhaps the most telling term is the word *doom*.

What is doom? Conventionally, doom is a decree or an ordinance: a directive.[28] Doom can also refer to judgment, law, the faculty of judging, or the final judgment that happens after the end of the world.[29] Yet doom is also what we *deem*— opinion or discernment.[30] Doom can mean fate, destiny, and in a stronger sense, death.[31] Finally, doom means justice, or even judge, one who dispenses justice.[32] Justice is a figure that Derrida calls synonymous with deconstruction, in that it is irreducibly futural: perfect justice can never be achieved now—there is always a remainder to come.[33] A good judge doesn't just mechanically dole out judgments, but paradoxically enforces and suspends the law at the same time.

Doesn't this rich range of meanings suggest something about the hyperobject? The hyperobject is indeed the bringer of fate, destiny, death. This destiny comes from beyond the (human) world, and pronounces or decrees the end of the world. This decree marks a decisive pivot in Earth history in which humans discern the nonhuman and thus reckon the fate of Earth with a greater justice. Or, just to go hog-wild Heidegger-style for a moment, doom comes from doom and dooms doom; this doom marks a decisive moment in which humans doom the nonhuman and thus doom the doom of Earth with greater doom.

Each political and ethical decision is made on the inside of a hyperobject, caught in the resonance of the zones that spell doom. Even cynicism becomes a species of hypocrisy in the grinding roar of the hyperobject. Cynicism is the worst hypocrisy: hypocrisy squared, since cynicism is hypocritical about its hypocrisy. The hypocrite understands that she is caught in her own failure. The cynic still hopes that if he vomits disgustingly enough, things will change. The cynic hopes: he is not beyond hope—he is a hypocrite. He is trying to escape doom.

Humans have entered an era of *hypocrisy*. Now I begin to argue that the time of hyperobjects is a time of *hypocrisy, weakness,* and *lameness.* I mean these terms very precisely. First we should try to understand hypocrisy. In Greek, *hypo* means *under, hidden,* or *secret,* while *krisis* means *judgment, determination,* or *discernment,* so we are still exploring the contours of *doom* when we think about hypocrisy. Hypocrisy is a "secret doom": convention tells us that this means that someone is hiding something, pretending. Hypocrisy is a pretense, an act. But it is also simply hidden doom, a message sent from somewhere obscure. Or a message that is secret in some sense: encrypted.

Hypocrisy comes from the Greek term for *delivery (hypokrisis).* An actor is a hypocrite. Remember that one sense of *doom* is a decree or ordinance: that which is delivered, a statute or statement, a phrase that stands. Delivery is the fifth aspect of traditional rhetoric (Aristotle, Quintilian): there is discovery (invention), arrangement (logic), style, memory, and delivery. Delivery is how a speech is embodied, how it is spoken, how it comes to exist for others. Demosthenes was once quizzed about what he thought was the most important part of rhetoric: he replied,

"Delivery." Upon being asked what the second most important part was, he replied, "Delivery"—and so on.[34] Demosthenes practiced his delivery by putting pebbles in his mouth and climbing steep hills while reciting his speeches. Delivery is physical.

What if we flipped this around, so that we could understand that *the physical is a form of delivery*? Think about it. A CD is a delivery. An MP3 is a delivery. A vinyl record is a delivery. A cassette tape is delivery. Each one has its own physicality. Each one is an object: not some merely neutral medium, but an entity in its own right. Now what if this green banker's lamp were a form of delivery? The lamp tells my eyes about the light that its green glass diffuses. The brass base of the lamp delivers the stem to the cherry wood desktop. The fluorescent light inside the lamp delivers the dusty photograph to me in such a way that I can see a reflection of my typing hands in the glass in the photo frame. We never hear the wind as such, only the wind in the chimney, the wind in the doorway.[35] The zone of one object crisscrosses with another's in the interobjective configuration space. Things are Aeolian, acousmatic: their timbre (timber, substance, matter) speaks of secret strangers.[36] A thing delivers another thing. Rain, sunburn, plastic bags, and car engines all deliver the doom of the hyperobject. They are its hypocrites. They lie about the hyperobject; they tell secrets.

The Aeolian properties of objects are well accounted for in OOO. OOO holds that there are real things, and that these real things are objects, every single one. We humans are objects. The thing called a "subject" is an object. Sentient beings are objects. Notice that "object" here doesn't mean something that is automatically apprehended by a subject. There are all kinds of objects that so-called subjects don't apprehend. Global warming existed long before human instruments started to detect it. For millions of years oil oozed around deep under the ocean. All kinds of objects apprehended it, of course. When we are conscious of something, we are on a continuum with rock strata and plankton that apprehend oil in their own way.

According to OOO, objects are Aristotelian, in some sense. One pleasant thing about OOO is that it refashions overlooked philosophy, such as Aristotle, Al-Ghazali, Husserl, and Zubiri. What is an Aristotelian object? Not a materialist one, for starters. If the first phase of my work on ecology was ecology without Nature, this one is ecology without matter. And for the same reasons. I've seen wood, I've seen photographs of atoms, I've seen clouds in diffusion chambers, I've seen drawings of wave packets. Sure. But have I ever seen matter? I'm starting to think that this thing called "matter" is like the thing called Nature or the thing called Santa Claus—you have to say you believe in it so as not to upset the kids. So when Mr. Spock claims to have found "matter without form," he is sadly mistaken.[37]

Don't get me wrong here by assuming that this position in any way advocates hostility to science. Far from it—this position is trying to incorporate contemporary science back into philosophy to "imagine that which we know," as Percy Shelley succinctly puts it.[38] OOO is able to cope with the three most progressive scientific views of our age, relativity, ecology, and quantum theory. It is simply that we really shouldn't leave ontology to scientism. Otherwise we end up with some New Age head-shop, lava-lamp ontology that defaults to a reductionist atomism.

In this sense, OOO begins to see beyond capitalism, if by that economic process we mean the positing of value in some mystical, ethereal beyond: the shadow world of capital. It's not the essence that's the trouble, so much as the positing of it in some beyond, some distant dimension over yonder: the metaphysical dimension of capital. With its mistrust of appearances, Marxist ideology theory also does this. All we poor saps can do is lament our lot, sitting around in the trashed world, the world that isn't even as real as the unseen one that truly determines us. This mode of thinking is not a fine-grained sieve, but a blunt instrument that reduces everything to an unspeakable powder.

According to OOO, objects have a very interesting property. We only see their sensual qualities, in interactions that spontaneously spawn new objects. Me smelling an oil spill is a whole new object in the universe. You can examine this object, as well as the oil and my nose. This object also has special properties. What are they? Just like all objects, hyperobjects *withdraw*. All objects are hidden from access in some sense. No other object, no finger, photon, or supercomputer, can possibly experience every single aspect of the object. Consider a coin. You can never see the other side of the coin *as* the other side. When you flip it over, the other side becomes *this* side. All objects are like that.

But hyperobjects make this withdrawn quality obvious. So how *do* we experience them at all? People love to churn out that hackneyed phrase, "Writing about music is like dancing about architecture." I always thought dancing about architecture sounded like a good idea. And in OOO terms, this is what all objects are doing with each other. After all, no object truly contacts another one. They really only share what Harman calls their "notes." So architecture "columns" (or whatever it does) about human relationships. And dogs sniff about trees (nicely, *about* can also mean *around*). And pencils pencil about pencil sharpeners.

Imagine a world where we could only play music if we wanted to "talk about" music. It would be like John Malkovich's nightmare world in *Being John Malkovich,* with music as Malkovich.[39] Music musics about music. Or as Joyce writes somewhere, "love loves to love love."[40] No. We clap about music, we dance about music, we play music about music, we write about music—all these things are *not the music* about which we are performing. Alvin Lucier's long thin wire vibrates about the people walking through the installation.[41] The storm storms concerning the chimney it blows through (Heidegger's nice example). The calculator calculates concerning the bank balance I'm anxious about. Think of how compatible OOO is with relativity. Einstein's train trains about the flash of lightning. The camera on the side of the track cameras about it. Now consider quantum theory. The photon photons about the electron. The birds bird about the BP oil slick, telling us about it in bird metaphors. And weather weathers about global warming. And writing writes about music. Just like dancing about architecture.

Why does the rain lie about the hyperobject, while telling secrets about it? Things get stranger still when we consider a single object—which is why reckoning hyperobjects as objectively present *(vorhanden)* is simply out of the question. Let us imagine, for the sake of argument, one single thing, alone—I know how difficult this is for us in an age in which even Chevron tells us every day that "everything is interconnected." One single banker's lamp. The banker's lamp delivers itself. The delivery is different from the deliverer. It is like the difference between the *I* that is writing this, and the *I* about which I am writing. So that I can say the following: "I am lying." "This sentence is false." Such sentences are Liars, the most famous of which is the liar paradox: "All Cretans are liars," says a Cretan. The Cretan is telling the truth and lying at the same time, and for the same reasons. The sentence is a hypocrite. It says one thing and does another. Objects are hypocrites, actors portraying themselves. They can't be justly represented. They emit blue notes that differ from themselves without difference. They lie—again: "What constitutes pretense is that, in the end, you don't know whether it's pretense or not."[42] Hyperobjects simply allow us to see this intrinsic, ontological level of hypocrisy, because they are just so much larger in scale than we are, both temporally and spatially. We see signs everywhere, but not the hyperobject as such. We see signs of doom, but the doom is nowhere objectively present. How easy it is for denialism to work its magic on Americans who are both very insecure and very nihilistic.

Gerard Manley Hopkins writes about delivery:

Each single thing does one thing and the same:
Deals out that being each one indoors dwells;
Selves, goes itself, crying *What I do is me, for that I came.*[43]

The richly knotted vocabulary hides and tells the truth at the same time. "Deals out": delivers. "That being indoors each one dwells": *dwells* here seems almost transitive—the thing "dwells" a secret "being indoors," dealing it out—pronouncing its doom, delivering it, telling the secret *(hypocrisis).* "Selves, goes itself," like "going green," "going berserk." This scholastic *haecceitas* ("thisness") appears to be simply a vivid version of the standard ontology (with "actuality" and bland substances), unless we recall that objects are hypocrites. How can you *go yourself*? You are already yourself. You can only "go yourself" if you are not yourself. You must be not-yourself at the same time as being yourself. When a thing cries, "What I do is me," the thing is saying "This sentence is false"; "I am lying." The piercing blue note that the object sends out is both major and minor, a perfect photograph and an opaque mask, a femme fatale behind whose eyes is a depth of mystery or a blank void, or not even nothing. Doom.

The hyperobject is a liar. We never see the hyperobject directly. We infer it from graphs, instruments, tracks in a diffusion cloud chamber, sunburn, radiation sickness, mutagenic effects, childbirth (Plate 3). We see the shadows of the hyperobject, gigantic patches of darkness that fleetingly slide across the landscape. We see shadows of humans engraved on a Japanese wall. We see rain clouds, mushroom clouds, we see the Oort Cloud at the edge of the Solar System. "The awful shadow of some unseen power."[44] We see figments and fragments of doom.

Waking up in the shadow of the unseen power of hyperobjects is like finding yourself in a David Lynch movie in which it becomes increasingly uncertain whether you are dreaming or awake. Humans are forced to confront phenomenological sincerity, the truth that "there is no metalanguage."[45] Far from being a cool T-shirt slogan, such a truth makes us extremely vulnerable. We have not traversed the curtain of illusion into a world of certainty, even if that world is a shiny process-relational upgrade, a happening of fluids and flows and rhizomes. The Liar sits in the corner wearing an enigmatic half-smile, smoking a cigarette with a look of vacancy, or is it profound depression, or just boredom—is he even alive? Does he have a mind? What does he know about us? What doesn't he know? As Laurie Anderson put it in her song "Born Never Asked," "What is behind that curtain?"[46] The play of illusion and concealment is a symptom of reality. Thus, some environmentalist rhetoric—the scorn for mediation, the anti-intellectualism—is part of the problem, not the solution. The further into the Great Acceleration we go, the more we shall need to confront feelings of unreality.

Here we encounter the deep reason why inside the hyperobject we are always in the wrong. Since we never encounter the hyperobject directly, since we are lower dimensional than it and exist with it in an interobjective aesthetic–causal space that includes $1 + n$ (withdrawn) entities, we are unable to get a purchase on it. Hyperobjects stick to us, like melting mirrors. They leak everywhere. They undulate back and forth, oozing spacetime all around them. They come in and out of phase with our quotidian existence. They interface with us in a slightly evil-seeming aesthetic dimension.

As I stated above, Kierkegaard argues that "against God, we are always in the wrong."[47] It is not possible for us to attain the perfect stance toward God. Indeed, attempting to do so might result in horrific violence or evil. The thought that against God, we are always in the wrong, is curiously relaxing and confidence-inspiring: we have nothing to lose. Kierkegaard calls this feeling "edifying," a term that is flavored with a dash of characteristically Protestant virtue. Kierkegaard's insight is also true for the human relationship with hyperobjects: as I wrote, *inside the hyperobject, we are always in the wrong*. We are in a state of hypocrisy with regard to hyperobjects—the hypocrisy fish eats the cynicism fish, just as the Darwin fish eats the Jesus fish on the back of some people's cars.

Beautiful soul syndrome, which Kierkegaard assaults remorselessly, is the default ideological mode of modernity. The beautiful soul sees reality "over yonder," separated from her by a thin pane of aestheticizing glass. Beautiful me over here, corrupt world over there. The beautiful soul is a Hegelian category, a stance toward the world that typifies the Romantic artist—she has no inkling that she herself is formally responsible for the corruption in the world that she sees. The gaze that sees evil "over yonder" *is evil*. So to get over beautiful soul syndrome is to realize that you are a hypocrite.

Marxists will argue that huge corporations are responsible for ecological damage and that it is self-destructive to claim that we are all responsible. Marxism sees the "ethical" response to the ecological emergency as hypocrisy. Yet according to many environmentalists and some anarchists, in denying that individuals have anything to do with why Exxon pumps billions of barrels of oil, Marxists are displacing the blame away from humans. This view sees the Marxist "political" response to the ecological emergency as hypocrisy. The ethics–politics binary is a true differend: an opposition so radical that it is in some sense insuperable. Consider this. If I think ethics, I seem to want to reduce the field of action to one-on-one encounters between beings. If I think politics, I hold that one-on-one encounters are never as significant as the world (of economic, class, moral, and so on), relations in which they take place.

These two ways of talking form what Adorno would have called two halves of a torn whole, which nonetheless don't add up together. Some nice compromise "between" the two is impossible. Aren't we then hobbled when it comes to issues that affect society as a whole—nay the biosphere as a whole—yet affect us all individually (I have mercury in my blood, and ultraviolet rays affect me unusually strongly)?

Yet the deeper problem is that our (admittedly cartoonish) Marxist and anarchist see the problem as hypocrisy. Hypocrisy is denounced from the standpoint of cynicism. Both the Marxist and the anti-Marxist are still wedded to the game of modernity, in which she who grabs the most cynical "meta" position is the winner: Anything You Can Do, I Can Do Meta. Going meta has been the intellectual gesture par excellence for two centuries. I am smarter than you because I can see through you. You are smarter than they are because you ground their statements in conditions of possibility. From a height, I look down on the poor fools who believe what they think. But it is I who believes, more than they. I believe in my distance, I believe in the poor fools, I believe they are deluded. I have a *belief about belief*: I believe that belief means gripping something as tightly as possible with my mind. Cynicism becomes the default mode of philosophy and of ideology. Unlike the poor fool, I am undeluded— either I truly believe that I have exited from delusion, or I know that no one can, including myself, and I take pride in this disillusionment.

This attitude is directly responsible for the ecological emergency, not the corporation or the individual per se, but the attitude that inheres both in the corporation and in the individual, and in the critique of the corporation and of the individual. Philosophy is directly embodied in the size and shape of a paving stone, the way a Coca Cola bottle feels to the back of my neck, the design of an aircraft, or a system of voting. The overall guiding view, the "top philosophy," has involved a cynical distance. It is logical to suppose that many things in my world have been affected by it—the way a shopping bag looks, the range of options on the sports channel, the way I think Nature is "over yonder." By thinking rightness and truth as the highest possible elevation, as cynical transcendence, I think Earth and its biosphere as the stage set on which I prance for the amusement of my audience. Indeed, cynicism has already been

named in some forms of ideology critique as the default mode of contemporary ideology.[48] But as we have seen, cynicism is only *hypocritical
hypocrisy.*

Cynicism is all over the map: left, right, green, indifferent. Isn't Gaian
holism a form of cynicism? One common Gaian assertion is that there is
something wrong with humans. Nonhumans are more Natural. Humans
have deviated from the path and will be wiped out (poor fools!). No one
says the same about dolphins, but it's just as true. If dolphins go extinct,
why worry? Dolphins will be replaced. The parts are greater than the
whole. A mouse is not a mouse if it is not in the network of Gaia.[49] The
parts are replaceable. Gaia will replace humans with a less defective
component. We are living in a gigantic machine—a very leafy one with
a lot of fractals and emergent properties to give it a suitably cool yet non-
threatening modern aesthetic feel.

It is fairly easy to discern how refusing to see the big picture is a form
of what Harman calls *undermining*.[50] Undermining is when things are
reduced to smaller things that are held to be more real. The classic form
of undermining in contemporary capitalism is individualism: "There
are only individuals and collective decisions are ipso facto false." But this
is a problem that the left, and environmentalism more generally, recognize well.

The blind spot lies in precisely the opposite direction: in how common ideology tends to think that bigger is better or more real. Environmentalism, the right, and the left seem to have one thing in common:
they all hold that incremental change is a bad thing. Yet doesn't the case
against incrementalism, when it comes to things like global warming,
amount to a version of what Harman calls *overmining*, in the domain of
ethics and politics? Overmining is when one reduces a thing "upward"
into an effect of some supervenient system (such as Gaia or consciousness).[51] Since bigger things are more real than smaller things, incremental steps will never accomplish anything. The critique of incrementalism
laughs at the poor fools who are trying to recycle as much as possible
or drive a Prius. By postponing ethical and political decisions into an
idealized future, the critique of incrementalism leaves the world just as
it is, while maintaining a smug distance toward it. In the name of the

medium-sized objects that coexist on Earth (aspen trees, polar bears, nematode worms, slime molds, coral, mitochondria, Starhawk, and Glenn Beck), we should forge a genuinely new ethical view that doesn't reduce them or dissolve them.

Cynicism is enabled by the left: "Since no one person's action will solve global warming, better to do nothing, or at most await the revolution to come." As I argued above, vegetarians, Prius owners, and solar power enthusiasts often encounter this logic. The trouble is, left cynicism maps perfectly both onto U.S. Republican do-nothing-ism and Gaian defeatism ("Gaia will replace us, like a defective component"). Nothing happens. Result? Global warming continues.

A Nietzschean tendency is at work within modernity. This Nietzscheanism strives for being "meta than thou." Cynicism is nothing other than the attitude inherent in what Heidegger calls the "ontotheological" stance of this Nietzscheanism: pure becoming floating in the void (nihilism).[52] Holding reality at a distance, it reifies reality into an objectively present block, then it explodes the block itself. No longer serving the purpose for which it was intended, Marxian critique is a specific mode of this Nietzschean tendency. To assert this is by no means to suggest that there is no social reality beyond capitalism. Yet this critique mode is not attuned to the time of hyperobjects, which brings cynicism to an end.

How do we overcome Nietzsche? We can't, because Nietzsche is the high priest of overcoming. As I've argued elsewhere, we have to creep lamely underneath Nietzsche and get away like that. Malcolm Bull has written a very powerful escape manual for lame creatures who want to exit Nietzschean modernity, entitled *Anti-Nietzsche*. Thinking needs to begin to set the bar incredibly low for solidarity between humans, and between humans and nonhumans—including non-"sentient" humans. Otherwise we become gatekeepers of solidarity, and remain within Nietzschean ontotheology—nihilism.[53]

The Romantic period was the beginning of the phase in which cynicism became the highest mode of thinking. Romantic-period art writes the manual on how to produce avant-garde products, starting an inflationary war in which successive waves of the avant-garde strive to overmaster their predecessors. This movement is deeply akin to the way in which philosophy gradually retreated into the possibility of the possibility of the possibility of . . . gradually eroding its ability to talk about reality, a self-inflicted wound of doubt and paranoia.[54]

Hegel says that the Owl of Minerva—the forward movement of history, which just is the progress of thinking—flies only at dusk.[55] The Owl of Minerva has become the Oil of Minerva. Yet the Romantic period was also the moment at which nonhuman beings emerged decisively on the human stage. Animal rights became thinkable, not simply as a mystical practice, but as a political one. Carbon began to spread around Earth, eventually ending up in the ice floes of the Arctic. The counternarrative to the Romantic period and beyond is the story of how the Oil of Minerva emerges from its invisible place in the human framing of things. The Oil of Minerva gradually convinces cynicism that it is only a disguised form of hypocrisy. It is to this story that we now turn, the story of how nonhumans finally convinced the most recalcitrant humans to let them into their thinking. We have arrived at the next moment of history, not by dint of our own efforts, but because the very inner logic of science ran up against a limit, revealing the uncanny futurality of objects for all to see.

The Age of Asymmetry

Modern life presents us with a choice between two options:

(1) The essence of things is elsewhere (in the deep structure of capital, the unconscious, atoms, evolution, the cosmic order, and so on);

(2) There is no essence.

Philosophies, like elections, have consequences. The restriction of this choice between these two options is one reason why Earth is in big trouble. The choice resembles having to pick between grayish brown and brownish gray.

Yet there is a third option:

(3) There is an essence, and it's right here, in the object resplendent with its sensual qualities yet withdrawn.

We are entering a new era of scholarship, where the point will not be to one-up each other by appealing to the trace of the givenness of the openness of the clearing of the lighting of the being of the pencil. Thinking past "meta mode" will bring us up to speed with the weirdness of things, a weirdness that evolution, ecology, relativity and quantum theory all speak about. This weirdness resides on the side of objects themselves, not our interpretation of them.

Even Pat Robertson and Richard Dawkins must use sunscreen to counteract the effects of ozone depletion. Hyperobjects have dragged humans kicking and screaming (when they feel anything at all, rather than being merely blank with denial) into an *Age of Asymmetry* in which our cognitive powers become self-defeating. The more we know about radiation, global warming, and the other massive objects that show up on our radar, the more enmeshed in them we realize we are. Knowledge is no longer able to achieve escape velocity from Earth, or more precisely, what Heidegger calls "earth," the surging, "towering" reality of things.[1] The dance-on-a-volcano idealism of Romantic philosophy and art has collapsed because we have discovered that the walls of the volcano are ever so much higher than we took them to be. We are no longer poised on the edge of the abyss, contemplating its vastness while leaning on a walking stick, like the character in the Friedrich painting who exemplifies the transcendental turn and the managerial power of the bourgeoisie (*Wanderer above the Sea of Fog,* 1818). Instead, like Wile E. Coyote in midair, we have discovered that we are already falling inside the abyss, which is not pure empty space, but instead the fiery interior of a hyperobject. Or we discover that the space we inhabit is not open and neutral, but is the interior of a gigantic iceberg whose seeming transparency was simply a matter of our less than adequate eyes. Flying through the universe in the space shuttle of modernity, we find out that we were driving with the breaks on, revving the engines while the fuselage lies rusting in a junkyard. We have woken up inside an object, like a movie about being buried alive. It is now the uncanny time of zombies after the end of the world, a time of hypocrisy where every decision is "wrong."

Should we feel terrified or liberated? Both. As the black metal band Wolves in the Throne Room say, "We are all hypocrites."[2] This is an astonishing thing for members of Earth First! to say. If even these people can admit that no ethical or political decision can be pure and free of compromise in the time of hyperobjects, then we are really making some progress. The asymmetry between action and reflection gives us a strong feeling of the uncanny. We know more than ever before what things are, how they work, how to manipulate them. Yet for this very reason, things become more, rather than less, strange. Increasing science is not increasing demystification. The ethical asymmetry is a function of an ontological asymmetry between humans and nonhumans.

Let's think about a philosopher who wrote at the beginning of the Anthropocene, when those carbon deposits were first laid down. Let's think about Hegel. Hegel's history of art is pretty telling when it comes to understanding what got us into the Anthropocene in the first place. Hegel sees art as a conversation between what we think we know and what materials we have at our disposal. Since what we think we know keeps upgrading, art moves (Hegel would argue that it must move "forward," but I'm not so sure about that), and without a reverse gear, since we can't unknow what we know. Hegel outlines a thoroughly teleological history of art, in which increasing human understanding gives rise to a transcending of art materials, and eventually to a transcending of art itself. By "materials" he means the "subject matter" of art, the aesthetic conventions, the paint, stone, and ink. The phases are the *Symbolic, Classical,* and *Romantic.* In the Symbolic phase, for example, a weak understanding (Hegel calls it Spirit) is dwarfed by materials. A thousand (for Hegel, inadequate) images of Spirit proliferate as Hindu gods, fetishes, and Buddhas: Hegel is thinking mainly of "Oriental" art.[3] But in this view a Gothic cathedral would also encapsulate the Symbolic phase: a huge mass of stone and glass, missing the sense that the God of the "beyond" died on the cross and is transmogrified into human being-together (the Holy Spirit). Nonhumans seem to possess godlike powers. Stones speak, the heavens shape human destiny.

I am not endorsing Hegel's views, least of all his teleology, the hide-and-seek game in which Spirit already knows where it is hiding, somewhere in Romantic-period Prussia. It is of great interest, this teleological vision: it is itself a symptom of modernity. In addition to allowing us to see something, it excludes something. What it excludes is a fourth possibility, perfectly predictable according to the inner logic of Hegel's history of art (again, I do not endorse this logic), but radically unspeakable within it. There is the possibility of a postromantic, or we might say (truly) post-modern phase, which I here call the Age of Asymmetry. How do we get there from here?

The Symbolic phase of art is unstable because all attitudes are unstable for Hegel: there is a gap between the idea and the attitude that it codes for. The attitude is the unconscious of the idea. When you figure out the attitude, it is now included on "that" side of what you are thinking. Then a new idea has been born, a fusion of the original idea and its accompanying attitude: the dialectical synthesis. Increasing knowledge (both practical and theoretical) increases Spirit's understanding of its materials, which reflects back on Spirit itself, developing its idea of itself. Thus, the Symbolic phase collapses into the Classical phase. In the Classical phase, there is a Goldilocks sweet spot in which there is a pleasant symmetry between Spirit and art materials.[4] A harmony emerges that a later age can only regard as an illusion. Humans and nonhumans meet each other halfway, generating all kinds of beautiful machinery. Mozart and Haydn sound sweetly neoclassical, their music embodying how the nonhuman no longer towers over the human, but the human doesn't fully comprehend the depths of its own inner space. Art focuses on what William Blake called "the human form divine."[5] But this "equilibrium" is actually unstable, since temporality is internal to thinking. It is not simply that customs and ideas change "in time." It is that there is a necessary movement within Spirit because of the gap between itself and its manifestations.

So the Classical phase collapses into the Romantic phase. Spirit's self-understanding far outstrips the materials of art at this point. Philosophy takes over the driver's seat. In this period, humans recognize the infinite depths of their inner space for the first time. It becomes radically impossible to embody this inner space in any nonhuman entity.[6] So Romantic art must talk about the failure to embody the inner space in outer things. Yet by failing this way, art ironically *succeeds* to talk about the inner space. Isn't the inner space precisely what can't be embodied? So the job of art is to fail better, or rather, more sublimely. A truly Christian art is now possible, because art can now express the ironic gap between the divine idea and fallen human flesh, embodied in the incarnation of Christ.[7] So, oddly, medieval cathedrals are less Christian than a Beethoven string quartet. From here on, art can only be about the failure of its materials to embody Spirit fully, precisely because Spirit is not reducible to those materials. The inner infinity discovered in the Kantian sublime and in the poetry of Wordsworth ranges over the world of things like a ghost in search of a destination. Art becomes deeply story-shaped, as artists realize that since they can't directly express Spirit, they must tell the story of the failure to express it. Music develops into the extreme chromaticism of Mahler, who explores every possible relationship between the notes of a tune. "Chromaticism" means the use of semitones, the smallest possible traditional Western interval between notes.

The story of art's failure to embody Spirit is recorded in the history of the avant-garde, which is also bound up with the history of the failure to change the objective social conditions of capitalism. The long march of the "isms" is the march of one form of Romanticism after another: Romanticism, realism, Impressionism, Expressionism . . . At the same time, art realizes that philosophy is now its big brother. At the very least, art needs manifestos and statements of purpose, philosophical explorations and justifications—because of its failure. We know more than we can embody and we can't put the genie back in the bottle.

In order to express the nonexpression of the inner life of the human, technologies were invented such as the piano, whose massive resonant interior can be heard when the sustain pedal is depressed. *Equal temperament* came to dominate modes of tuning, because it enabled music to wander around in a consistent world, no matter how much chromaticism was employed. Now in order to attain equal temperament, you have to detune the piano strings a little bit. The relationships between them are not based on whole number ratios. If they were—a tuning called *just intonation*—then wild dissonances and interference patterns between sound waves would result: the *wolf tones*. Equal temperament fudges the ratios a little bit. The endless journey of musical matter in search of Spirit happens in a coherent world of equal temperament fudge, like a sepia painting or photograph.

So, ironically, Beethovenian expressions of the rich inner life of Spirit are bought at the price of the enslavement of nonhuman beings—piano strings—to a system that turns them into fudge. Likewise, conductors arose to command the orchestra like a boss commanding workers in a factory. Gone were the genteel classical days when an orchestra conducted itself through the agency of the lead violinist, an arrangement that rather elegantly expresses the Goldilocks harmony between Spirit and materials that exemplifies that earlier era.

What happens next is something like the Master–Slave dialectic that Hegel explores in the *Phenomenology of Spirit*.[8] The Master commands the Slave, but by working on the Master's things, the Slave gains power and is eventually able to break free. But what happens next was unthinkable for Hegel. Hegel thought that art was going to be irony and inner life from his time on out because of the gap between Spirit and materials. Art came bundled with manifestos such as Wordsworth's *Preface to Lyrical Ballads* or Breton's *Surrealist Manifesto*: a quasi-philosophical statement of intent, which decenters the art by providing a way to think about it, dislocated from experiencing it directly.

The Romantic period is the very advent of the Anthropocene, when a layer of carbon is deposited by human industry throughout Earth's top layers of crust. It doesn't seem like a random coincidence, the epochal event of carbon deposits in Earth; the invention of pianos, gigantic slabs of hollow wood wound with strings tightened with industrially made nuts and bolts; the invention of the factory-like orchestra with its managerial conductor; and the dominance of equal temperament, spearheaded by the age of the piano. Equal temperament allowed the piano to dominate, to become a general musical instrument, much like the steam engine— recall that James Watt's 1784 patent specified that it was a general purpose machine—as is its descendant, the universal Turing machine known as the computer. While a steam engine can be harnessed to a wide variety of machines (a train or loom, for example), a computer can pretend to be any machine at all.

Yet what has happened so far during the epoch of the Anthropocene has been the gradual realization by humans that they are not running the show, at the very moment of their most powerful technical mastery on a planetary scale. Humans are not the conductors of meaning, not the pianists of the real: a truth that is common both to poststructuralist and to speculative realist thought, despite their stated differences.

Let us explore the history of that nonhuman Romantic hero, the piano. It was as if composers began not so much to impose their will on pianos as become their operators, servants, or technicians, in a playful parody of the fate of the industrial worker, "an appendage of the machine."[9] Composers stopped listening to their inner space and started tuning to the inner space of the piano, its physicality, its timbre. We could describe the extreme Romanticism, shading into Expressionism, of Scriabin and then Schoenberg, Berg, and Webern, as the way in which human inner space was evacuated through the logic of storytelling as such. Atonal music was a kind of Weimar Republic of sound, in which a protosocialist democracy made all notes equal. Serialism then proceeded to reduce the narrative sequence to an algorithmic process, a computation of patterns strictly based on the twelve-tone row.[10] Žižek makes a very perceptive statement about how atonal music begins to show the shadow side of the human self—it is paramusic, contacting the vortex of drives beneath the dialectic of desire, releasing them as an undead sound, a spectral materiality that no longer tells stories.[11] But this was also a moment of liberation for another physicality, a nonhuman kind. Piano strings were beginning to be set free.

Gradually the inside of the piano freed itself from embodying the inner life of the human being, and started to resonate with its own wooden hollowness. There is a long yet traceable history between the first uses of the piano sustain pedal in the Romantic period, and the long, frightening boom from the inside of the piano at the end of The Beatles' "A Day in the Life."[12] John Cage liberated piano strings from sounding like a piano, by placing other objects on them, domestic items that might surround pianos in normal circumstances, items such as rubber bands and screws. These objects, which created the "prepared piano," were not meant to express Cage's inner self; they had their own anarchic autonomy. It is as if they were allowed to occupy the inner space of the piano. In Cage's *Sonatas and Interludes,* all kinds of fresh timbres emerge from the strings: muffled gongs, twangs, beeps. In the same way, AMM guitarist Keith Rowe constructs musical hyperobjects by allowing electric guitar strings to resonate with all kinds of sounds that are not intended by the human operating them. Indeed, Rowe's term for silence, which is just a human refraining from making a sound, is *un-intention,* since "silence" is only when humans stop making sounds.[13] The improvisations of Rowe allow nonhumans to jut through the art into human space.

Then La Monte Young, a student of John Cage, took the next step. He liberated the strings of the piano from equal temperament, reverting to the just intonation that had been abandoned to create the Romantic world of sepia fudge. To return the strings to just intonation was indeed an act of justice, a "doom." In justly tuned piano wires, we hear the doom of wire and wood. It was Young, first of the New York Minimalists, who used sound to end Romantic storytelling. Serialism had deconstructed the Romantic narrative by feeding what Webern calls the *Strukturklang,* the ghostly, spectral–material sound of structure as such, back into the music. Cage had gone further and fed household objects into pianos. Instead of coming up with a new tune, Young decided to work directly with tuning. Young's *The Well-Tuned Piano* explodes the tradition begun by Bach's *Well-Tempered Clavier,* organizing music not around a journey but around the vibrations of strings tuned to whole number ratios, ratios that allow ears to hear a dizzying height of crystal clear harmonics within any one note. This is the music of attunement, not of stories. Young's drone music, accompanied by Marian Zazeela's light pieces, happen for days at a time, sometimes longer, as human voices try to tune to a sine wave that is as pure as possible. The world of sepia, the consistency that enables the world as such to be, is brought to an end by vibrant colors that clash and interfere with one another, like lines in a painting by Napangati or Riley.

A string vibrates in a piano. Since it's tuned to whole number ratios, the sound is clear and transparent, as if it were infinite, even though the string itself is finite. Yet the sound is specific, colorful, vivid: far more vivid than the topped and tailed, sepia sound of an equally tempered string. It cannot tell a story so easily, because piano strings that are not curtailed by equal temperament are unable to allow music to wander in the possibility space of effortless modulation between keys, an unre-stricted movement that is in direct proportion to the hobbling of the strings themselves, like the bound feet of Chinese women. If you try to change key, you create wolf tones, extra vibrations that oscillate wildly, spoiling the smoothness of the possibility space. Wolf tones are named precisely to evoke the nonhuman, the wild animal that must be domes-ticated to be of use.

What are we hearing when we hear a justly tuned piano, playing the slow single notes and clusters that Young favors? We are hearing the piano as object, as open to its nonhumanness as is possible for humans to facilitate. The pianist becomes the medium—in the spiritualist sense—for the piano. Thus *The Well-Tuned Piano* is a cycle that is over five hours long, defying the human mind to make a story out of it. It is a loving work of restorative justice, allowing the piano to sound without reference to the human. Young's previous music, in particular the sets of instructions to release a butterfly into the hall, or to push the piano until it goes through the wall, or to push and pull tables and chairs to emit shrieking harmonics, are algorithmic recipes for involving nonhumans in musical space. They are more or less versions of what Cage had already laid out in *4' 33"*, a piece designed for an open-air amphitheater. But *The Well-Tuned Piano* is a deliberate attunement to a nonhuman, the most significant musical nonhuman of the Anthropocene.

This brings us to the subject of Young's music of attunement and drones. Young uses sine-wave generators so accurate that they only have an error once per calendar year. Young tries to live inside these sonic fields for as long as possible. What are we hearing when we enter Young's Dream House in New York City (at 275 Church St.), where these generators create crisscrossing interference patterns that shift as we move? We are hearing the equipment itself, we are hearing "music" that is a tuning to the equipment, and not the other way around. Rather than the equipment delivering the music, the music delivers the equipment. Likewise, Young's drone pieces are tunings, like Indian classical music, which winds around a central motif, with the voice or the sitar trying to attune itself to the divine. Strings and generators have been liberated from telling a human story. They tell their own story, pronounce their own doom.

Tuning to tuning as such: doesn't this remind us of the loop-like quality of meditation or contemplation, mocked in the Hegelian lineages of Western modernity as narcissistic navel gazing? For it is Hegel who above all wants to paper over the Kantian phenomenon–thing gap. Since I can think this gap, there is no gap—this is a too-short parody of Hegel's idealism. Simply allowing the gap to exist would plunge me into the night in which all cows are black, the dreaded pure negation of A = A. Hegel pathologizes this loop as a primitive form of consciousness that he calls Buddhism, an orientalist inscrutability that approaches the status of "object"—something that must be mastered, overcome, manipulated, changed. Raw materials. Yet what is an object other than the truth of A = A, which is strangely, spectrally in-difference, a loop that resembles "This sentence is false"? This sort of loop is not totally static, just as a night with black cows is not totally blank or opaque: after all, there are cows in the dark . . . An object, according to our understanding of hyperobjects, consists precisely of a rift between its appearance and its essence. Yet the appearance of a piano string is not the appearance of a plastic bag. A piano string is . . . a piano string: A = A. Yet this A can unleash not-A, insofar as all kinds of high-frequency sounds that are normally suppressed in equal temperament can be coaxed from the string, if only it is tuned according to a whole number ratio. The "equals A" is, as Derrida remarks in a discussion of the copula, a minimal difference within A as such, a difference that turns a self-swallowing snake into a Möbius strip.

So when modern music starts to go into a loop, beginning with late Romanticism, what emerges is a spectral physicality denied by Hegel and celebrated by his contemporary opponent, Schelling. The release of the vampiric remainder of sound at first seems uncanny and horrific, but the pure colors of Young's just intonation are its direct descendant. The meditative, contemplative lineage into which Young deliberately plugs, the bhakti of devotion, in which one attunes to God in physical form (as the guru), and via physical forms (such as drones and chanting), is the Western descendant of Theosophy and the Victorian fascination for the spectral as spiritual, as a parareligious realm not wedded to the Christian narrative and the Christian love of narrativity.

Hegel's disavowal of the richness of A = A has a long history in the Christian suppression of its more meditative forms (demonized as "Gnoticism"). The attempt to eliminate contemplative practices in the West is readily discernible in the history of religious interference with music. It is significant that Pope Gregory, who developed rules for sacred music, banned the augmented fourth, the infamous *diabolus in musica*. The augmented fourth chord is considered sacred in Hindu music, precisely because it allows the ear to access a vast range of harmonics, a range that evokes a hugely expanded sense of what in musical language is called timbre: the material that generates a sound, such as the wood and strings and open body of a sitar. What resonates in just intonation, for example—music based on whole number harmonic intervals, such as Indian music—is a profound range of materiality. It is like the "diabolical," ghoulish materiality of atonal music, but colored brilliant violet, magenta, and viridian. The singing of Sanskrit syllables, such as "OM" (a sound that Hinduism and Buddhism associate with the material universe as such), evokes the materiality of the singing body and of the breath that circulates within and outside that body while it remains alive. These syllables are made to vibrate with as subtle and as profound a range of harmonics as possible, evoking the vastness of the universe. Devotional singing, then, is a form of hyperobject, one that meets the intimacy with the other and with the distant future that hyperobjects such as plutonium force on us.

The aesthetic realm, the realm of causality, is demonized in Western thought: it is precisely seen as a demonic force from a beyond that is immanent rather than outside the universe. No wonder then that there is a connection between the vampiric sound of atonal music and the spiritual sound of La Monte Young. Recognition of the uncanny nonhuman must by definition first consist of a terrifying glimpse of ghosts, a glimpse that makes one's physicality resonate (suggesting the Latin *horreo*, I bristle): as Adorno says, the primordial aesthetic experience is goose bumps.[14] Yet this is precisely the aesthetic experience of the hyperobject, which can only be detected as a ghostly spectrality that comes in and out of phase with normalized human spacetime.

We discover in the contemplative singing practices of India an expanded materialism that tunes the singer and the listener to the precise timbre of the voice and the body, and to the resonant frequencies of the ambience in which the music is played. In so doing, expanded materialism shows the way to bring the hyperobject into human social and philosophical space. This materialism is designed precisely to "bring the gods to mind," to achieve the intimacy of devotion (bhakti) that is also practiced in esoteric Buddhism.[15] La Monte Young hit upon the notion of attending to matter in a contemplative way when he sought a radical break with Western music in the early 1960s. Young decided that the only way to evoke a truly new music was to stop the narrative flow that is normative in Western music, to pull the emergency break and bring to a shuddering halt the predictable journeys around the world of diatonic harmony and equal temperament. His *Trio for Strings* of 1958 is probably the first minimalist musical composition. Hanging like monoliths in huge, gorgeous swathes of silence, the trio's lapidary chords evoke something more threatening, more intimate and vast, than the repetitive riffing of the later minimalists Steve Reich and Philip Glass. It is significant that Reich and Glass have been far more successful in the bourgeois world of luxury products than Young, whose work demands a level of passion and commitment—and free time—that would probably embarrass and irritate, not to mention disturb, the average middle-class concertgoer.

Young's interest in tones as such began with a fascination with the sound of the transformer in his turtle's aquarium, the hum of the electrics that kept the environment habitable: the sound of the nonhuman. And so he produced *15 VIII 65: Day of the Antler from The Obsidian Ocelot, The Sawmill and The Blue Sawtooth High-Tension Line Stepdown Transformer Refracting The Legend of The Dream of The Tortoise Traversing The 189/98 Lost Ancestral Lake Region Illuminating Quotients from The Black Tiger Tapestries of The Drone of The Holy Numbers*. This astonishing title is evidently a hypertitle, full of objects. Adjunct to the sonic space traced in the piece, Young's partner Marian Zazeela's calligraphy begins to reveal the tracery of unmeaning that language supposedly transcends. Zazeela places writing in structures that employ a fourfold bilateral symmetry, turning script into the illegible arabesque it already is. These fractal squiggles, reminiscent of sound waves seen on oscilloscopes, mark the performance space, illuminated with magenta and blue lights that clash in a way analogous to the way in which notes in an augmented fourth clash, producing a supersaturated abundance of radiation. What is this music other than art in the Age of Asymmetry? In other words, the music is a two-pronged attempt both to bring hyperobjects into human aesthetic–causal (social, psychic, philosophical) space, and to open that space to the wider world, or rather to the charnel ground after the end of the world; that is, to create a musical–social space for a while (hours and days) in which the project of attunement to the non-human is performed.

Attunement is precisely how the mind becomes congruent with an object.[16] Young and Zazeela bring tuning to the forefront of art by having the music "tune" itself, insofar as singers and instruments play a fluid sequence of adjustments to a drone. Attunement opens the supposed here and now of light and sound into an infinite "lightyears tracery" (Young's phrase), a nowness of harmonic frequencies, vibration within vibration, the infinite in matter, on this side of things; an immanent beyond. A sonic ecology without presence, without the present.

Singing the syllable "AH" (as Young and Zazeela do on *31 VII 69 10:26–10:49pm: Map of 49's Dream The Two Systems of Eleven Sets of Galactic Intervals Ornamental Lightyears Tracery,* side 1 of the so-called *Black Album*) involves breath, vocal chords, the air around the body, and so on. This is not a realm of abstract presence, not a "world," no *Gesamtkunstwerk* phantasmagoria of Wagnerian "total art." Working directly on sound and light, on tones as such, reveals the emptiness and vastness of timbre, its groundless difference. Young's and Zazeela's New York Dream House is not natural, but super-natural, extra-natural, more natural than natural. It is bound to its materiality.

Young's art allows us to encounter the timbre and determinacy of things; and at the very same time, and for the very same reasons, the depth of things. The art object strives to attune itself to hyperobjectivity. One of La Monte Young's algorithmic compositions from 1960 involves playing a chord "for as long as possible." The future that this art opens up is highly relevant to enabling us to cope with hyperobjects. Art in this mode approaches an aesthetic transcendence of normative human limits, yet not as Schopenhauer predicted in his ascetic and sclerotic version of Buddhism, an escape from samsara into a realm of soothing contemplation.[17] This contemplation is hot, intense, passionate and compassionate, intimate with death and poison, staking its place in the charnel ground, coexisting with specters and structures, with the mathēsis that tunes human cognition to the withdrawn thing. Is this not exactly what we need in order to live alongside hyperobjects? We shall be playing the game of coexistence for a very long time.

The nonhuman, already right here in social space, is finally acknowledged in the Age of Asymmetry. The nonhuman is no longer simply an object of knowledge (calculable and predictable), but is known by humans as a being in its own right, through a tricky ruse of reason itself, which now knows *too much* about nonhumans. We only hear a limited amount of the piano string. We only see a constrained amount of the electromagnetic spectrum. We know that the sounds and the lights tower into our perceptual realm through depths and heights immeasurable to our everyday experience. Thus, we get a somewhat metaphorical, yet vivid, taste of how all entities are profoundly withdrawn.

The Age of Asymmetry resembles the Symbolic phase, in that materials now gain a new "life." But humans can't unknow what they know. We know about quarks and sine waves and Beethoven and the Anthropocene. So the Age of Asymmetry is not a return to animism as such, but rather ~~animism~~ *sous rature* (under erasure).[18] It's called the Age of Asymmetry because within human understanding humans and nonhumans face one another equally matched. But this equality is not like the Classical phase. There is no Goldilocks feeling in the Great Acceleration era of the Anthropocene. The feeling is rather of the nonhuman out of control, withdrawn from total human access. We have even stopped calling nonhumans "materials." We know very well that they are not just materials-for (human production). We have stopped calling humans Spirit. Sure, humans have infinite inner space. But so do nonhumans. So does that piano note at the end of "A Day in the Life." So the Age of Asymmetry is also like the Romantic phase, because we have not lost the sense of inner space. This feeling of inner space has only expanded, since we now glimpse it in nonhumans. Some even find it in other "higher" primates, some in all sentient beings, and some (the real weirdos such as myself) in all beings whatsoever: eraser, black hole singularity, ceramic knife, molasses, slug.

From within the Romantic phase, we can already begin to detect the footprints of nonhumans in the very fact of irony, the one ingredient that appears to suck us into the vacuum of our inner space. The default position of Romanticism—which has been going on from about 1776 to now—is irony. Irony is the aesthetic exploitation of gaps, or as I have sometimes called it in undergraduate classes, *gapsploitation*. To be more precise, irony is the exploitation of a gap between $1 + n$ levels of signification. Irony means that more than one thing is in the vicinity. Irony is the echo of a mysterious presence. For there to be irony, something must already be there.

We can see in this phenomenon of irony stemming from an awareness of $1 + n$ levels the seeds of Romanticism's dissolution. But this knowledge is only available to us now in the time of hyperobjects. Recall the discussion of interobjectivity. Remember how hyperobjects point out how things share a weird sensual space in which everything is entangled. When you encounter a phenomenon in this sensual space, $1 + n$ entities are withdrawn in order for this encounter to take place. Irony is the footprint of at least one other entity, an inner ripple, a vacuum fluctuation that indicates the distorting presence of other beings.

So, strangely, irony has not gone anywhere, but has increased in potency and poignancy. Irony has lost its "postmodern" (I would prefer to say "late modern") edge, its T-shirt sloganeering. Irony has become the feeling of waking up inside a hyperobject, against which we are always in the wrong. The full truth of Romantic irony, in which the narrator realizes that she is part of the story and that "there is no metalanguage," is fully born not in the Romantic period, surprisingly, but in the Age of Asymmetry.[19] Asymmetric irony is when we "save the Earth" but have no idea exactly why. "They were going to make me a major for this, and I wasn't even in their Army anymore" *(Apocalypse Now)*;[20] or, "The vicissitudes of this life are like drowning in a glass pond."[21] Irony multiplies everywhere, since no being's appearance fully exhausts its essence. Irony becomes the experience of total sincerity, of being Jonah in the whale realizing that he is part of the whale's digestive system, or Han Solo and Leia inside the gigantic worm they think is the surface of an asteroid.

Consider the absurd politics of MAD (Mutually Assured Destruction) that held the world in the weird oppressive peace of the Cold War. Behind the face-off between the United States and the Soviet Union, do we not also glimpse an aspect of the Age of Asymmetry, in which humans coexist with a hyperobject, nuclear materials? Have humans not been forced since 1945 to contemplate a world without them, not simply in the abstract, but next week, ten years from now, in my children's lifetime? It is hyperobjects whose presence guarantees that we are in the next moment of history, the Age of Asymmetry. With their towering temporality, their phasing in and out of human time and space, their massive distribution, their viscosity, the way they include thousands of other beings, hyperobjects vividly demonstrate how things do not coincide with their appearance. They bring to an end the idea that Nature is something "over yonder" behind the glass window of an aesthetic screen. Indeed, this very concept of Nature is itself a product of the Romantic phase. Hyperobjects likewise end the idea that things are lumps of blah decorated with accidents, or not fully real until they interact with humans.

Art in the Age of Asymmetry must thus be a *tuning* to the object. Uncannily, the Platonic idea returns: art as attunement to the realm of demons. In the *Ion* Socrates and the rhapsode Ion imagine art to be the transmission of some demonic energy, as if Muse, poet, poem, rhapsode and audience were connected like magnets.[22] This really isn't too far from the idea of an electromagnetic field as such. Faraday and Maxwell imagined electromagnetic fields permeating the universe. The same can be said for gravitational fields. They are never completely nullified. In addition, one can see the Cosmic Microwave Background from the "beginning" of the universe in TV snow. Art becomes tuning to the depth of these fields.

The existence of this field, itself a hyperobject, seriously upsets the applecart of art as modernity defines it. Westerners have spent two centuries supposing that one could *be a genius*. Now the older idea of *having genius* (as with the Greek *daimon*, intermediary spirit) is returning. Genius is no longer a production of my inner space, but a collaboration between my inner space and at least one other entity. There is indeed something like a *genius loci,* we have found, not because we can stultify ourselves and unlearn science and throw away electric engines in favor of carts—but because we can't. Art becomes a collaboration between humans and nonhumans, or as Negarestani puts it, "complicity with anonymous materials."[23] When you write a poem you are making a deal with some paper, some ink, word processing software, trees, editors, and air. You have to wonder whether your poem about global warming is really a hyperobject's way of distributing itself into human ears and libraries. Art becomes an attunement to the demonic: Felix Hess allows us to hear the sound of air pressure fluctuations over the Atlantic by recording sounds from microphones placed on a window, then speeding up the recording to a more-than-human speed (see the section "Temporal Undulation"). Rather than "being" a genius, you "have" it, because art is an attunement to a demonic force coming from the nonhuman and permeating us: as we all know we have all been strafed by radiation, for example. In Negarestani's *Cyclonopedia,* the "anonymous materials" of oil and deep geological strata spring to demonic life, as if philosophy were a way not so much to understand but to summon actually existing Cthulhu-like forces, chthonic beings such as Earth's core, which Negarestani imagines as locked in conflict with a tyrannical sun, like Greek Titans.[24] In China Miéville's *Perdido Street Station,* a city becomes a sentient being, while in *The Scar,* a floating city is made out of a gigantic assemblage of captured ships.[25]

There is another reason why art becomes an attunement to the demonic. The more we know about an object, the stranger it becomes. Conversely, the more we know about an object, the more we realize that what call *subject* is not a special thing different from what we call *object.* According to evolution, I look and quack enough like a human to pass on my DNA. This "satisficing" is enough to make me a human. A computer program looks and quacks enough like a person in a Turing Test, which is enough to make it a person. So in turn I look and quack like a person. Life 2.0 is possible; so "original life" is Life 1.0, artificial already. Life is made of non-life, so that replicant molecules such as DNA, RNA, and some silicates are neither alive nor non-alive, but rather they are more like the undead, persisting ironically by reproducing themselves in the very attempt to erase their disequilibrium. Eliminative materialists, who say that this means that smaller or simpler things such as nucleotides and quarks are more real than medium-sized things such as amoebae, horses, and minds, are in denial about the necessarily spectral properties of things in the Age of Asymmetry. Something about being is inherently spooky, disturbingly uncertain. "What constitutes pretense is that, in the end, you don't know whether it's pretense or not"[26] *Object* does not mean *objectified*. Rather it means *totally incapable of objectification*. It's clear that we only ever see footprints of hyperobjects. But in some sense we only see footprints of pencils, penguins, and plastic explosive.

Art, then, must attune itself to the demonic, interobjective space in which causal–aesthetic events float like genies, nymphs, faeries, and djinn. Something like a return to sensationalism or sentimentality seems to work, with added layers of irony and weirdness, as in the movies of David Lynch where, as Žižek observes, fire really burns and light itself hurts your eyes, where songs are the most beautiful songs you have ever heard and emotions passed over in daily life take on a horrifying, uncanny hue.[27]

In the previous section, we saw that the time of hyperobjects is an age of a precisely defined hypocrisy. Now we shall add to the (truly) post-modern human portfolio another specific category: *weakness*. Weakness determines the capacity for tuning. Just as hypocrisy flies in the face of a Nietzschean tendency within modernity, so weakness ends the search for ultimate men and supermen. Modernity is like the dinosaur, rendered extinct by some planet-scale cataclysm. Small, weak mammals crawled out from the wreckage.

The time of hyperobjects is a time of weakness, in which humans are tuned to entities that can destroy them: "'Well, what's your name?' you ask him. 'Odradek,' he says. 'And where do you live?' 'No fixed abode,' he says and laughs; but it is only the kind of laughter that has no lungs behind it. It sounds rather like the rustling of fallen leaves."[28] Kafka uncannily blends Nature writing ("the rustling of fallen leaves") with a claustrophobic indoor confrontation between a human and a nonhuman. The figure is the same that Coleridge uses in *The Rime of the Ancient Mariner*, which talks about "brown skeletons of leaves" in a way that provokes thoughts of undead beings.[29] The sound of trees resonates, but not in the expected way, to soothe or inspire a soul. Odradek, the contemporary object par excellence, is just there. We are powerless to explain him. Yet somehow he was invited into our home. Odradek is a physical anomaly, like a drought or an unexpected tornado, or a mutant leaf bug with legs coming out of its eyes, born near Chernobyl. His very name has obscure origins: "Some say the word Odradek is of Slavonic origin, and try to account for it on that basis. Others again believe it to be of German origin, only influenced by Slavonic. The uncertainty of both interpretations allows one to assume with justice that neither is accurate, especially as neither of them provides an intelligent meaning of the word."[30] When does global warming stop and start? When did the Anthropocene begin? The decisive dates (1784, 1945) and the vivid news stories (relating earthquakes and fires) belie the undisclosed vagueness, yet realness, of the hyperobject. The very feeling of wondering whether the catastrophe will begin soon is a symptom of its already having begun. Besides, hyperobjects are too viscous, too nonlocal and molten, too interobejctive to be specified in the way we commonly think objects should be pinned down. The properties of hyperobjects provide an open window for denialist "skeptics" who use the tricks the tobacco industry has used for years: asserting that probability is not a guarantee of causality (even though science is nothing more than a collection of statistically significant data). Large, complex systems require causality theories that are not deterministic. The oppressive drive to repeat the epistemological thrills and spills of the correlationist era by returning to Humean skepticism is itself a symptom that the nonhumans are already here.

Consider Sheryl St. Germain's poem "Midnight Oil," written in response to the BP Deepwater Horizon oil spill of 2010:

> how to speak of it
> this thing that doesn't rhyme
> or pulse in iambs or move in predictable ways
> like lines
> or sentences
>
> how to find the syntax
> of this thing
> that rides the tides
> and moves with the tides and under the tides
> and through the tides
> and has an underbelly so deep and wide

even our most powerful lights
cannot illuminate its full body

this is our soul shadow,
that darkness we cannot own
the form we cannot name

and I can only write about it at night
when my own shadow wakes me, when I can feel
night covering every pore and hair follicle, entering eyes
and ears, entering me like Zeus, a night I don't want
on me or in me, and I dream of giving birth
to a rusty blob of a child who slithers out of me,
out and out and won't stop slithering, growing and darkening,
spreading and pulsing between my legs
darkening into the world

what it might feel like to be a turtle, say,
swimming in the only waters you have ever known
swimming because it is the only way you move through the world
to come upon this black bile
a kind of cloying lover
a thing that looks to you
like a jellyfish, so you dive into it and try to eat it
but it covers your fins so they can't move as before
and there is a heaviness on your carapace and head
that wasn't there before, and you are blind
in the waters of your birth[31]

Notice how the poem is indented, justified to the right, not the left of
the page, as if a gigantic force had reversed the normal right–left polarity.
The poem seems to stick to a viscous object just off the edge of the right-
hand side of the page. Far from foregrounding the human subject's supposed priority to things, this inversion of normal lineation truly makes
the poem a response, in the deep sense of *tuning*.

Hyperobjects only make clear what is already the case: humans are weak, since they sincerely tune to the entities that crowd around them, unable to bootstrap themselves into the geostationary orbit of metalanguage. The inner logic of the Great Acceleration ensures that in "touching the real" with the scanning tunneling microscope of objective presence, humans lose track of it immediately.[32] Some contemporary ecological art tries to create cognitive maps of relationships between coexisting things. Yet if things are somehow irreducibly withdrawn, if they have an inevitable shadow side, such cognitive maps can only skate over the surface of things. The Age of Asymmetry ends the beautiful-soul syndrome of modernity. It is now no longer possible to maintain the aesthetic distance necessary for the "going meta" moves of the beautiful soul.

Romantic art exemplified by Wordsworth is the manual for the mapping approach, whose avant-garde edge is what I shall call *constructivism*. Constructivism views the artwork as a machine for upgrading the mind of the viewer. The machine is complex enough and distracting enough to unhinge one's habitual patterns and encourage new cognitive maps to be drawn. The map, or the compendium, of Benjamin's convolutes (the Arcades Project), the volume with two or three columns of prose (Derrida's *Glas*), and the online text peppered with hypertext links all derive from this Wordsworthian approach. Constructivism is fundamentally Romantic: it gives us too much to know, and Spirit floats free of things like a ghost. The wish of constructivism is an if-only: if only I could displace you enough, dear reader, the world would change.

Some art objects talk directly about hyperobjects. Consider the poignant graffiti and guerilla installations of British artist Banksy. When a child rides the mechanical dolphin in Banksy's piece *Pier Pressure,* a song plays, the familiar English "Oh I do like to be beside the seaside . . . "; only the dolphin is swimming in an ocean of oil. Banksy's dolphin ride is designed to provoke disgust and gallows humor.[33] The repurposed fairground ride is a good example of constructivism. It forces us to think. It's the late grandchild of Wordsworthian aesthetic strategies Likewise, Shelley, the first Wordsworthian of the next generation, styled himself as a hyper-Wordsworth who would do the same thing only better, and was more committed to radical politics.

What about art that takes the hyperobject as its form? Are there any hyper-art-objects that perform the terrifying ooze of oil? As I argued previously, our position vis-à-vis these objects is like trying to get closer to the moon by running toward it, all the while forgetting that you are on the surface of Earth. The viscosity is a direct product of increasing information. The more data we have about hyperobjects the less we know about them—the more we realize we can *never* truly know them. As we've seen, hyperobjects are *viscous*: we can't shake them off; they are stickier than oil and as heavy as grief. The closer we get, the less we know. Yet we can't break free of them no matter how far away we retreat. We are stuck to hyperobjects, as if they enacted Sartre's nightmare, "the sugary death of the For-itself," evoked when I plunge my hand into a jar of honey.[34] But it's really much worse than that. We can't assert a transcendental metaphysics in the face of hyperobjects. They won't let us. They keep getting stuck to us. It was precisely our fantasies of transcendental smoothness and presence that summoned them into being. It was our drive to see and know everything that made us discover their oily presence, everywhere. *Modernity's nihilism is confronted by its specter, the nothingness of the thing.*

This curious phenomenon confirms that we have entered an ecological era. A few moments ago we were delighting in our ironic free play. Now it seems we're stuck to the mirror. This sticking occurs as a function of our attempt to realize the dream of progress, to see ourselves in the mirror of the end of history. Our very attempt to achieve escape velocity from our physical and biological being has resulted in being stuck to Earth. Rather than the total disintegration of the subject à la Fredric Jameson, or the vertiginous freedom of deconstruction, what we have is the creepy awareness that we are stuck to objects forever: we can't un-know what we know.

Like Anansi and the Tar Baby, there is no way to break free from hyperobjects. It becomes impossible to achieve pure detached irony. Viscosity reinforces itself in the very attempt to break free from it: we are enmeshed in A = A, which turns out not to be the night in which all cows are black, but a strange sticky Möbius strip. So we find ourselves incapable of the quizzical, man-in-space postmodernism of the 1980s.

Knowing more about hyperobjects is knowing more about how we are hopelessly fastened to them. Hyperobjects have done what two and a half decades of postmodernism failed to do, remove humans from the center of their conceptual world (there's that term again).

What we end up with is a situation in which it becomes impossible to maintain aesthetic distance. This distance is the main factor in producing the concept *Nature*. So the curious phenomenon arises in which Nature dissolves just as hyperobjects start to ooze uncannily around us. "Objects in mirror are closer than they appear." Viscosity is what compels us, what puts us in the *zone* of *the imperative* (Lingis's term). In this zone, choice is not the protocol of moral action. The viscosity of hyperobjects haunts us. It looms into our social, psychic, and ecological space. Or rather, we discover that it was already looming. Ontologically (and temporally) prior to our conceptual probing, hyperobjects are here, like the ghosts in *The Sixth Sense*.

This leads us to consider an approach that is precisely the converse of constructivism. The approach is the weird little sister of the rather masculine constructivist strategy. Let us call it *the object-oriented approach*. If objects subtend their relations, not as substantial blah decorated with accidental candy, but as sparkling realities withdrawn from access, the constructivist approach can only go so far. The inventor of the object-oriented approach was John Keats, who exemplifies a minor tradition within modernity, a tradition that has flirted with objects and is thus vilified as naïve, kitsch, or commodity-fetishist. When Wordsworth heard some of Keats's poem *Endymion,* he took offense, muttering sarcastically, "A very pretty piece of Paganism." His infantilizing, feminizing remark was right on the money. Wordsworth saw the threat. Keats had discovered a totally new move within modern consumerist possibility space. He was not playing in Wordsworth-space at all, the space of open form, of complex machines that upgrade the subject. Instead, he went straight to the object, trying not to upgrade the reader's mind but to melt it.

We need to get out of the persuasion business and start getting into the magic business, or the catalysis business, or the magnetizing business, or whatever you want to call it. Using reason isn't wrong. But with objects this huge, this massively distributed, this counterintuitive, this transdimensional, it's not enough simply to use art as candy coating on top of facts. We can't just be in the PR business. Percy Shelley put it beautifully when he wrote, "We [lack] the creative faculty to imagine that which we know."[35] That was back in 1820, and it's only gotten worse. Consider the heavy hydrocarbons that subtend the soil of the Lago Agrio oil field in Ecuador, a black fudge hyperobject that oozes into drinking water, with unknown and under-studied mutagenic and carcinogenic effects. We do not need to keep on parsing the data like Chevron, the defendants in the lawsuit on behalf of the people affected by the contaminated soil. Such parsing of data would be using the very same tactic as the gigantic corporation, the strategy of producing endless maps and graphs.

What we need is more like what Judge Nicolás Zambrano finally did in the case, which was to suspend the endless construction of (necessarily incomplete statistical) data, and specify that precisely because there is a gap in our knowledge—what do these heavy hydrocarbons do exactly?— to determine that the best action is to act as if the threat were real. To specify them not as assemblages of relations but as a *unit*, as an entity with unknown powers, a unique entity consisting of all kinds of other entities, all kinds of complex hyrocarbons, but an entity nonetheless, just like any other in its Tardis-like inconsistency. To respect the Kantian gap between phenomenon and thing on which modernity and modern science is based. And yet to respect it still more than the deniers, who endlessly look for more data, more proof. This is a philosophical war, a war that Blake calls a "mental fight."[36] The tactic of Judge Zambrano was in effect to specify the oil as an entity in its own right rather than as an assemblage or set of relations: an object-oriented tactic. Precisely because the hyperobject is withdrawn—it is mathematizable to humans as reams and reams of data—its appearance is in doubt: its appearance as cancer, its appearance as sores covering the body of a newborn baby.[37] And for *precisely this reason,* precaution must be the guiding principle. No further proof is required, since the search for proof is already contaminated by an unwillingness to acknowledge the hyperobject, an unwillingness we may readily call denial.

The burden of proof is shifted to the defendant: Chevron must now prove that oil does *not* have a harmful effect.[38] This is a judo move within a post-Humean age in which scientific causality just is statistical. Toxicity is a category that emerges from the Humean science of statistical causality. You can't directly specify it since there is no single criterion for it—its object withdraws, yet every day we see people dying of cancer from the mutagenic effects of radiation and hydrocarbons. Moreover, only about twenty-five of the thousands of hydrocarbons in existence on Earth have been studied as to their toxic effects. So Chevron can parsimoniously claim that there is no proof. Figuring out exactly what the causal links are, even if possible, would result in further delay and further damage to nonhuman and human life. It is like Lingis and the cigarette in the sequoia forest. Reasoning as the search for proof only delays, and its net effect is denial. This doesn't mean that a cigarette is an umbrella, or that the effects of heavy aromatic hydrocarbons are to cause cotton candy to sprout on banana trees. It means that things are liars who tell the truth, like "This sentence is false"; the larger the things are, the more obvious this feature becomes. Ethics and politics in a post-modern age after Hume and Kant must be based in attunement to directives coming from entities, which boils down to accepting and listening to true lies. Any ethical or political decision thus feels like an uncanny leap into a void, where we are unsure of ourselves, precisely *because* there is so much data.

The trouble with the PR approach, or the reason-only approach (its twin in some ways), is that human beings are currently in the denial phase of grief regarding their role in the Anthropocene. It's too much to take in at once. Not only are we waking up inside of a gigantic object, like finding ourselves in the womb again, but a toxic womb—but we are responsible for it. And we know that really we are responsible simply because we can understand what global warming is. We don't really need reasons—reasons inhibit our responsible action, or seriously delay it. No neonatal or prenatal infant is responsible for her mother's toxic body. Yet that is the situation we find ourselves in—on the one hand terrifyingly regressing, on the other hand, enragingly implicating. It's like the joke about the man who ended up in an asylum as he was paranoid that he was being stalked by a gigantic chicken. Upon being released, he returns a few weeks later, sweating and terrified. The chief psychiatrist tries to reassure him: "But you *know* that there is no chicken." "I know that," says the man—"But try telling that to the chicken." The urgent question of our age is, how do we convince the chicken—in particular, the American chicken—that she doesn't exist? In other words, how do we talk to the unconscious? Reasoning on and on is a symptom of how people are still not ready to go through an affective experience that would existentially and politically bind them to hyperobjects, to care for them. We need art that does not make people think (we have quite enough environmental art that does that), but rather that walks them through an inner space that is hard to traverse.

What is required, then, is to renew the object-oriented approach pioneered by Keats. Drop or supplement the Nature strategy—why is constructivism a Nature strategy in the lineage of Rodchenko and Naum Gabo? Because Nature art creates machines that change attitudes, paradoxical devices that upgrade human consciousness, changing people's relations with one another and with nonhumans. Their raw material is the viewer's or reader's conceptual mind. Why? Because Wordsworth, "poet of Nature," as Shelley calls him, wrote the manual on this strategy. This affects all kinds of art practice including concept art and performance art, and even agriculture as performance art (as in the work of Wendell Berry). The art object as geographical text. You think you know what Nature is—all it requires is some good PR. You get into the convincing business. You are working in the configuration space of advertising. To many, dropping the Nature–constructivist approach in favor of an object-oriented approach will look like an abandonment of Nature. It is—but it is by no means an abandonment of Earth or of things in their weird vibrancy. Far from it. Let's consider some examples.

The sound art of Francisco Lopez evokes the hyperobject in an object-oriented way. *La Selva* is an immensely powerful example.[39] Lopez achieved it by using simple equipment: place just two good mikes in the Amazon jungle, hit record, stop. The result is far from an ambient rendering or simulation of the real. By using loops and careful equalization, recordings of Nature tend to evoke a comforting sense of being surrounded. What we hear in *La Selva* is a threatening, solid wedge of

sound. Lopez summons the jungle as a discrete unit, a *quantum* incapable of being divided further. Since there are real objects, I contend,
some metaphors for them are better than others—and Lopez's translation of the jungle into MP3 form is an excellent translation, based at any
rate on my personal experience of the Amazon rainforest. In the jungle,
lifeforms abolish all sense of aesthetic distance. They are in your face—
you need to keep them away, frequently, to avoid fatal disease. The temperature is roughly human body temperature, constantly, so it becomes
hard at the level of deep sensation to maintain a boundary between where
one's skin stops and where the rainforest starts. And the jungle as a unit
is present—this is not to argue that it's a whole that is greater than the
sum of its parts (a Gaian whimsy). You do not experience the jungle as
a gigantic benevolent machine made of tiny replaceable components.
Rather, the jungle is an entity that comes right up to your skin and penetrates it, beaming through you like x-rays. Lopez forces us to confront
the rainforest in this manner.

Consider Robert Ashley's *She Was a Visitor*.[40] Ashley intones the
phrase "She was a visitor" into a microphone. The audience begins to
pronounce whatever phoneme of the phrase an individual chooses. The
piece becomes a massively distributed pronunciation of "She was a visitor," split into sonic chunks. It spine chillingly captures the alien presence of the strange stranger, the notion of entities as irreducibly uncanny.
There is an echo of the Greek tragic chorus and the protagonist, as Ashley's voice speaks over the hissing, clicking ocean of syllables. "She was
a visitor" becomes strange. Perhaps she was a visitor to my house. Perhaps she was a visitor to the concert hall. Perhaps she was a visitor from
another planet. She gives us a glimpse of the futural essence of a thing.
Likewise, the phrase itself becomes a "visitor," an alien being that rus-
tles like a rainforest around Ashley. In the mouths of the audience, the
phrase becomes a hyperobject—distributed, yet there—like the image
in a Magic Eye picture that can only be glimpsed anamorphically, yet is
distributed throughout the picture plane, like a hologram. The past of
she was melts into the future, the *future future*, the unknown unknown.

John F. Simon's *Every Icon* is an algorithmic piece, easily found online.[41]
Every Icon is software code that causes the microprocessor to produce

every possible icon capable of being made out of a small grid, which consists of a series of cells that can be black or white. When left to run, given sufficient energy, and given a universe whose duration is very different from our own, *Every Icon* executes what it says in the title over the course of ten trillion years. Or, as the accompanying text puts it succinctly:

Given:
An icon described by a 32 × 32 grid.
Allowed:
Any element of the grid to be colored black or white.
Shown:
Every icon.

Like Ashley's *She Was a Visitor,* this is a disturbingly futural work. The fact that the algorithm will stop, but only after 1012 years, conveys the futurality of the hyperobject: very large finitude makes infinity humiliatingly easy, as I've argued earlier. Smith's piece shows how hyperobjects make clear the reality of *execution*—what algorithms do when they run.[42] Each momentary state of *Every Icon* is not *Every Icon*, because that is the execution of an algorithm. Without an object-oriented theory of objects at hand, the fact that each moment of *Every Icon* is not *Every Icon* might cause us to imagine there was a Sorites paradox at work: the ancient paradox of the heap, in which if I place a grain of sand next to another, it is not a heap—and if I repeat this process, even tens of thousands of times, each time I check, there will be no heap, since adding one grain does not make a heap. If no moment of *Every Icon* is the work itself, then suddenly there is no work! The work *withdraws,* precisely because it *executes,* a fact that is more significant than its duration. *Every Icon* is ignoring us humans in its moment-to-moment procedural unfolding.[43] The fact that we only see flickering pieces of a hyperobject is an indication of a hyperobject's reality, not of its nonexistence.

The work of Jarrod Fowler exemplifies the object-oriented approach. Fowler is a percussionist working in what he conceptualizes as the creation or discovery of *non-music,* a category that evokes François Laruelle's notion of non-philosophy, an attempt to see philosophy within a wider configuration space. In this sense, Fowler's music includes the absolute absence of music as well as the presence of noise. Yet these theories become almost insignificant when one is confronted by the actual sound of his pieces *Percussion Ensemble* and *P.S.,* which consist of vast samplings of layer upon layer of percussion pieces. This layering gives rise to what feels like a forest of glittering shards of broken glass stretching as far as the ear can see.[44] I wrote the sleeve note for *P.S*:

> To generate, or rather to discover from within music itself, substances that resist not only classification as music, but music as such. To locate music as a small island of pseudo-consistency in a gigantic ocean of *nonmusic,* after François Laruelle. To locate noise as the infinitesimal subsidence of this island into the ocean, much bigger than noise, quiet, sound and silence.
>
> To force music to think about itself, as music. To see thinking about music as distorted by what is exterior to thought, and even to human being. To discover, with a slightly uncanny horror, that the wall between human being and nonhuman is the appearance of the nonhuman itself. To realize that this wall of resistance is a symptom of what the philosopher Quentin Meillassoux calls *hyperchaos.*
>
> To delineate through this method a working model of causality itself, which operates by what Jarrod Fowler calls *rhythmicity.* To investigate beats, which break up sonic continua: one beat as the miniscule flicker of causality. To realize that this causality floats on top of and emerges from the ocean of rhythmicity. To see, to hear that there is only this ocean, continually sampling itself, breaking itself up into itself. To announce this inherently contradictory reality in a sonic form as dialetheia, doubletruth: $p \land \neg p$.[45]

In the ears, however, the music becomes a hyperobject, literally consisting of layers of beats and no-beats that offer dizzying perspectives of phasing, high-dimensional sound (and non-sound). What we don't have here is a postmodern pastiche. What we have is a musical hyperobject, a truly new entity. Imagine summing all the waves of all the rhythms in the universe and constructing a musical hyperobject of the highest possible complexity—this would be the Platonic ideal (yet substantial and immanent) of this "non-music."

Now, though enormous, this sum is necessarily incomplete! Why? Because of the determinacy of the objects in the universe, including the transmission media. For a beat to exist, at least *one* frequency is always "left out" of the perceived beat—no music can ever be complete precisely because there is an interaction between waves plus at least one wave that is canceled out. To hear a beat at all, something must be erased. So there really can be no "beyond" in which the absolute sum could be "heard": a fact that is very similar to Cantor's diagonal proof of transfinite sets. What Fowler's music demonstrates, then, is a *weird realism* in which objects are uncanny, futural, and slightly threatening. They exist in an interobjective space that emerges from the coexistence of $1 + n$ objects, as we saw in the section on phasing.

Most environmentalist art is constructivist, not object oriented, for the simple reason that constructivism has been the dominant mode of art in modernity. Another strange fact: the art that emerges at the inception of the Anthropocene is not fully capable of addressing it. The 350.org movement places the number 350 on gigantic surfaces, such as beaches, that are photographed from above. Like the Nazca Lines in in Peru, they cannot be seen fully from ground level. Three hundred and fifty is the number of parts per million CO_2 that is deemed acceptable to avoid disastrous global warming. This graffiti is designed to change your mind. Or consider the geographical map-like piece *Wellness over Time,* by Marije de Haas (Plate 4). A detailed map of artists' responses to the Arctic is drawn to supplement maps of physical space, including a cross section of isotherms influenced by the pioneering work of Humboldt. Comically, there is a variable (and appropriate symbol) for bowel problems along with affective states, diet, and so on. The constructivist work is a *map*, trying to give us more, ever more, even too much, so that we can't take it all in.

In 2011 some artists and architects and other scholars in Sydney were trying to come up with ways to do an exhibition about hyperobjects.[46] I suggested purchasing some space aboard a satellite that passed over the exhibition space in its orbit. The idea is put about that something has been placed in a locked container aboard the satellite, something known only to a few people, but with some unspecified significance to do with hyperobjects. Then when the satellite passes over the exhibition, it photographs people entering. When people enter the museum, they give their e-mail addresses. At some randomly generated point after people leave, the satellite sends them a photograph of themselves entering the museum. I wanted the artwork to be as threatening as possible. But such a piece remains within a constructivist framework.

By contrast, consider Chris Wainwright's, *Red Ice 3,* a photograph of an iceberg in red light (Plate 5). To achieve this, Wainwright simply photographed the iceberg with a red flash. As Wordsworth sneered, the feminine is in play. The iceberg looks like the femme fatale Judy in Hitchcock's *Vertigo,* when she is flooded with red light and we realize with creepy horror that she is indeed the woman from the earlier part of the film. The ocean no longer looks deep and fishy, but more like a rippling layer of latex. By heightening the artificiality, Keats-style, something of the object as such intrudes into human social and psychic space. By tinting the mirror pinkish red, objects within it are realized to be "closer than they appear." The sudden disappearance of the background pushes the iceberg forward like an actor in a drama or a figure in an Expressionist painting.

Without a background, without Nature, without a world, the iceberg haunts us. There is a weird effect of withdrawal and disturbing intimacy all at once, like the pull focus, another favorite Hitchcock technique. David Lynch movies and Chris Wainwright's iceberg, or the dreampop of Slowdive or Lush, are differently resonant than a constructivist map. This resonance contains a vital ecological truth, because the object-oriented art of the Age of Asymmetry forces us to coexist with nonhumans—coexist without an agenda. Now we may see how astonishing it is that Napangati was able to combine a *map* (constructivism) with a *device* (object-oriented art) in *Untitled 2011* (Plate 1), which I discussed in "Phasing" in part 1.

Object-oriented art confronts us with the possibility of accommodating ourselves to things that are viscous and sticky and slow. Art that sticks to us and flows over us. To this extent, Pink Floyd were not the first space rockers. They were the first exponents of viscous pop. Their very name conjured up the huge bowl full of pink jello into which their fans dived when they played live in 1967. Their early light show, the first to use the oil wheel, covered the band in oozing light. We could read this not as metaphorical for trippy space but as literal oil and radiation, covering their bodies, impossible to slough off. The oil slides developed by Peter Wynne-Wilson speak to a phenomenological truth called *sincerity*. There is no way to jump outside sensual objectivity, because when you try, you find yourself slap in the middle of another one. As has been said many times, *there is no metalanguage*.[47] Irony becomes just another way of sticking to hyperobjects. Or, in the words of Buckaroo Banzai, "Wherever you go, there you are."[48] Sincerity eats irony.

Consider Brenda Hillman's poem "Styrofoam Cup," a poem whose title's play with Greek announces in advance that this will be some kind of remix of Keats's *On a Grecian Urn*:

> thou still unravished   thou
>
> thou,   thou bride
>
>
> thou unstill,
> thou unravished   unbride
>
>
> unthou   unbride[49]

On the one hand, the poem is a commentary on disposable culture with its less-than-visible waste, in which mountains of Styrofoam form a hyperobject of their own. On the other hand, by including the "waste" within the poem, by returning to the commodity's afterlife outside human use, Hillman shows us, similarly to Keats and his urn, how objects are not exhausted by our use, but rather persist beyond it, beyond the grave. The cup haunts the poetic space, just as the Grecian urn seems to haunt Keats with its "leaf-fring'd legend" that "haunts about [its] shape" (5). The poem takes the first line of Keats's ode, "Thou still unravish'd bride of quietness," and repeats it (as in industrial production), while distorting and as it were "crushing" it (like casual hands crumpling a Styrofoam cup).[50] The space around the lines becomes part of the poem, puffed up like Styrofoam itself. It is as if wherever we look, we find pieces of Styrofoam, pieces of poetry lines—waste made visible. The cup, the poem, and the first line are eminently repeatable and disposable. But this does not get rid of the cup: it keeps returning weirdly, as if reincarnated or zombified, as if no amount of crushing and reuse would "ravish" it. It maintains an uncanny opacity, an opacity that extends beyond presence, to an uncanny realm in which it is shot through with nothingness, an "unbride"—undead, "unthou." This is the Keatsian, object-oriented strategy par excellence. In this strategy, a strange pull focus effect occurs whereby irony's attempt to achieve escape velocity from sincerity is constantly thwarted, resulting in bigger and bigger physicality, like the expanding puffiness of Styrofoam.

Comora Tolliver's *Pod* installation is a disturbing, wonderful exploration of our current ecological crisis (Plate 6).[51] Rather than rely on worn-out Nature-speak, Tolliver cuts to the heart of the matter and renders the strange mixture of intimacy, grief, and overwhelmingness that is the current reaction to global warming and the Sixth Mass Extinction Event—an extinction triggered by human activity, the sixth major one on Earth (the last was about 66 million years ago). *Pod* is entirely covered with Mylar. At first glance it says, "Covering the world with plastic brought this about, this destruction, this commodification, this need to preserve now threatened with extinction." It also references the radiation-resistant foil covering the Lunar Module around the time Pink Floyd were oozing through their powerful PA system. Like any truly great work of art, however, *Pod* is a dialectical image that says a lot more than that. The threshold of *Pod* vibrates with form and color so much that nonhumans, such as dogs, take fright and run.

Pod is a seed bank turned into the visual equivalent of a huge wall of guitar feedback. Inside the Pod is a grave-like hollow in which dead flowers float in water. It's as if the Pod contains a grave for the now dead concept of Nature, a plastic fetish disguised as the real thing. For Tolliver, by contrast, Mylar is a distorting mirror held up to our non-Nature, a mirror that refuses to reflect the human but instead reaches out to destroy us. In this sense the floating flowers at the grave-like core of *Pod* are the most artificial things in the entire installation. The threshold as well as the interior melts with vibrant Mylar dripping with paint. So reflective is the surface and so intense the light that the paint seems in places to stand out from the surface down which it drips in fronds and tentacles. It is as if background and foreground have been shockingly suspended, leaving us with a hallucinatory, psychotic experience that is at once intensely real yet at the same time uncannily withdrawn and unspeakable. Like the gigantic oceans of sound produced by musicians such as Spacemen 3, Sunn O))), or La Monte Young, Tolliver's work is literally staggering, inducing neurological shock in the same way Bridget Riley makes you see your own optic nerve. Tolliver replicates the viscosity of hyperobjects.

The jaw dropping loveliness of the colors that seem to melt in pure space evokes a world that is far too close to be called a world, an ecological real that is right under our skin—it is our skin. We find ourselves like prisoners waking up inside the ecological mesh of lifeforms. There was no outside. The interstitial space of the *Pod* entrance screams, "You are already inside this." It's a monument to the beginning of history. How arrogant that we thought it was the end when the Berlin Wall came down.

Marina Zurkow's *Mesocosms* are two digital pieces that last over 140 hours. One is based in Northumbria, the other in Wink, Texas, the site of a petroleum sinkhole (Plate 7). One starts the animation and lets it run, and turns one's attention to it coming and going as one does with the weather—this compels us to see how boredom and anxiety are intrinsic to the scalar shift required to think about hyperobjects. There is a strange dislocation: the temporal scale of the animations disturbs, while the images resemble familiar pictures in a Nature coloring book. Yet amid the charming familiarity, strange things happen. In the Northumberland animation, a portly naked man gets up and walks out of the screen into the blank or void space on either side. A strange planet rises off in the horizon. In the Wink, Texas, animation gorgeous butterflies float in slow motion while disconcertingly small people (children?) in hazmat suits crawl across the landscape. Yet these strange events occur alongside the ordinary. The stars come out. It rains.

A mesocosm is an ecologist's term for a slice of an ecosystem that one has isolated in order to study. Zurkow's *Mesocosms* evoke uncanny feelings of being-with other things, lifeforms, horizons, the void around the frame. To adapt a phrase of Derrida's, there appears to be no outside-mesocosm: it is as if things considered to be Nature and Nature art are still there (the sky, a tree, a butterfly, and the charming, children's style of illustrating them) while things considered not to be (voids, hazmat suits, weird overlapping speeds) coexist alongside, eating Nature away slowly, gently and thus with true remorselessness. In Zurkow's *Elixir* series, we watch the human as a fragile essence in a crystal decanter, storm-tossed in waves or billowing clouds (Plate 8). There is a little world of liquids within the decanter, and a vast ocean without, so that each bottle is a mise en abyme of a larger nonhuman space. Inside each bottle, a cartoon human flaps artificial wings, or surfs. The fragile glass decanters, containing their cartoon line drawing humans in their bottled worlds, are correlationist ships in bottles, storm tossed inside the hyperobject of climate. Each bottle is a swollen glass head full of dreams, adrift in a real world.

A ne plus ultra of the object-oriented approach is JLiat's found sound piece, a series of straightforward recordings of the hydrogen bomb tests in the Pacific.[52] Words fail to describe the horror with which I heard the first few seconds of the sound of the Bravo test, "the worst radiological disaster in US history," as JLiat's home page puts it. After those first few seconds, I had to tear the headphones off my head. There's something about hearing that sound, that actual sound. It has been sampled and translated of course into an MP3, yet it is a sample of the real sound of a real object, a massive bomb. Hearing it rather than seeing it, in a tiny movie image on YouTube behind the aestheticizing glass screen of your computer, restores to the aesthetic dimension a trauma and a pain that we edit out at our peril. Hearing it, in other words, restores not full presence but *spectral intimacy* to the thing. This is the promise of the object-oriented approach: not a back-to-Nature erasure of art's mendacity—that would be a denial of the Kantian gap between phenomenon and thing—but a strange reinforcement of the gap that brings us into intimacy, into coexistence with strangers, which is ecological being-with.

Ecological awareness is without the present. The "As I write . . . " trope of *ecomimesis* is, without admitting it, an elegy to this totally lost presence.[53] "As I write these words, snow is gently falling outside my hut at the edge of the forest," is an inverted acknowledgment of the towering realities of the Anthropocene. The calls for a restoration of a balance that never existed on Earth—Earth being the name for a text of geotrauma—are desperate attempts to put the genie back in the bottle; or rather the twin genies of Anthropocenic reason and Anthropocenic human force. The perverse triumphalism that rubbernecks the sadistic victory of Gaia over lifeforms deemed improper—the viral human—is a futile attempt to master the irreducible uncanny futurality of things: all things—a Styrofoam cup that lasts for five hundred years, a dog dosed with strontium-90 encased in a block of concrete for forty years, the shadow of a human impressed on a Hiroshima wall—an image eerily reproduced in Yves Klein blue in 1961 (Figure 15).[54]

A more genuine acknowledgment of what is happening—the opening for humans of the Rift between essence and appearance, the vanishing of the present and of presence—is the work of Butoh, the Japanese "dance of darkness" that was invented in the wake of Hiroshima.[55] In Butoh, the human body no longer floats as if weightless in abstract space, but is pressed down from all sides by a horrible gravity, the spacetime emitted by a gigantic object, preventing the human from achieving escape velocity. The waves of other beings distort the human face into sickening masks of itself—faces that are already heavily made up to appear masklike. The body is powdered with ash as if from the fallout of an atomic bomb.[56] Cinders, ash, the trace, the shadow of a holocaust.[57]

Reality in the Anthropocene is becoming more vivid and "unreal," spectral. Without a world, without Nature, nonhumans crowd into human space, leering like faces in a James Ensor painting or the faces of Butoh dancers. The difference between a face and a mask (in the Greek, *prosō-pon*) collapses. Without presence, habitual, ontically given coordinates of meaningfulness dissolve. This irreducible unreality is a *symptom*

FIGURE 15. Human atomic shadow (with ladder), Hiroshima, Japan. A human blocks the wall from being totally bleached by the propagation of heat from the blast. In light of this image one might reverse Foucault's quip (at the end of *The Order of Things*) that the figure of man will vanish like an image drawn in sand on the seashore. Hyperobjects make clear the far more disturbing fact that what is called human continues after the end of the (human) world. Here the human is literally a shadow on a much larger physical structure, a shadow of the conversion of matter to energy.

of reality as such with which the weird realisms (speculative realism, object-oriented ontology) are beginning to cope as emergent features of the uncanny intersection of geotrauma and human history. Covered in ash, the human dances, caught in a horrible physicality: physicality without a beyond, without an outside, without presence.

Ecological coexistence is with ghosts, strangers, and specters, precisely because of reality, not in spite of it. The coexistence of beings, without an agenda, is predicated on what I call *lameness*. *Lameness* is the third human attunement to the time of hyperobjects, the first two being *hypocrisy* and *weakness*. Like hypocrisy and weakness, lameness has a very specific significance here. The fundamental reason for lameness has to do with a special property of any given entity that is particularly visible in the case of hyperobjects. An object fails to coincide with its appearance-for another object, no matter how accurate that appearance-for. There is thus a lameness within every object, a lameness that constitutes the very being of the object as such. In order to exist, an object must fail to coincide with itself totally. Existence, contra Alain Badiou, is not consistency but rather a fragile inconsistency.[58] Every object exhibits this ontological inconsistency, but hyperobjects make it especially obvious. A tornado is not global warming. A mountain is not planet Earth. Tissue scars from x-rays are not radiation. A child is not the biosphere.

The lameness applies to humans, who now stand within the resonance of hyperobjects. There is a fissure between how we appear and what we are, a fissure this study has called *the Rift*. The "inner space" that Kant and others opened up in the Romantic period is only a distant and inverted caricature of the Rift, like a photographic negative. The Rift guarantees that inner space, no matter how deep or vivid or sensitively attuned, is hermetically sealed from other entities. The Kantian experiences of beauty and the sublime are inner echoes of other beings, just as the synthetic judgment that these experiences underwrite is a footprint of these other beings.[59] Even correlationism maintains a tenuous umbilical link with nonhuman realities. When hyperobjects are fully exposed to human being, the power and freedom of the Romantic sublime inverts itself into contemporary lameness. It is not an unpleasant reversal, unless you really need to be on top all the time. Indeed, the "saving power" that Hölderlin speaks of is truly the saving lameness of the Rift: the way in which all things, humans no exception, are hobbled from within by an ontological gap. Spirit now no longer floats in the zero gravity of inner space. Instead, humans find nonhumans pressing in on all sides, in the charnel ground at the end of the world.

Art in these conditions is grief-work. We are losing a fantasy—the fantasy of being immersed in a neutral or benevolent Mother Nature—and a person who is losing a fantasy is a very dangerous person. In no sense then should art be PR for climate change. Have you ever considered the possibility of doing PR for a relentless army of zombies?

Every aspect of hyperobjects reinforces our particular lameness with regard to them. The viscosity that glues us to the hyperobject forces us to acknowledge that we are oozing, suppurating with nonhuman beings: mercury, radioactive particles, hydrocarbons, mutagenic cells, future beings unrelated to us who also live in the shadow of hyperobjects. The nonlocality of hyperobjects scoops out the foreground–background manifolds that constitute human worlds. The undulating temporality that hyperobjects emit bathes us in a spatiotemporal vortex that is radically different from human-scale time. The phasing of hyperobjects forcibly reminds us that we are not the measure of all things, as Protagoras and correlationism promise. And like a wafting theater curtain, interobjectivity floats in front of objects, a demonic zone of threatening illusion, a symptom of the Rift between essence and appearance.

The object-oriented approach that frees hyperobjects for our being-with them is Keatsian, in that it is a type of *rest*. Keats writes that, resting in a room, he absorbs the qualities of those around him, like a chameleon: when "not himself goes home to himself," because the identity of everyone in the room has pressed upon him and annihilated his identity:

> As to the poetical Character itself . . . it is not itself—it has no self—it is every thing and nothing—It has no character—it enjoys light and shade; it lives in gusto, be it foul or fair, high or low, rich or poor, mean or elevated. It has as much delight in conceiving an Iago as an Imogen. What shocks the virtuous philosop[h]er, delights the camelion Poet. . . . A Poet is the most unpoetical of any thing in existence; because he has no Identity—he is continually in for—and filling some other Body—The Sun, the Moon, the Sea and Men and Women who are creatures of impulse are poetical and have about them an unchangeable attribute—the poet has none; no identity—he is certainly the most unpoetical of all God's Creatures. . . . It is a wretched thing to confess; but it is a very fact that not one word I ever utter can be taken for granted as an opinion growing out of my identical nature—how can it, when I have no nature? When I am in a room with people if I ever am free from speculating on creations of my own brain, then not myself goes home to myself: but the identity of every one in the room begins [*for so*] to press upon me that, I am in a very little time an[ni]hilated.[60]

Resting is an aesthetic event. Most of our comportment to hyperobjects looks like "rest" right now in various forms: stunned silence, denial, obsessive compulsive behaviors (endless 350s on beaches) that sum to rest across the surface of Earth (when you see them from a high-enough dimension). Meditation or contemplation is the quintessence of rest in this sense. It does not have to be obsessive or stunned, however. "Rest" simply means the way in which thinking handles what Husserl calls "intentional objects." Rest could be an attunement to the nonhuman, coexisting with their necessary spectrality. Thinking is already, in itself, a relation to the nonhuman, insofar as the logical content of one's thought is independent of the mind thinking it.[61] In this sense thinking is intrinsically contemplative. Thus, when in meditation the mind takes itself as its own object of rest, the withdrawn, secret quality of the mind itself becomes poignant. Consider again Hillman's "Styrofoam Cup": the distorted repetition is a form of contemplative attunement to the cup as such, just as Keats seems to turn the Grecian urn around for inspection. The uncanny thing is that the more one does such a task, the less immediately graspable an object becomes—precisely because we become more and more intimate with it. Such contemplation is far from simplistically apolitical, far from a retreat from things.

Philosophical reflection on the hyperobject is also a form of rest. There are various dimensions of this rest—mindfulness, awareness, simple letting-be—that are equally fascinating. Rest in this "positive" sense suggests a deep acceptance of coexistence. Since Keats is not (ontically given) Keats but is a symbiotic community of all the impressions of others on his chameleon-like skin, what can he do but rest with that? Is this a receptiveness only to subjective impressions? Yes, but in a modified sense. "Subjective impression" is far more than a merely whimsical or self-centered interpretation of a thing, but an attunement to a thing's reality. This attunement might be distorted in some way, but in order to be distorted there has to be a reality, an always-already going on. Does this receptivity reduce objects to relations? No. My aesthetic–causal impression of something *is not that something,* by definition. This becomes obvious in the case of hyperobjects: the cold wet things I feel plopping on my head are not global warming, yet they are. Moreover, since all entities are chameleon poets in this sense—since Keats and a chameleon and a piece of chalcedony are all doing the same thing—all entities are "resting."

What have we witnessed in this book? Radiation, hydrocarbons, global warming, and a number of other hyperobjects. Along with them, we have seen the emerging reactions to hyperobjects as genuine non-human entities that are not simply products of a human gaze. Hyperobjects are not just the stuff of charts and simulations, but rather are a huge objects consisting of other objects: global warming comprises the sun, the biosphere, fossil fuels, cars, and so on. Thus, hyperobjects spell the end of environmentalisms that employ Nature (a tool of modernity) against modernity, fighting fire with fire, matter with matter, the present with the present. To say the least, it is a surprising situation. One might have thought that seeing ecology as connected feedback loops would "undermine" (reduce downward) and "overmine" (reduce upward) all entities on this planet into systems or material processes or discursive effects.[62] And one might have thought that it was environmentalism and ecocriticism that pushed us out of modernity. But in effect that was the last gasp of hot air inside the plane of modernity. What waited outside was a hyperobject, and it is responsible for pushing us out of the plane: we are now in the Age of Asymmetry. This age is marked by the birth of speculative realisms that oppose the correlationist circle that emerged at the time of the Anthropocene.

As we reach the end of this book, can we explore the Age of Asymmetry a little more carefully still? Human inner space is profound and vast. We can comprehend infinity: we can comprehend the transfinite, as Cantor showed with his astonishingly simple diagonal proof that we can discern infinities larger than the infinity of rational numbers. When I say "inner depth," I don't mean a dimensional "inside," as if what I am talking about lives inside the human skull. There is no necessary implication of psyche or soul or self. The closest is the thinking of Heidegger on Dasein, being-in-the-world. By "world" Heidegger certainly doesn't mean something that environmental philosophers want him to mean:

a set of comforting or inspiring or ennobling beings that surround us. Dasein is profoundly uncanny. Dasein is the being after the end of the world, if *world* is what this book means by that term.

The inner depth and strangeness of the human is real and is articulated by many philosophers and artists, in particular Sophocles, whose chorus from *Antigone* is the epigraph of this part of the book: "Many are the disturbing beings in existence, but none is more disturbing than man."[63] This passage fascinated Heidegger.[64] The neuter plural term *deina* suggests fear and weirdness combined: it's where the first part of the word dinosaur comes from; Deimos was the brother of Phobos (fear). The best word is "dreadful": Deimos is the demon of dread, while Phobos is the demon of panic. Dread is existentially prior to panic: panic is starting to be a flight or fight situation, based on dread.

What makes humans the most dreadful is their ecological power. The uncanniness of human being is that it stirs up the oceans, divides the rocks, and ploughs up the soil. The chorus in *Antigone* sings of this in a powerfully disturbing way. Antigone is about a woman who goes beyond the law in the name of a transcendent law. Antigone is an uncanny human who is even prepared to go outside the physical and normative boundaries of the Greek city-state.

There is just one problem with the idea that humans are *to deinotaton* (the most dreadful thing): all beings have a dreadful depth. The very term *to deinotaton,* a neuter noun, brings to light that dreadfulness is thing-like. My depth is not the uncanniness of this paperweight, a Perspex sphere in which floats a magnified dandelion in full puff, each tiny hair visible and startling. A small rainbow hangs at the top of the sphere and the fluorescent light of the banker's lamp is reflected in it upside down. I do not interpret the paperweight as an emergent property of a fizzing buzz of dots or flecks of light and color: this actual paperweight unleashes its power, seducing me with its compelling roundness and softness. Yet I am unable to grasp the essence of the paperweight, whether I use the paperweight, ignore it, or contemplate it for the rest of my life. Things are "standoffish," as Stanley Cavell puts it, borrowing from a line of thinking in Emerson's essay "Experience": "I take this evanescence and lubricity of all objects, which lets them slip through our fingers then when we clutch hardest, to be the most unhandsome part of our condition."[65]

This seems like an understanding of things that the time of hyperobjects has enabled. I mean this in the fullest possible sense, so just to be clear, let me restate it in stronger terms. Nonhuman beings are responsible for the next moment of human history and thinking. It is not simply that humans became aware of nonhumans, or that they decided to ennoble some of them by granting them a higher status—or cut themselves down by taking away the status of the human. These so-called posthuman games are *nowhere near posthuman enough* to cope with the time of hyperobjects. They are more like one of the last gasps of the modern era, its final pirouette at the edge of the abyss. The reality is that hyperobjects were already here, and slowly but surely we understood what they were already saying. They contacted us.

Hyperobjects profoundly change how we think about any object. In a strange way, every object is a hyperobject. But we can only think this thought in light of the ecological emergency inside of which we have now woken up. Heidegger said that only a god can save us now.[66] As we find ourselves waking up within a series of gigantic objects, we realize that he forgot to add: *We just don't know what sort of god.*

Notes

INTRODUCTION

1. Timothy Morton, *The Ecological Thought* (Cambridge, Mass.: Harvard University Press, 2010), 130–35.

2. *Local manifestation* is philosopher Levi Bryant's term for the appearance of an object. See *The Democracy of Objects* (Ann Arbor, Mich.: Open Humanities Press, 2011), 15.

3. In some sense, the idea of *weakness* is an expansion of Vattimo's proposal for a weak thinking that accepts the human–world gap, and which moves through nihilism. Gianni Vattimo, *The Transparent Society*, trans. David Webb (Baltimore: Johns Hopkins University Press, 1994), 117, 119.

4. Jacques Lacan, *Écrits: A Selection*, trans. Alan Sheridan (London: Tavistock, 1977), 311.

5. I derive this line of thinking from Graham Harman, *Guerrilla Metaphysics: Phenomenology and the Carpentry of Things* (Chicago: Open Court, 2005), 101–2.

6. Henry David Thoreau, *The Maine Woods*, ed. Joseph J. Moldenhauer (Princeton, N.J.: Princeton University Press, 2004), 71.

7. The atmospheric chemist Paul Crutzen devised the term *Anthropocene*. Paul Crutzen and E. Stoermer, "The Anthropocene," *Global Change Newsletter* 41.1 (2000): 17–18; Paul Crutzen, "Geology of Mankind," *Nature* 415 (January 3, 2002): 23, doi:10.1038/415023a.

8. Karl Marx, *Capital*, trans. Ben Fowkes, 3 vols. (Harmondsworth: Penguin, 1990), 1:499.

9. The decisive study of situatedness is David Simpson, *Situatedness; or Why We Keep Saying Where We're Coming From* (Durham, N.C.: Duke University Press, 2002), 20.

10. Timothy Morton, *Ecology without Nature: Rethinking Environmental Aesthetics* (Cambridge, Mass.: Harvard University Press, 2007), 33.

11. Jacques Derrida, "Hostipitality," trans. Barry Stocker with Forbes Matlock, *Angelaki* 5.3 (December 2000): 3–18; Morton, *Ecological Thought*, 14–15, 17–19, 38–50.

12. See Trinity Atomic Website, http://www.cddc.vt.edu/host/atomic/trinity/ trinity1.html.

13. Bruno Latour, *We Have Never Been Modern*, trans. Catherine Porter (Cambridge, Mass.: Harvard University Press, 2002).

14. Martin Heidegger, *Being and Time*, trans. Joan Stambaugh (Albany: State University of New York Press, 1996), 83–85.

15. Arthur Eddington, *The Nature of the Physical World* (New York: Macmillan, 1928), 276.

16. Heidegger, *Being and Time*, 191.

17. See David Simpson, "Romanticism, Criticism, and Theory," in *The Cambridge Companion to British Romanticism*, ed. Stuart Curran (Cambridge: Cambridge University Press, 1993), 10.

18. Immanuel Kant, *Critique of Pure Reason*, trans. Norman Kemp Smith (Boston: St. Martin's Press, 1965), 84–85.

19. Heidegger, *Being and Time*, 196.

20. Heidegger, *Being and Time*, 193.

21. Heidegger, *Being and Time*, 208.

22. Martin Heidegger, *Phenomenological Interpretations of Aristotle*, trans. Richard Rojcwicz (Bloomington: Indiana University Press, 2001), 23.

23. Friedrich Nietzsche, *The Gay Science*, trans. and ed. Walter Kaufmann (New York: Vintage, 1974), 125.

24. William Blake, "The Divine Image," in *The Complete Poetry and Prose of William Blake*, ed. D. V. Erdman (New York: Doubleday, 1988).

25. Quentin Meillassoux, *After Finitude: An Essay on the Necessity of Contingency*, trans. Ray Brassier (London: Continuum, 2010), 119–21.

26. José Ortega y Gasset, *Phenomenology and Art*, trans. Philip W. Silver (New York: Norton, 1975), 63–70; Harman, *Guerrilla Metaphysics*, 39, 40, 135–43, 247.

27. Graham Harman, "Critical Animal with a Fun Little Post," *Object-Oriented Philosophy* (blog), October 17, 2011, http://doctorzamalek2.wordpress.com/2011/10/17/critical-animal-with-a-fun-little-post/.

28. The term *irreduction* is derived from the work of Bruno Latour and Graham Harman. Graham Harman, *Prince of Networks: Bruno Latour and Metaphysics* (Melbourne: Re.press, 2009), 12.

29. Karl Marx, *The Communist Manifesto*, in *Selected Writings*, ed. David McLellan (Oxford: Oxford University Press, 1977), 12; William Shakespeare, *Macbeth* (New York: Washington Square Press, 1992), 19.

30. Morton, *Ecological Thought*, 121.

31. Martin Heidegger, *Contributions to Philosophy: (From Enowning)*, trans. Parvis Emad and Kenneth Maly (Bloomington: Indiana University Press, 1999), 283–93. See also Joan Stambaugh, *The Finitude of Being* (Albany: State University of New York Press, 1992), 139–44.

32. I am inspired to use this phrase by the innovative arguments of the Heideggerian philosopher Iain Thomson in *Heidegger, Art, and Postmodernity* (Cambridge: Cambridge University Press, 2011), and "Heidegger's Aesthetics," in *The Stanford Encyclopedia of Philosophy*, ed. Edward N. Zalta, summer 2011 ed., http://plato.stanford.edu/entries/heidegger-aesthetics/.

33. Lacan, *Écrits*, 311.

34. Thing theory is the invention of Bill Brown. See the special issue of *Critical Inquiry*, "Things" (Fall 2001).

35. *Wall•E*, directed by Andrew Stanton (Pixar Animation Studios, 2008).

VISCOSITY

1. Richard Dawkins develops the concept in *The Extended Phenotype: The Long Reach of the Gene* (Oxford: Oxford University Press, 1999), 1–2.

2. *Twin Peaks*, directed by David Lynch et al. (ABC, 1990); *Twin Peaks: Fire Walk with Me* (CIBY Pictures, 1992).

3. Perhaps the most vivid account of the politics of this agency to date has been Jane Bennett, *Vibrant Matter: A Political Ecology of Things* (Durham, N.C.: Duke University Press, 2004), 21.

4. Plato, *Ion*, trans. Benjamin Jowett, http://classics.mit.edu/Plato/ion.html.

5. Ursula Heise, *Sense of Place and Sense of Planet: The Environmental Imagination of the Global* (New York: Colombia University Press, 1982), 84.

6. Immanuel Kant, *Critique of Judgment*, trans. Werner S. Pluhar (Indianapolis: Hackett, 1987), 445–46.

7. Jean-Paul Sartre, *Being and Nothingness: An Essay on Phenomenological Ontology*, trans. and ed. Hazel Barnes (New York: Philosophical Library, 1984), 610, 609.

8. Sartre, *Being and Nothingness*, 609.

9. Debora Shuger, "'Gums of Glutinous Heat' and the Stream of Consciousness: The Theology of Milton's *Maske*," *Representations* 60 (Fall 1997): 1–21.

10. Reza Negarestani, *Cyclonopedia: Complicity with Anonymous Materials* (Melbourne: Re.press, 2008), 29.

11. Negarestani, *Cyclonopedia*, 87–97, 98–100, 101–6.

12. Julia Kristeva, *Powers of Horror: An Essay on Abjection*, trans. L. S. Roudiez (New York: Columbia University Press, 1982), 3–4.

13. I derive the phrase "revenge of Gaia" from James Lovelock, *The Revenge of Gaia: Earth's Climate Crisis and the Fate of Humanity* (New York: Basic Books, 2007).

14. E. V. Klass et al., "Reconstruction of the Dose to the Victim as a Result of Accidental Irradiation in Lia (Georgia)," *Atomic Energy* 100.2 (2006): 149–53; Richard Stone, "The Hunt for Hot Stuff," *Smithsonian* 33.12 (March 2003): 58; PBS, Transcript of "Dirty Bomb," *Nova*, February 25, 2003, http://www.pbs.org/wgbh/nova/transcripts/3007_dirtybom.html; NTI, "Radiothermal Generators Containing Strontium-90 Discovered in Liya, Georgia," January 15, 2002, http://www.nti.org/db/nistraff/2002/20020030.htm.

15. Steven A. Book, William L. Spangler, and Laura A. Swartz, "Effects of Lifetime Ingestion of 90Sr in Beagle Dogs," *Radiation Research* 90 (1982): 244–51.

16. John Donne, *Holy Sonnets 14,* in *Major Works: Including Songs and Sonnets and Sermons,* ed. John Carey (Oxford: Oxford University Press, 2000).

17. The line is from the *Bhagavad Gita,* trans. Swami Nikhilananda (New York: Ramakrishna-Vivekananda Center, 1944), 11.32. The term *shatterer* rather than *destroyer* first appeared in "The Eternal Apprentice," *Time,* November 8, 1948, http://www.time.com/time/magazine/article/0,9171,853367-8,00.html.

18. Ortega y Gasset, *Phenomenology and Art,* 63–70; Harman, *Guerrilla Metaphysics,* 39, 40, 135–43, 247.

19. Harman, *Guerrilla Metaphysics,* 135–36.

20. Ulrich Beck, *Risk Society: Towards a New Modernity* (London: Sage, 1992), 19–22.

21. Robert Parker, *Miasma: Pollution and Purification in Early Greek Religion* (Oxford: Oxford University Press, 2001), 5–9.

22. Harman, *Guerrilla Metaphysics,* 247.

23. Lacan, *Écrits,* 311.

24. David Bohm and Basil Hiley, *The Undivided Universe: An Ontological Interpretation of Quantum Theory* (London: Routledge, 1995), 18–19, 23.

25. See Anton Zeilinger, *Dance of the Photons: From Einstein to Quantum Teleportation* (New York: Farrar, Straus, and Giroux, 2010), 236.

26. Bohm and Hiley, *Undivided Universe,* 28–38.

NONLOCALITY

1. Ian Bogost, *Unit Operations: An Approach to Videogame Criticism* (Cambridge, Mass.: MIT Press, 2008), 4–15.

2. See Levi Bryant, "Let's Talk about Politics Again!—Ian Bogost," *Larval Subjects* (blog), September 17, 2012, http://larvalsubjects.wordpress.com/?s=Bogost.

3. This is a version of an argument in Meillassoux, *After Finitude,* 82–85.

4. David Bohm, *Quantum Theory (New York: Dover, 1989),* 99–115.

5. Bohm, *Quantum Theory,* 158–61.

6. Bohm, *Quantum Theory,* 139–40, 177.

7. Bohm, *Quantum Theory,* 493–94.

8. Alejandro W. Rodriguez et al., "Theoretical Ingredients of a Casimir Analog Computer," *Proceedings of the National Academies of Sciences* (March 24, 2010), www.pnas.org/cgi/doi/10.1073/pnas.1003894107.

9. David Bohm, *Wholeness and the Implicate Order* (London: Routledge, 2008), 219.

10. Bohm, *Quantum Theory,* 177.

11. Bohm, *Quantum Theory,* 139–40.

12. David Bohm, *The Special Theory of Relativity* (London: Routledge, 2006), 155.

13. Bohm, *Quantum Theory,* 118.

14. Dawkins, *Extended Phenotype*, 156; Joan Roughgarden, *Evolution's Rainbow: Diversity, Gender, and Sexuality in Nature and People* (Berkeley: University of California Press, 2004), 26–27.

15. Yuri Aharanov and David Bohm, "Significance of Electromagnetic Potentials in the Quantum Theory," *Physical Review* 115.3 (August 1, 1959): 485–91; Alain Aspect, Philippe Granger, and Gérard Roger, "Experimental Realization of Einstein-Podolsky-Rosen-Bohm *Gedankenexperiment*: A New Violation of Bell's Inequalities," *Physical Review Letters* 49.2 (July 2, 1982): 91–94; Anton Zeilinger et al., "An Experimental Test of Non-Local Realism," *Nature* 446 (August 6, 2007): 871–75; L. Hofstetter et al., "Cooper Pair Splitter Realized in a Two-Quantum-Dot Y-Junction," *Nature* 461 (October 15, 2009): 960–63.

16. Albert Einstein, Nathan Rosen, and Boris Podolsky, "Can Quantum-Mechanical Description of Reality Be Complete?" *Physical Review* 47 (1935): 777–80.

17. Anton Zeilinger et al., "Distributing Entanglement and Single Photons through an Intra-City, Free-Space Quantum Channel," *Optics Express* 13 (2005): 202–9; Villoresi et al., "Experimental Verification of the Feasibility of a Quantum Channel between Space and Earth," *New Journal of Physics* 10 (2008): doi:10.1088/1367-2630/10/3/033038; Fedrizzi et al., "High-Fidelity Transmission of Entanglement over a High-Loss Freespace Channel," *Nature Physics* 5 (June 24, 2009): 389–92.

18. Edward Casey, *The Fate of Place: A Philosophical History* (Berkeley: University of California Press, 1997), 106–16.

19. John Bell, "On the Einstein Podolsky Rosen Paradox," *Physics* 1 (1964): 195–200.

20. Elisabetta Collin et al., "Coherently Wired Light-Harvesting in Photosynthetic Marine Algae at Ambient Temperature," *Nature* 463 (February 4, 2010): 644–47.

21. Aaron D. O'Connell et al., "Quantum Ground State and Single Phonon Control of a Mechanical Ground Resonator," *Nature* 464 (March 17, 2010): 697–703.

22. O'Connell et al., "Quantum Ground State," 701.

23. Collin et al., "Coherently Wired Light-Harvesting," 644–47; Erik M. Gauger et al., "Sustained Quantum Coherence and Entanglement in the Avian Compass," *Physical Review Letters* 106 (January 28, 2011): doi:10.1103/PhysRevLett.106.040503.

24. Arkady Plotnitsky, *Reading Bohr* (Dordrecht: Springer, 2010), 35.

25. Anthony Valentini, *Quantum Theory at the Crossroads: Reconsidering the 1927 Solvay Conference* (Cambridge: Cambridge University Press, 2009), vii–xi.

26. Bohm and Hiley, *Undivided Universe*, 28–38.

27. Bohm, *Wholeness*, 246–77.

28. Bohm, *Wholeness*, 21.

29. Bohm, *Wholeness*, 14.

30. Harman, *Guerrilla Metaphysics*, 83.

31. Bohm, *Quantum Theory*, 139.

32. Graham Harman, *Tool-Being: Heidegger and the Metaphysics of Objects* (Chicago: Open Court, 2002), 129–33.

33. Bohm, *Quantum Theory,* 158–61.

34. See Einstein, Rosen, and Podolsky, "Can Quantum-Mechanical Description?," 777–80.

35. Backward causation is favored by Phil Dowe in *Physical Causation* (New York: Cambridge University Press, 2000), 176–86.

36. See, for example, Bohm, *Wholeness,* 246–77.

37. Petr Hořava, "Quantum Gravity at a Lifshitz Point," March 2, 2009, arXiv: 0901.3775v2 [hep-th].

38. Aaron O'Connell, "Making Sense of a Visible Quantum Object," TED Talk, March 2011, http://www.ted.com/talks/aaron_o_connell_making_sense_of_a_vis ible_quantum_object.html.

39. Science Daily, "Quantum Mechanics at Work in Photosynthesis: Algae Familiar with These Processes for Nearly Two Billion Years," February 3, 2010, http://www.sciencedaily.com/releases/2010/02/100203131356.htm?sms_ss=blogger.

40. Bohm, *Wholeness,* 183, 187–88, 244.

41. Bohm, *Wholeness,* 192, 218–71.

42. Craig Hogan, "Spacetime Indeterminacy and Holographic Noise," October 22, 2007, arXiv:0706.1999v2 [gr-qc]; Craig Hogan, "Holographic Noise in Interferometers," January 8, 2010, arXiv:0905.4803v8 [gr-qc]; Raphael Bousso et al., "Predicting the Cosmological Constant from the Causal Entropic Principle," September 15, 2007, hep-th/0702115; Raphael Bousso, "The Holographic Principle," *Review of Modern Physics* 74 (2002): 825–74.

43. James Boswell, *Boswell's Life of Johnson* (London: Oxford University Press, 1965) 333.

44. John Hersey, *Hiroshima* (New York: Vintage Books, 1989).

45. Hersey, *Hiroshima,* 20.

46. *Empire of the Sun,* directed by Steven Spielberg (Warner Bros., 1987).

47. Heidegger, *Contributions to Philosophy,* 283–93. See also Stambaugh, *Finitude of Being,* 139–44. Robert Oppenheimer's line is from the *Bhagavad Gita,* 11.32. As stated earlier, the term "shatterer" rather than "destroyer" first appeared in "The Eternal Apprentice," *Time.*

48. Martin Heidegger, "The Question Concerning Technology," in *Basic Writings: From Being and Time to The Task of Thinking,* ed. David Krell (New York: HarperCollins, 1993), 307–41.

49. William Wordsworth, *The Prelude,* in *The Major Works: Including the Prelude,* ed. Stephen Gill (Oxford: Oxford University Press, 2008), lines 330–412.

50. Sigmund Freud, *The Ego and the Id,* trans. Joan Riviere, rev. and ed. James Strachey (New York: Norton, 1989), 24; Sigmund Freud, "A Note on the Mystic Writing Pad," in *The Standard Edition of the Complete Psychological Works of Sigmund Freud,* trans. and ed. James Strachey (London: Hogarth Press, 1953), 19:225–32; Jacques Derrida, "Freud and the Scene of Writing," *Writing and Difference,* trans. Alan Bass (London: Routledge and Kegan Paul, 1978), 246–91.

51. Timothy Morton, "Some Notes towards a Philosophy of Non-Life," *Thinking Nature* 1 (2011): http://thinkingnaturejournal.files.wordpress.com/2011/06/to wardsnonlifebytimmorton.pdf.

52. Nick Land, *Fanged Noumena: Collected Writings, 1987–2007* (Falmouth: Urbanomic, 2011), 335, 448. See also Negarestani, *Cyclonopedia*, 26, 72.

53. Negarestani, *Cyclonopedia*, 70; see also 13–14, 16–21.

54. Negarestani, *Cyclonopedia*, 27.

55. Negarestani, *Cyclonopedia*, 26.

56. Martin Heidegger, "The Origin of the Work of Art," in *Poetry, Language, Thought,* trans. Albert Hofstadter (New York: Harper & Row, 1971), 15–86.

57. William K. Wimsatt and Monroe C. Beardsley, "The Intentional Fallacy," *Sewanee Review* 54 (1946): 468–88.

58. Ray Brassier, *Nihil Unbound: Enlightenment and Extinction* (New York: Palgrave, 2010), 48.

Temporal Undulation

1. Levi Bryant, "Hyperobjects and OOO," *Larval Subjects* (blog), November 11, 2010, http://larvalsubjects.wordpress.com/2010/11/11/hyperobjects-and-ooo/.

2. *Das Rad,* directed by Chris Stenner, Arvid Uibel, and Heidi Wittlinger (Georg Gruber Filmproduktion, Filmakademie Baden-Württemberg, 2001).

3. Felix Hess, *Air Pressure Fluctuations* (Edition RZ, 2001).

4. Harman, *Guerrilla Metaphysics,* 86.

5. Theodor Adorno, *Aesthetic Theory,* trans. and ed. Robert Hullot-Kentor (Minneapolis: University of Minnesota Press, 1997), 65; Theodor Adorno, "The Idea of Natural History," *Telos* 60 (1984): 111–24.

6. David Archer, *The Long Thaw: How Humans Are Changing the Next 100,000 Years of Earth's Climate* (Princeton, N.J.: Princeton University Press, 2008); David Archer, "How Long Will Global Warming Last?," http://www.realclimate.org/index.php/archives/2005/03/how-long-will-global-warming-last/.

7. Kant, *Critique of Judgment,* 519–25.

8. See Morton, *Ecological Thought,* 40, 118.

9. *Plastic Bag,* directed by Ramin Bahrani (Noruz Films and Gigantic Pictures, 2009).

10. Casey, *Fate of Place,* 106–12.

11. Blaise Pascal, *Pensées,* trans. A. J. Krailsheimer (New York: Penguin, 1966), 201:95.

12. Bohm, *Special Theory of Relativity,* 189–90.

13. Albert Einstein, *The Meaning of Relativity* (Princeton, N.J.: Princeton University Press, 2005), 30.

14. Einstein, *Meaning of Relativity,* 63.

15. Bohm, *Special Theory of Relativity,* 156, 189–90, 204–18.

16. Bohm, *Wholeness,* 12–13.

17. Alphonso Lingis, *The Imperative* (Bloomington: Indiana University Press, 1998), 25–37.

18. Einstein, *Meaning of Relativity,* 61.

19. Timothy Morton, *Realist Magic: Objects, Ontology, Causality* (Ann Arbor, Mich.: Open Humanities Press, 2013), 26, 36, 40–41, 56–62.

20. Meillassoux, *After Finitude*, 119–21.

21. Iain Hamilton Grant, *Philosophies of Nature after Schelling* (London: Continuum, 2008), 204.

22. H. P. Lovecraft, "The Call of Cthulhu," in *The Dunwich Horror and Others,* ed. S. T. Joshi (Sauk City, Wisc.: Arkham House, 1984), 139.

23. Meillassoux, *After Finitude*, 7.

24. Bohm, *Special Theory of Relativity,* 91–96, 129.

25. NASA Science News, "NASA Announces Results of Epic Space-Time Experiment," http://science.nasa.gov/science-news/science-at-nasa/2011/04may_epic/.

26. Casey, *Fate of Place*, 106–16; Latour, *We Have Never Been Modern.*

27. Ar-Razi, *Doubts against Galen*, in *Classical Arabic Philosophy*, trans. John Mcginnis and David C. Reisman (Indianapolis: Hackett, 2007), 53.

28. Graham Harman, "Aristotle with a Twist," in *Speculative Medievalisms: Discography*, ed. Eileen Joy, Anna Klosowska, and Nicola Masciandaro (New York: Punctum Books, 2012) 227–53.

29. Percy Shelley, *A Defence of Poetry*, in *Shelley's Poetry and Prose*, ed. Donald H. Reiman and Neil Fraistat (New York: Norton, 2002), 509–35 (535).

30. Camille Parmesan, "Ecological and Evolutionary Responses to Recent Climate Change," *Annual Review of Ecology, Evolution, and Systematics* 37 (2006): 637–69.

PHASING

1. Percy Shelley, "Hymn to Intellectual Beauty," in *Shelley's Poetry and Prose,* ed. Donald H. Reiman and Neil Fraistat (New York: Norton, 2002), lines 1–2.

2. Percy Shelley, *Mont Blanc, Poetry and Prose*, lines 1–2. See Steven Shaviro, "The Universe of Things," *Theory and Event* 14.3 (2011): doi:10.1353/tae.2011 .0027.

3. Walter Benjamin, "The Work of Art in the Age of Mechanical Reproduction," in *Illuminations*, ed. Hannah Arendt, trans. Harry Zohn, (London: Harcourt, Brace, and World, 1973), 217–51.

4. Edward Burtynsky, *Manufactured Landscapes: The Photographs of Edward Burtynsky* (New Haven, Conn.: Yale University Press, 2003); *Manufactured Landscapes,* directed by Jennifer Baichwal (Foundry Films, National Film Board of Canada, 2006).

5. Martin Heidegger, *What Is a Thing?*, trans. W. B. Barton and Vera Deutsch, analysis by Eugene T. Gendlin (Chicago: Henry Regnery, 1967), 102–3.

6. Kant, *Critique of Pure Reason*, 84–85.

7. The Beatles, "A Day in the Life," *Sgt. Pepper's Lonely Hearts Club Band* (Parlophone, 1967).

8. See Bryant, *Democracy of Objects*, 208–27.

9. The most important of these sources is *In Contradiction: A Study of the Transconsistent* (Oxford: Oxford University Press, 2006).

10. In "Auguries of Innocence," *The Complete Poetry and Prose of William Blake,* ed. David V. Erdman (New York: Doubleday, 1988).

11. *Star Wars 4: A New Hope,* directed by George Lucas (Twentieth Century Fox, 1977).

INTEROBJECTIVITY

1. Morton, *Ecological Thought,* 14–15.

2. Heidegger, *Being and Time,* 64, 70, 73, 95, 103, 111, 187, 333, 348. I use Harman's apt translation "contexture."

3. When I wrote *The Ecological Thought,* it was unclear to me which one of the two entities that study disclosed—the *mesh* and the *strange stranger*—had priority. It now seems clear that the strange stranger has ontological priority. For a full discussion, see Morton, *Realist Magic,* 24, 75, 140.

4. *Oxford English Dictionary,* s.v. "mesh," n.1 a, b, http://www.oed.com.

5. Lawrence M. Krauss, Scott Dodelson, and Stephan Meyer, "Primordial Gravitational Waves and Cosmology," *Science* 328.5981 (May 2010): 989–92.

6. *Oxford English Dictionary,* s.v. "mesh," http://www.oed.com.

7. See, for example, Michael E. Zimmerman and Sean Esbjörn-Hargens, *Integral Ecology: Uniting Multiple Perspectives on the Natural World* (Boston: Shambala, 2009), 216.

8. Heidegger, *Being and Time,* 127–28, 254–55.

9. Alan M. Turing, "Computing Machinery and Intelligence," in *The Philosophy of Artificial Intelligence,* ed. Margaret A. Boden (Oxford: Oxford University Press, 1990), 40–66.

10. Herbert A. Simon, *The Sciences of the Artificial* (Cambridge, Mass.: MIT Press, 1996), 51–53.

11. Grant, *Philosophies of Nature,* 27–30.

12. Heidegger, "Origin," 15–86.

13. Stephen M. Feeney et al., "First Observational Tests of Eternal Inflation: Analysis Methods and WMAP 7-year Results," *Physical Review D* 84.4 (2011): doi:10.1103/PhysRevD.84.043507.

14. Shelley, *Defence of Poetry,* 509–35 (522).

15. George Spencer-Brown, *Laws of Form* (New York: E. P. Dutton, 1979); Niklas Luhmann, *Social Systems,* trans. John Bednarz and Dirk Baecker (Stanford, Calif.: Stanford University Press, 1996), 65–66, 275.

16. Jacques Derrida, *Dissemination,* trans. Barbara Johnson (Chicago: University of Chicago Press, 1981), 54, 104, 205, 208, 222, 253.

17. Shelley, *Defence of Poetry,* 522.

18. John Ruskin, *The Seven Lamps of Architecture* (London: Smith, Elder, 1849), 125.

19. See my argument in *Ecology without Nature,* 138.

20. Meillassoux, *After Finitude,* 7.

21. Morton, *Realist Magic,* 212–13.

22. Aristotle, *Physics,* trans. Robin Waterfield (Oxford: Oxford University Press, 2008), Book 4 (especially 105–8); see also 26, 34–35.

23. *Empire of the Sun,* directed by Stephen Spielberg; J. G. Ballard, *Empire of the Sun* (Cutchogue, N.Y.: Buccaneer Books, 1984).

24. *The Day After,* directed by Nicholas Meyer (ABC, 1983); *The Day after Tomorrow,* directed by Roland Emmerich (Centropolis Entertainment, 2004).

25. Gillian Beer, introduction to *The Origin of Species,* by Charles Darwin (Oxford: Oxford University Press, 1998), vii–xxviii (xxvii–xviii).

THE END OF THE WORLD

1. Morton, *Ecological Thought,* 28, 54.

2. Aristotle, *Metaphysics,* trans. Hugh Lawson-Tancred (London: Penguin, 1999), 158–59.

3. Harman, *Tool-Being,* 127.

4. Roman Jakobson, "Closing Statement: Linguistics and Poetics," in *Style in Language,* ed. Thomas A. Sebeok (Cambridge, Mass.: MIT Press, 1960), 350–77.

5. Harman, *Tool-Being,* 21–22.

6. *The Two Towers,* directed by Peter Jackson (New Line Cinema, 2002).

7. Anon, "Residents Upset about Park Proposal," *Lakewood Sentinel,* July 31, 2008, 1; "Solar Foes Focus in the Dark," *Lakewood Sentinel,* August 7, 2008, 4.

8. Marx, *Capital,* 1:556.

9. Martin Heidegger, "The Question Concerning Technology," in *The Question Concerning Technology and Other Essays,* trans. William Lovitt (New York: Harper & Row, 1977), 17.

10. See, for instance, Heidegger, " Origin," 15–86.

11. Harman, *Tool-Being,* 155.

12. Pierre Boulez, *Répons* (Deutsche Grammophon, 1999); *Boulez: Répons,* directed by Robert Cahen (Colimason, INA, IRCAM, 1989), http://www.heure-exquise.org/video.php?id=1188.

13. Stephen Healey, "Air Conditioning," paper presented at the Materials: Objects: Environments workshop, National Institute for Experimental Arts (NIEA), Sydney, May 19, 2011.

14. David Gissen, *Subnature: Architecture's Other Environments* (New York: Princeton Architectural Press, 2009), 79; "Reflux: From Environmental Flows to Environmental Objects," paper presented at the Materials: Objects: Environments workshop, NIEA, Sydney, May 19, 2011.

15. R&Sie, *Dusty Relief,* http://www.new-territories.com/roche2002bis.htm.

16. Neil A. Manson, "The Concept of Irreversibility: Its Use in the Sustainable Development and Precautionary Principle Literatures," *Electronic Journal of Sustainable Development* 1.1 (2007): 3–15, https://sustainability.water.ca.gov/documents/18/3407876/The+concept+of+irreversibility+its+use+in+the+sustainable.pdf.

17. Fernand Braudel, *Civilization and Capitalism, 15th–18th Century,* trans. S. Reynolds, 3 vols. (Berkeley: University of California Press, 1982–84).

18. Aristotle, *Metaphysics,* 213, 217.

19. Marx, *Capital,* 1:620.

20. Burtynsky, *Manufactured Landscapes*; *Manufactured Landscapes,* directed by Jennifer Baichwal (Foundry Films, National Film Board of Canada, 2006).

21. Slavoj Žižek, *Enjoy Your Symptom! Jacques Lacan in Hollywood and Out* (New York: Routledge, 2001), 209.

22. ABCnews, "Oil From the BP Spill Found at Bottom of Gulf," September 12, 2010, http://abcnews.go.com/WN/oil-bp-spill-found-bottom-gulf/story?id=1161 8039.

23. Bryant, *Democracy of Objects*, 208–27.

24. Mary Ann Hoberman, *A House Is a House for Me* (New York: Puffin Books, 2007), 27.

25. Hoberman, *House*, 34, 42–48.

26. Harman, *Tool-Being*, 68–80.

27. The phrase is Graham Harman's: *Guerrilla Metaphysics*, 23, 85, 158, 161.

28. Stambaugh, *Finitude of Being*, 28, 53, 55.

29. An exemplary instance is Rocky Flats Nuclear Guardianship: http://www.rockyflatsnuclearguardianship.org/.

30. Thomas A. Sebeok, *Communication Measures to Bridge Ten Millennia* (Columbus, Ohio: Battelle Memorial Institute, Office of Nuclear Waste Isolation, 1984).

31. *Into Eternity,* directed Michael Madsen (Magic Hour Films and Atmo Media, 2010).

32. Susan Garfield, "'Atomic Priesthood' Is Not Nuclear Guardianship: A Critique of Thomas Sebeok's Vision of the Future," *Nuclear Guardianship Forum* 3 (1994): http://www.ratical.org/radiation/NGP/AtomPriesthd.txt.

33. Heidegger, *Contributions to Philosophy*, 13.

34. See Timothy Clark, "Towards a Deconstructive Environmental Criticism," *Oxford Literary Review* 30.1 (2008): 45–68.

35. Stambaugh, *Finitude of Being*, 93.

36. Derek Parfit, *Reasons and Persons* (Oxford: Oxford University Press, 1984), 355–57, 361.

37. Parfit, *Reasons and Persons*, 309–13.

38. Jacques Derrida, "Hostipitality," trans. Barry Stocker with Forbes Matlock, *Angelaki* 5.3 (December 2000): 3–18 (11).

39. Donna Haraway, *When Species Meet* (Minneapolis: University of Minnesota Press, 2007), 19, 27, 92, 301.

40. Rob Nixon, *Slow Violence and the Environmentalism of the Poor* (Cambridge, Mass.: Harvard University Press, 2011), 2.

41. Emmanuel Levinas, *Totality and Infinity: An Essay on Exteriority,* trans. Alphonso Lingis (Pittsburgh: Duquesne University Press, 1969), 160, 258; *Otherwise than Being: Or Beyond Essence,* trans. Alphonso Lingis (Pittsburgh: Duquesne University Press, 1998), 3.

42. Franz Kafka, "The Cares of a Family Man," in *Metamorphosis, In the Penal Colony, and Other Short Stories* (New York: Schoken Books, 1995), 160.

43. Kafka, "Cares," 160.

44. Kafka, "Cares," 160.

45. Chögyam Trungpa, *Glimpses of Abidharma* (Boston: Shambhala, 2001), 74; Heidegger, *Being and Time*, 171–78.

46. *The Matrix,* directed by the Wachowski brothers (Village Roadshow Pictures and Silver Pictures, 1999).

47. Radical Joy for Hard Times, "What Is an Earth Exchange?," http://www.rad icaljoyforhardtimes.org/index.php?option=com_content&view=article&id=79& Itemid=29. A slide show of the 2010 Global Earth Exchanges can be found at http://www.radicaljoyforhardtimes.org/index.php?option=com_content&view= article&id=55&Itemid=5.

48. Morton, *Ecological Thought,* 38–50.

49. "Cosmic Origins: A Series of Six Lectures Exploring Our World and Ourselves," University of Arizona College of Science, http://cos.arizona.edu/cosmic/.

50. I refer to the movie *The Island President,* directed by Jon Shenk (Samuel Goldwyn Films, 2011), about Mohamed Nasheed, president of the Maldives, whose islands are being inundated by the effects of global warming.

HYPOCRISIES

1. Talking Heads, "Once in a Lifetime," *Remain in Light* (Sire Records, 1980).

2. Horst Rittel and Melvin Webber, "Dilemmas in a General Theory of Planning," in *Developments in Design Methodology,* ed. N. Cross (Chichester: J. Wiley & Sons, 1984), 135–44.

3. Kelly Levin et al., "Playing It Forward: Path Dependency, Progressive Incrementalism, and the 'Super Wicked' Problem of Global Climate Change," http://environment.research.yale.edu/documents/downloads/0-9/2010_super_wicked_levin_cashore_bernstein_auld.pdf.

4. Søren Kierkegaard, "The Edifying in the Thought That Against God We Are Always in the Wrong," in *Either/Or: A Fragment of Life,* ed. Victor Eremita, trans. and intro. Alastair Hannay (London: Penguin, 1992), 595–609 (597, 602, 604).

5. This paradox has a rich history in the thinking of Žižek. See, for instance, *Tarrying with the Negative: Kant, Hegel, and the Critique of Ideology* (Durham, N.C.: Duke University Press, 1998), 193–96.

6. Heidegger, *Contributions to Philosophy,* 29, 67–68, 94–96.

7. Parfit, *Reasons and Persons,* 355–57.

8. Parfit, *Reasons and Persons,* 281.

9. Arthur Rimbaud to Paul Demeny, May 15, 1871, in *Rimbaud: Complete Works, Selected Letters: A Bilingual Edition,* ed. Seth Whidden, trans. Wallace Fowlie (Chicago: University of Chicago Press, 2005), 374.

10. Beck, *Risk Society,* 19–22.

11. Parfit, *Reasons and Persons,* 371–77.

12. Jacques Derrida, *The Animal That Therefore I Am,* ed. Marie-Louise Mallet, trans. David Wills (New York: Fordham University Press, 2008), 136.

13. Jacques Lacan, address given at MIT, quoted in Sherry Turkle, *Psychoanalytic Politics: Freud's French Revolution* (New York: Basic Books, 1978), 238.

14. Lingis, *Imperative,* 173, 221–22.

15. Lingis, *Imperative,* 26–38.

16. Harman, *Guerrilla Metaphysics,* 36–37.

17. Lingis, *Imperative,* 29.

18. Jacques Lacan, *Le seminaire, Livre III: Les psychoses* (Paris: Editions de Seuil, 1981), 48.

19. Hakim Bey, *The Temporary Autonomous Zone* (Brooklyn, N.Y.: Autonomedia, 1991), http://hermetic.com/bey/taz_cont.html.

20. Graham Harman, "The Theory of Objects in Heidegger and Whitehead," in *Towards Speculative Realism: Essays and Lectures* (Ropley: Zero Books, 2010), 22–43; Graham Harman, "Object-Oriented Philosophy," in *Towards Speculative Realism*, 93–104.

21. Adorno, *Aesthetic Theory*, 331.

22. Eliane Radigue, *Biogenesis* (Metamkine, 1996).

23. Heidegger, *Being and Time*, 127.

24. Heidegger, *Being and Time*, 5, 22–23, 62–71.

25. John Cleese and Graham Chapman, "The Argument Sketch," *Monty Python's Flying Circus*, "The Money Programme," series 3, episode 3 (November 2, 1972).

26. This is the title of one of Lacan's seminars, "Le séminaire de Jacques Lacan, Livre XXI: Les non-dupes errent" (unpublished).

27. Morton, *Ecology without Nature*, 109–23.

28. *Oxford English Dictionary*, s.v. "doom," n.1, http://www.oed.com.

29. *Oxford English Dictionary*, s.v. "doom," n.2, 3b, 5, 6, 7, http://www.oed.com

30. *Oxford English Dictionary*, s.v. "doom," n.3a, http://www.oed.com.

31. *Oxford English Dictionary*, s.v. "doom," n.4a, b, http://www.oed.com.

32. *Oxford English Dictionary*, s.v. "doom," n.8, 10, http://www.oed.com.

33. There is a very good summary of this in the entry "Jacques Derrida," in *The Stanford Encyclopedia of Philosophy*, ed. Edward N. Zalta, fall 2011 ed., http://plato.stanford.edu/archives/fall2011/entries/derrida/.

34. Quintilian, *Institutio Oratorica* 11.3, http://penelope.uchicago.edu/Thayer/E/Roman/Texts/Quintilian/Institutio_Oratoria/11C*.html#3.

35. Heidegger, " Origin," 15–86.

36. Morton, *Ecology without Nature*, 34–47.

37. "Return to Tomorrow," *Star Trek*, season 2, episode 20, first broadcast February 9, 1968.

38. Shelley, *Defence of Poetry*, 509–35 (530, 533).

39. *Being John Malkovich*, directed by Spike Jonze (USA Films, 1999).

40. James Joyce, *Ulysses* (Harmondsworth: Penguin, 1983), 331.

41. Alvin Lucier, *Music on a Long Thin Wire* (Lovely Music, 1979).

42. Lacan, *Le seminaire, Livre III*, 48.

43. Gerard Manley Hopkins, "As Kingfishers Catch Fire, Dragonflies Draw Flame," in *The Major Works*, ed. Catherine Phillips (Oxford: Oxford University Press, 2009).

44. Shelley, *Hymn to Intellectual Beauty*, line 1.

45. Lacan, *Écrits*, 311.

46. Laurie Anderson, "Born Never Asked," *Big Science* (Warner Bros., 1982).

47. Kierkegaard, "The Edifying in the Truth, 595–609.

48. Peter Sloterdijk, *Critique of Cynical Reason* (Minneapolis: University of Minnesota Press, 1988). See also Slavoj Žižek, *The Sublime Object of Ideology* (London: Verso, 1997), 28–33.

49. Arne Naess, *Ecology, Community, and Lifestyle: A Philosophical Approach* (Oslo: University of Oslo Press, 1977), 56.

50. Harman, *Guerrilla Metaphysics,* 79, 185.

51. Graham Harman, *The Quadruple Object* (Ropley: Zero Books, 2011), 7–18.

52. Heidegger, *Contributions to Philosophy,* 27, 78, 80, 83; "On the Question of Being," in *Pathmarks,* ed. William McNeill (Cambridge: Cambridge University Press, 1998), 291–322 (311, 313).

53. Malcolm Bull, *Anti-Nietzsche* (London: Verso, 2011), 11–13.

54. Harman, "Object-Oriented Philosophy," 93–104.

55. Georg Wilhelm Friedrich Hegel, *Hegel: Elements of the Philosophy of Right,* trans. H. B. Nisbet (Cambridge: Cambridge University Press, 1991), 23.

The Age of Asymmetry

1. Heidegger, *Contributions to Philosophy,* 54, 265. See Stambaugh, *Finitude of Being,* 60, 129.

2. Bradley Smith, "Interview with Wolves in the Throne Room 2006," *Nocturnal Cult,* June 10, 2006, http://www.nocturnalcult.com/WITTRint.htm.

3. *Hegel's Aesthetics: Lectures on Fine Art,* trans. T. M. Knox, 2 vols. (Oxford: Oxford University Press, 2010), 1:408; Hegel, *Introductory Lectures on Aesthetics,* trans. Bernard Bosanquet (London: Penguin, 1993), 82–84.

4. Hegel, *Aesthetics,* 1:301, 309–310, 1:427–42; Hegel, *Introductory Lectures,* 84–85.

5. Blake, "The Divine Image."

6. Hegel, *Introductory Lectures,* 85–86; Hegel, *Aesthetics,* 1:516–29.

7. Hegel, *Aesthetics,* 1:530–39.

8. Georg Wilhelm Friedrich Hegel, *Hegel's Phenomenology of Spirit,* trans. A. V. Miller (Oxford: Oxford University Press, 1977), 111–19.

9. Marx and Engels, *Manifesto,* 227.

10. See Susan McClary, *Conventional Wisdom: The Content of Musical Form* (Berkeley: University of California Press, 2001), 63–108.

11. Slavoj Žižek, "The Abyss of Freedom," in Slavoj Žižek and Friedrich Schelling, *The Abyss of Freedom / Ages of the World,* (*Ages of the World,* trans. Judith Norman) (Ann Arbor: University of Michigan Press, 2007), 46–48.

12. The Beatles, "A Day in the Life."

13. In David Toop, *Haunted Weather: Music, Silence, and Memory* (London: Serpent's Tail, 2004), 239–40.

14. Adorno, *Aesthetic Theory,* 331.

15. Laurie L. Patton, *Bringing the Gods to Mind: Mantra and Ritual in Early Indian Sacrifice* (Berkeley: University of California Press, 2005), 1–14.

16. Martin Heidegger, *What Is Philosophy?*, trans. and intro. Jean T. Wilde and William Kluback (Lanham, Md.: Rowan and Littlefield, 2003), 77–91.

17. Arthur Schopenhauer, *The World as Will and Representation*, trans. E. F. J. Payne, 2 vols. (New York: Dover, 1969), 1:411–12.

18. This position is somewhat similar to the one found in Chuck Dyke, "Natural Speech: A Hoary Story," in *How Nature Speaks: The Dynamics of the Human Ecological Condition,* ed. Yrjö Haila and Chuck Dyke (Durham, N.C.: Duke University Press, 2006), 66–77.

19. Lacan, *Écrits,* 311.

20. *Apocalypse Now,* directed by Francis Ford Coppola (American Zoetrope, 1979).

21. Chögyam Trungpa, "Instead of Americanism Speak the English Language Properly," in *The Elocution Home Study Course* (Boulder, Colo.: Vajradhatu, 1983), 3.

22. Plato, *Ion,* http://classics.mit.edu/Plato/ion.html.

23. The subtitle of his *Cyclonopedia.*

24. Negarestani, *Cyclonopedia,* 195–207.

25. China Miéville, *Perdido Street Station* (New York: Ballantine, 2001); China Miéville, *The Scar* (New York: Random House, 2004).

26. Lacan, *Le seminaire, Livre III,* 48.

27. *The Pervert's Guide to Cinema,* directed by Sophie Fiennes, presented by Slavoj Žižek (P Guide Ltd., 2006).

28. Kafka, "Cares," 160.

29. Samuel Taylor Coleridge, "The Rime of the Ancient Mariner," in *Samuel Taylor Coleridge: The Major Works,* ed. H. J. Jackson (Oxford: Oxford University Press, 2008), line 533.

30. Kafka, "Cares," 160.

31. Permission to print this poem was granted by the author.

32. Colin Milburn, *Nanovision: Engineering the Future* (Durham, N.C.: Duke University Press, 2008), 83.

33. Banksy, *Pier Pressure,* http://www.youtube.com/watch?v=4hjIuMx-N7c.

34. Sartre, *Being and Nothingness,* 609.

35. Shelley, *Defence of Poetry,* 509–35 (530).

36. Blake, "And Did Those Feet in Ancient Time," line 13.

37. From the documentary *Crude,* directed by Joe Berlinger (Entendre Films, Radical Media, Red Envelope Entertainment, Third Eye Motion Picture, First Run Pictures, 2009).

38. Suzana Sawyer, "The Toxic Matter of Crude: Law, Science, and Indeterminacy in Ecuador and Beyond," lecture, Rice University, November 29, 2012.

39. Francisco Lopez, *La Selva* (V2_Archief, 1998).

40. Robert Ashley, *She Was a Visitor, Automatic Writing* (Lovely Music, 1979).

41. John F. Simon, *Every Icon* (1997), http://numeral.com/eicon.html.

42. I am grateful to Robert Jackson for discussing this with me. See "What the Hell Is a Hyperobject?," http://robertjackson.info/index/2010/10/what-the-hell-is-a-hyperobject/.

43. See Robert Jackson, "Some Notes on 'The Art of the Real,'" http://robert jackson.info/index/2010/12/some-notes-on-the-art-of-the-real/.

44. Jarrod Fowler, *Percussion Ensemble* (Senufo Edition 6, 2011); Jarrod Fowler, *P.S.* (Leaving Records, 2011), http://leavingrecords.com/releases/lrfo10-p-s/.

45. Timothy Morton, sleeve note for Jarrod Fowler, *P.S.* (Leaving Records, 2011), available for download at http://leavingrecords.com/releases/lrfo10-p-s/.

46. Timothy Morton, David Gissen, and Douglas Kahn, roundtable discussion at the conference Materials Objects Environments, NIEA, University of New South Wales, http://ecologywithoutnature.blogspot.com/2011/05/materials-objects-envir onments.html.

47. Lacan, *Écrits,* 311.

48. *The Adventures of Buckaroo Banzai across the Eighth Dimension,* directed by W. D. Richter (20th Century Fox, 1984).

49. Brenda Hillman, "Styrofoam Cup," from *Cascadia* (Middletown, Conn.: Wesleyan University Press, 2001). Reproduced by permission of the author.

50. John Keats, *The Complete Poems,* ed. Barnard, John, 2nd ed. (London: Penguin, 1987).

51. Comora Tolliver, *Pod,* http://www.comoratolliver.com/installation.html.

52. JLiat, *bravo,* 18:45:00.0 28 February 1954 (GMT) Bikini Atoll, http://www .jliat.com/.

53. Morton, *Ecology without Nature,* 29–78.

54. Book, Spangler, and Swartz, "Effects of Lifetime Ingestion," 244–51.

55. Nanako Kurihara, "The Most Remote Thing in the Universe: Critical Analysis of Hijikata Tatsumi's Butoh Dance" (PhD diss., New York University, 1996).

56. Sondra Fraleigh, *Butoh: Metamorphic Dance and Global Alchemy* (Urbana: University of Illinois Press, 2010), 61.

57. Derrida wrote about cinders constantly. Examples are too numerous, but see Jacques Derrida, *Cinders,* trans. Ned Lukacher (Lincoln: University of Nebraska Press, 2001).

58. Alain Badiou, "Towards a New Concept of Existence," *The Symptom* 12 (Fall 2011): http://www.lacan.com/symptom12/?p=116. Morton, *Realist Magic,* 199–200.

59. Immanuel Kant, *Critique of Pure Reason,* trans. Werner S. Pluhar (Indianapolis: Hackett, 1996), 201, 202, 232–37.

60. John Keats to Richard Woodhouse, October 27, 1818, in *John Keats: Selected Letters,* ed. Robert Gittings and Jon Mee (Oxford: Oxford University Press, 2002), 147–48.

61. Edmund Husserl, *Logical Investigations,* trans. J. N. Findlay, vol. 1 (New York: Routledge, 2008). The entire book is essential for understanding this point, but the "Second Investigation" is particularly pertinent.

62. Harman, *Quadruple Object,* 7–18.

63. Sophocles, *Antigone,* ed. Martin D'Ooge (Boston: Ginn, 1888), 52.

64. Martin Heidegger, *Introduction to Metaphysics,* trans. Gregory Fried and Richard Polt (New Haven, Conn.: Yale University Press, 2000), 156–76.

65. Stanley Cavell, *This New Yet Unapproachable America: Lectures after Emerson after Wittgenstein* (Albuquerque: Living Batch Press, 1989), 86–88; Ralph Waldo Emerson, "Experience," in *Essential Writings,* ed. Brooks Atkinson and Mary Oliver (New York: Modern Library, 2000), 307–26 (309). I am grateful to Cary Wolfe for talking about this with me.

66. Martin Heidegger, "Nur noch ein Gott kann uns retten," interview in *Der Spiegel,* May 1976, 193–219.

Index

TIMOTHY MORTON is Rita Shea Guffey Chair of English at Rice University. He is the author of several books, including *The Ecological Thought* and *Ecology without Nature*.

(continued from page ii)